CW00952578

16
AIR ASSAULT
BRIGADE

The AgustaWestland Apache AH.1 attack helicopter provides 16 Air Assault Brigade with its main airborne firepower. (*AgustaWestland*)

16 AIR ASSAULT BRIGADE

The History of Britain's Rapid Reaction Force

by

Tim Ripley

Pen & Sword
AVIATION

First published in Great Britain in 2008 by
Pen & Sword Aviation
An imprint of
Pen & Sword Books Ltd
47 Church Street
Barnsley
South Yorkshire
S70 2AS

Copyright © Tim Ripley, 2008

ISBN 978 1 84415 743 3

A CIP catalogue record for this book is
available from the British Library

Printed and bound in Thailand
By Kyodo Nation Printing Services Co., Ltd

Pen & Sword Books Ltd incorporates the Imprints of Pen & Sword Aviation,
Pen & Sword Family History, Pen & Sword Maritime, Pen & Sword Military,
Wharncliffe Local History, Pen & Sword Select, Pen & Sword Military Classics,
Leo Cooper, Remember When, Seaforth Publishing and Frontline Publishing

For a complete list of Pen & Sword titles please contact
PEN & SWORD BOOKS LIMITED
47 Church Street, Barnsley, South Yorkshire, S70 2AS, England
E-mail: enquiries@pen-and-sword.co.uk
Website: www.pen-and-sword.co.uk

Contents

Acknowledgements   7

Introduction   9

Chapter 1 16 Air Assault Brigade, January 2008   15

Chapter 2 British Army and Air Mobility   41

Chapter 3 24 Airmobile Brigade to Bosnia   57

Chapter 4 16 Air Assault Brigade and JHC Formed   69

Chapter 5 By Helicopter to Kosovo   83

Chapter 6 Sierra Leone, 2000   101

Chapter 7 Exercise Eagle's Strike, 2000   113

Chapter 8 Operation Essential Harvest   127

Chapter 9 Afghanistan, 2002   145

Chapter 10 Invading Iraq, 2003   153

Chapter 11 The Queen's Apaches   179

Chapter 12 A Fatal Blow?   195

Chapter 13 Exercise Eagle's Strike, 2005   205

Chapter 14 Afghanistan, 2006   219

Chapter 15 The Future of 16 Air Assault Brigade   261

Index   269

Notes

For ease of recognition the place names used throughout are those in general usage in the international media. Many locations in the Middle East and Balkans have multiple spellings in local languages so confusion often arises.

Dedication

This book is dedicated to young Fergus Ripley who has already shown a keen interest in flying helicopters after watching several of the famous 'Whooka, Whooka' of the RAF above our house.

Acknowledgements

This book has only been possible thanks to the help of scores of members of the British and allied armed forces who have recounted their experiences or provided assistance to the author on his numerous visits to operational theatres. Many are named below but many others asked to remain anonymous. They know who they are – many thanks to you all.

A special thanks must also go to Dr Amanda Cahill, AKA Mrs Ripley, for her support and understanding during the long process of writing this volume. It would not have been possible without her.

Ploce 1995, 24 Airmobile Brigade: Brig Robin Brims; Lt Col John Greenhalgh, AAC; Lt Col Roger Brunt, R ANGLIAN; Maj Gerry Bartlett, PWRR; Major Mark Proffley, RLC; WCO Ian McKluskie, RAF, SHF.

Kosovo 1999: WCO Wayne Gregory and Sqn Ldr Paul Bartlett SHF HQ; Maj Richard Leakey 659 Sqn AAC; Maj Rupert Hibbert HQ KFOR; Maj Andrew Venus HQ KFOR; Lt Col Robin Hughes UK PIC (press information centre) Pristina; Lt Col George M Bilafer, 6-6 CAV; Lt Col Bruce McQuade, 408 Sn Canadian AF; Flt Lt Jeff Lindsay, 27 Squadron; Paul Beaver KFOR Media Pool.

PJHQ/Sierra Leone 2000: Admiral Sir Ian Garnett CJO; Lt Col Neil Salisbury, Chief of Staff, JFHQ; Lt Col Tony Cramp, JFHQ; Lt Cdr Garry Lydiate, JFHQ; Col Stuart Green PJHQ.

Exercise Eagle's Strike 2000, 16 Brigade: Brig Peter Wall, Maj Dave Reynolds, WCO Gavin Davey.

Macedonia 2001: Lt Col Duncan Francis; Capt Alex Dick; Flt Lt Al Richie, 16 Brigade; Lt Col 'Chip' Chapman 2 PARA; Maj Dennis Griffin, Task Force Hunter; Andrew Venus, OSCE; Ingemar Ingemarsson, NATO; Paul Bernard; Pete Haslam; Paul Sykes and Simon Wren, UK MoD; Mr and Mrs Andrew Testa; Christian Jennings; Nick Wood.

Iraq 2003: DCC (RAF); WCO Ian Tofts, PIC Qatar; Gp Capt Al Lockwood; RAF PIC Kuwait, Spokesman Gp Capt John Fynes; WCO Mike Cairns and Steve Dargan.

Ali Al Salem AB: Gp Capt Andy Pulford, JHF; WCO Paul Lyall, 33 Sqn; WCO David Prowse, 18 Sqn.

British Army PIC Kuwait, Lt Col Rob Partridge; PIC Qatar, Major Will MacKinnley.

JHC/AAC: AVM David Niven; Maj Gen Gary Coward; Lt Col Paul Beaver.

RAF Odiham: WCO Andy Lawless; Sqn Ldr Steve Carr, 18 (Bomber) Sqn.

Exercise Eagle Strike 2005, 16 Brigade: Brig Ed Butler; Lt Col Richard Felton; Lt Col

Dave Reynolds Geoff Meade, Sky News; Paul Wood, BBC News.

Afghanistan 2006, UK TF: Brig Ed Butler; Capt Drew Gibson; Lt Col Dave Reynolds, RAF; ACM Glenn Torpy; WCO Jon Ager; WCO Alisa Gough Strike Command DCC; Sqn Ldr Dan Startup, 27 Squadron; WCO Nick Laird MoD; Gp Capt Mark Roberts DCOMBRITFOR (AIR); Wg Cdr Mark Knight OC 904 EAW; WCO Ian Duguid, OC IV Squadron; Sqn Ldr Martin Balshaw, OC C-130 Det; WCO Trevor Field, RAF DCC MoD.

CDISS

Pauline Elliott; Col Richard Connaughton.

PHOTOGRAPHIC CREDITS

Patrick Allan; Bob Morrison; Teddy Neville; Andy Lawless; Kate Roberts, BAE Systems; Geoff Russell, AgustaWestland; USMC; US DoD; Canadian Ministry of National Defence.

The author has made every effort to trace the copyright owners of all the images but if any are incorrectly attributed this will be corrected in subsequent editions.

INTRODUCTION

Kandahar Airfield, Afghanistan, 24 September 2006

Down the flight line at the massive NATO airbase in the barren desert of southern Afghanistan a pair of British Army Air Corps (AAC) Apache attack helicopters were returning from a mission, empty weapon pylons indicating that they had seen serious action a few miles away where Canadian and British forces were mopping up Taliban resistance after the conclusion of Operation Medusa. At the other end of the base, RAF Harrier jump jet pilots were walking around their aircraft in preparation for the third close air support mission of the day to protect British paratroopers defending isolated district centres in war-torn Helmand province. Nearby, RAF engineers and army air dispatch experts were packing pallets of water, food and ammunition to be parachuted out of the back of C-130 Hercules transports to the besieged paratroopers under the cover of darkness that night.

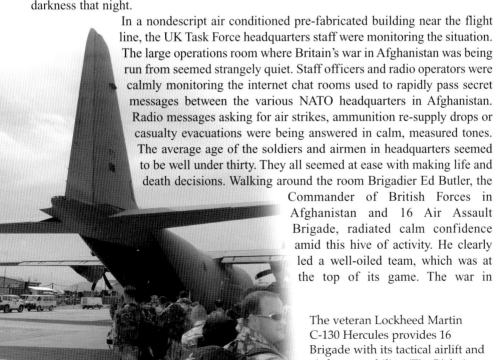

In a nondescript air conditioned pre-fabricated building near the flight line, the UK Task Force headquarters staff were monitoring the situation. The large operations room where Britain's war in Afghanistan was being run from seemed strangely quiet. Staff officers and radio operators were calmly monitoring the internet chat rooms used to rapidly pass secret messages between the various NATO headquarters in Afghanistan. Radio messages asking for air strikes, ammunition re-supply drops or casualty evacuations were being answered in calm, measured tones. The average age of the soldiers and airmen in headquarters seemed to be well under thirty. They all seemed at ease with making life and death decisions. Walking around the room Brigadier Ed Butler, the Commander of British Forces in Afghanistan and 16 Air Assault Brigade, radiated calm confidence amid this hive of activity. He clearly led a well-oiled team, which was at the top of its game. The war in

The veteran Lockheed Martin C-130 Hercules provides 16 Brigade with its tactical airlift and airdrop capability. *(Tim Ripley)*

Afghanistan was not yet over but the Brigadier and his troops were soon to head home. They had fought a series of pitched battles and proved, if anyone still doubted it, that the British Armed Forces had at last mastered the use of the helicopter in high intensity combat.

In the summer of 2006 British AAC and RAF helicopter crews found themselves in the forefront of a series of desperate battles to help paratroopers of 16 Air Assault Brigade isolated in walled compounds called district centres. Throughout the summer of 2006 the troops and helicopter crews of 16 Brigade battled against overwhelming odds to keep several thousand Taliban fighters at bay. By the autumn, both sides had drawn back and a pause descended over the bloody Afghan battlefields.

The first phase of the Battle of Helmand proved a tough test of 16 Brigade and its reliance on helicopters and other air support to compensate for its lack of heavy armoured vehicles and artillery. A few months later the Brigade's personnel were awarded an unprecedented number of decorations for gallantry, including two Victory Crosses, for their time in Afghanistan. This illustrated dramatically the intensity of the fighting as well as the bravery and determination of the Brigade's personnel.

While the award of a series of prestigious decorations to members of the Parachute Regiment won much publicity, the Afghan operations awards list in 2006 also included a raft of awards to helicopter pilots, crewmen, forward air controllers, aeromedics and Harrier pilots. This was graphic recognition that 16 Brigade was a true air manoeuvre force that depended on brave and skilled aviators from both the AAC and RAF for its success.

The honing of 16 Air Assault Brigade into the British Armed Force's elite rapid reaction formation that specialises in using helicopters and transport aircraft, backed by airborne firepower, to carry out what are termed air manoeuvre operations has been a long and

The RAF Boeing Chinook HC.2
heavy-lift helicopters are the mainstay
of 16 Brigade's rotary wing support
forces. *(Tim Ripley)*

tortured process. This book charts that process, which stretches back to the 1956 Suez crisis when helicopters were used to ferry assault troops ashore from aircraft carriers off the Egyptian coast.

This promising start in utilising the unique attributes of the helicopter – the ability to land and take off vertically – was soon lost. It was nearly three decades until the British Army formed its first specialised air mobile brigade, even through the Americans were soon using helicopters on an unprecedented scale during the Vietnam war in the 1960s and 1970s. Shortages of money, resistance from existing regiments and corps, along with inter-Service rivalry between the RAF and Royal Navy, were the main causes of the British Army's failure to move more aggressively to utilise helicopters in combat.

The British military helicopters were in the forefront of combat operations in the Middle and Far East in the 1960s, Northern Ireland from 1969 to 2007 and the Falklands in 1982. However, the lack of a dedicated air mobile force meant that hard learnt expertise and experience were quickly lost when units were retuned to conventional duties after conducting helicopter operations. The exception to this was the Royal Marines who had their own dedicated Commando Helicopter Force, which became highly skilled at projecting combat power ashore by helicopter during amphibious operations. The British Army clearly suffered through not having a comparable organisation.

While a shortage of resources was a major part of the British Army's inability to fully embrace air mobile operations, there was also a strong reluctance from a significant part of the Service's senior hierarchy to get its mind around the potential of the helicopter. An often-used phrase in the 1980s was, 'moving by helicopter is not an act of war, you know'. The inference was that on a Central European battlefield – packed full of tens of thousands of tanks, armoured personnel carriers and self-propelled artillery – lightly armed helicopter-borne troops would get slaughtered before they could achieve any effect. At the height of the Cold War in the 1970s and 1980s, many senior British NATO commanders only thought in terms of any future war with the Soviets being a bloody war of attrition that would evitable result in a unwinnable nuclear exchange.

The fact that the RAF's helicopter force was multi-roled to provide mobility for logistic support for the army and RAF Harrier jump jet squadrons deployed to field sites, meant that there were often competing demands for the limited number of large transport or support helicopters throughout the 1970s and 1980s.

This changed in the mid-1980s when the British Army formed an experimental air mobile brigade to act as a kind of air portable 'speed bump'. The role of the brigade's helicopters was to rapidly move large numbers of infantry armed with anti-tank guided missiles to block any breakthrough by Red Army tank divisions. This was the start of the recognition that air mobility might play a part in future operations.

Battalions of the Parachute Regiment have spearheaded all of 16 Brigade's major operations. *(Tim Ripley)*

The 1991 Gulf Conflict was a major watershed for the British Army's interest in helicopters after it saw what the US Army and Marine Corps attack helicopters achieved during the brief '100 hour war' against Iraq.

Although the next fifteen years saw dramatic progress in the development of UK air mobile forces, it proved a hard struggle. In the post Cold War era, cutbacks in defence spending meant it was a constant battle to win resources to buy new helicopters and other capabilities. The mid-1990s did see a spike in investment in helicopters and other capabilities, including sixty-seven AH-64 Apache attack helicopters, twenty-two EH101 Merlin and fourteen CH-47 Chinook helicopters and twenty-five new C-130J tactical air lifters. Barely had this equipment been ordered than budget cuts and procurement mistakes meant the delivery of this equipment to frontline users became a long and tortuous process.

The weakness of the UK's air mobile and strategic airlift equipment was highlighted dramatically during the ill-fated deployment of 24 Airmobile Brigade to Bosnia in 1995. Four years later the paratroopers and Gurkhas of 5 Airborne Brigade conducted a daring air mobile operation to open the NATO move into war-torn Kosovo. This operation was clearly a sign of things to come and showed a new confidence on the part of UK air manoeuvre commanders.

The past decade saw the formation of 16 Brigade as the British Armed Forces' centre of air manoeuvre excellence. This term is now used by the UK military to encompass air mobility or movement by helicopter, airborne operations by parachute and air transport moves by tactical airlift aircraft. The Brigade has been in action almost constantly since its formation in 1999. A large part of the Brigade was committed to action in Sierra Leone the following year. In 2001, it spearheaded NATO's successful intervention in Macedonia to separate government troops and Albanian rebels. The next year it was in Afghanistan and in 2003 the Brigade was in the thick of fighting in Iraq. Elements of the Brigade then took turns contributing to occupation duty in Iraq as well as peacekeeping missions in the Balkans and Northern Ireland

These early operations were conducted largely with legacy equipment and it was not

Tim Ripley and one of Saddam Hussein's T-55 tanks in Al Amara, Iraq, 2003. *(Tim Ripley)*

until 2005 that new hardware, such as the Apache and Merlin helicopter, was in widespread use. The 2006 operation in Afghanistan saw 16 Brigade put its newfound combat capabilities to dramatic effect.

In the months after returning from Afghanistan, the Brigade moved into a new period of re-equipment, acquiring Bowman digital radios and more Apaches. These new capabilities are intended to enhance its combat power ahead of the Brigade's next deployment to Afghanistan in 2008. Other new capabilities including unmanned aerial vehicles and airborne stand-off radar sensors are being brought on line in time for deployment to Afghanistan with 16 Brigade.

All this suggests that 16 Air Assault Brigade will continue to be at the forefront of the British Army's expeditionary operations. It is almost certain that its soldiers and aviators will be earning many more medals in the conflicts of the coming decade.

For more than a decade I have followed the development of British air manoeuvre forces in trouble spots around the world, at their bases and headquarters in the UK, at defence industry conferences, helicopter factories around the world and Ministry of Defence briefings.

This book is based largely on my own observations of the battles and campaigns fought by 16 Air Assault Brigade – and its predecessor brigades. My observations range from the dusty helicopter landing pads at Ploce in Croatia in 1995, through to flying into weapon collection points in Macedonia in 2001, walking the deadly streets of Al Amara in Iraq in 2003 and to watching waves of Apaches and Harriers taking off to attack the Taliban in Afghanistan in 2006. In between my travels to operational theatres, I was able to see 16 Brigade put its innovative tactics to the test in a series of exercises around the UK.

During this time I have been able to speak to scores of soldiers and officers of 16 Brigade about their experiences, including interviewing a number of the Brigade's commanders, as well as senior officers of the Joint Helicopter Command and Permanent Joint Headquarters. The military personnel quoted by name in the following chapters were all speaking at public events, such as press briefings or interviews conducted 'on the record' in the presence of media operations officers or 'minders'. Many others wanted to contribute to this book anonymously because their comments might be considered 'off message' by the Ministry of Defence and Downing Street 'spin machines'. Even though many friends in the UK Armed Forces have reviewed my text, any errors and omissions are mine alone.

In many ways the story of 16 Brigade is also the story of Britain's wars in the post-Cold War era. It starts with success in peacekeeping operations in the Balkans and Africa. The past decade has seen the portion of the UK's national wealth devoted to defence continue to decline in real terms and this has been translated into the delay or cancellation of many military procurement projects. From the experiences of 16 Brigade in Iraq and Afghanistan since 2003, the implications of this are becoming increasingly clear. Britain's Armed Forces are fighting the country's wars without many items of key battle-winning equipment. These shortcomings are only being compensated for by the military prowess and battlefield bravery of our servicemen and women or the mistakes of our enemies.

Tim Ripley
January 2008

CHAPTER 1

16 Air Assault Brigade, January 2008

'16 Air Assault Brigade is the newest and largest Brigade in the British Army' is how Brigadier Mark Charlton-Smith, the current Commander 16 Air Assault Brigade, introduces his formation on its website. He continues:

> What makes 16 Brigade unique is not only that it is the Army's primary rapid reaction formation but that it is equipped and manned so it can be used in any eventuality, whether evacuation tasks and humanitarian operations, through to warfighting, should that ever be necessary in the future. The combination of air assault troops, parachute troops and helicopters makes it one of the most flexible and usable formations in any modern army in the world. 16 Air Assault Brigade is

RAF Boeing Chinook HC.2 heavy-lift helicopters move 16 Air Assault Brigade vehicles during Exercise Eagle's Strike 2005. *(Tim Ripley)*

the most exciting formation in the Army and we are the cutting edge of the military.

The Brigadier's enthusiasm for his command is not surprising. Leading the British Army's only air manoeuvre force is one of its most prestigious appointments. Outside the secretive world of the UK's Special Forces, 16 Air Assault Brigade is the most battle-hardened and combat-ready formation in the British Armed Forces.

Not only does the Brigade contain three Army Air Corps (AAC) aviation regiments, two of which are equipped with the British Army's newest and most powerful weapon system – the AgustaWestland Apache AH.1 attack helicopter – but it also contains two elite battalions of the Parachute Regiment. These forces have some of the best training available in the British Army lavished on them and a significant part of 16 Brigade's soldiers is held at high readiness to respond to sudden crises around the world as part of the UK's Joint Rapid Reaction Force (JRRF). As well as boasting some of the British Army's best units, it is also supported by helicopters and transport aircraft of the Royal Air Force to move it into action. At the heart of 16 Brigade is the ethos of 'going by air to battle', whether by parachute, helicopter or air transport. The British Armed Forces attribute the term air manoeuvre to this combination of capabilities, rather than airborne or air mobile operations, which refer respectively to parachute drops and helicopter-borne only activity.

As Brigadier Charlton-Smith hinted at, a posting to 16 Air Assault Brigade is not for those expecting a routine life in a backwater garrison. The Brigade's major units have participated in every major British military overseas deployment since Kosovo in 1999 and as this book goes to press in the autumn of 2008, it is making its final preparations before returning to Afghanistan for its third tour in the Central Asian country.

Deploying on operations is a way of life for the Brigade's soldiers. 'It's what we do' was the comment of one Parachute Regiment sergeant major when being questioned by journalists in Afghanistan in 2006 about the regularity of the Brigade's overseas tours of duty. Almost everything the Brigade does is orientated about being ready, should the call come to go into action. As one of the UK's main 'theatre entry' forces, 16 Brigade's soldiers have become used to being the first British troops on the ground in a new war zone. The ability to think on their feet and quickly find solutions to new problems has held them in good stead over the past decade.

Every since the British Army's Airborne Forces came into existence in 1940, they have been at the cutting edge of tactical innovation. They pioneered military parachuting in the British Armed Forces and then the employment of gliders. Today's 16 Brigade is no different. It used the attack helicopters in action for the first time in British military history and in the 2003 Iraq war fought an innovative air-land battle to defeat an Iraqi armoured division with artillery fire and air strikes alone.

16 Brigade is also unique in that it was the first modern British Army brigade to boast a near fixed or permanent brigade order of battle after it was formed in 1999. Up until 2004, all the infantry battalions and armoured regiments of the British Army moved every two to five years as part of what was known as the 'arms plot'. This was designed to liven up the careers of soldiers during the Cold War by giving them a variety of postings. For 5 Airborne and 24 Airmobile Brigades, 16 Brigade's direct predecessors, it meant many of their major units were never attached long enough to build up real experience expertise in airborne or air mobile operations before they were posted to another brigade.

16 Air Assault Brigade Badge and Historical Lineage

16 Air Assault Brigade was formed on 1 September 1999. It draws upon the historical traditions of 16 Independent Parachute Brigade, which was the UK's sole airborne formation from the late 1940s until 1977 when the brigade was disbanded. This in turn was formed after World War Two from the famous 1st and 6th Airborne Divisions, bringing together their numerical designations.

The new Brigade's badge draws on the traditions of both the paratroopers of the Airborne Forces and the aviators of the Army Air Corps (AAC). The 'Striking Eagle' design was adapted from the emblem of the Special Training Centre, Lochailot, Scotland, which was used to train Special Forces and Airborne troops between 1943 and 1945.

The maroon and light blue colours of the badge represent the Airborne and AAC constituent elements of the Brigade.

Since 1999, 16 Brigade has had a degree of organisational stability previously unknown in modern British Army experience and the result has been the building up of a degree of tactical expertise in air manoeuvre that is unprecedented. Most members of the Brigade staff and members of its major units are now veterans of numerous wars and operations over the past decade. Time and again over the past decade, the 'Toms' of the Parachute Regiment have flown into action in helicopters crewed by the same RAF pilots and loadmasters. They have shared the same lengthy tours away from home, living in the same desperate conditions and been shot at at the same time. Perhaps more significantly, the RAF helicopter crews have always been on hand to fly into harm's way to lift out wounded paratroopers. This level of familiarity with each other is otherwise unknown in the British armed forces, outside the Special Forces, and means when 16 Brigade deploys on operations it does so with a verve and confidence that is the envy of every other British Army brigade. This Brigade *esprit de corps* is a major factor in its success.

The 2004 Defence Review proposed to stop the 'arms plot' by the end of the decade and permanently assigned major combat units to individual brigades. But 16 Brigade led the way and the rest of the British Army is some way behind in building up the same degree of brigade spirit.

Another important element of the Brigade's success has been its strong connections to the UK's Special Forces community. A significant number 16 Brigade's personnel have served with the Special Forces at some point in their military careers. This means the

The Lead Airborne Task Force jumps into action over West Freugh. *(Bob Morrison)*

senior leadership of 16 Brigade and its major units all have unprecedented exposure to UK Special Forces operations, equipment and procedures. The UK Special Forces have been some of the most innovative users of helicopters in combat operations and their procedures and tactics have strongly influenced how 16 Brigade operates.

For the junior ranks, service in 16 Brigade is seen as a stepping stone to service in the Special Forces. The exposure of these young soldiers to so many Special Force veterans is a great spur to them developing their military expertise in a bid to try to pass the famous Special Forces selection test.

With some 8,000 personnel under its command in peacetime, 16 Brigade is the largest brigade-sized formation in the British Army. In peacetime the bulk of the Brigade is based in a number of barracks around Colchester in Essex, with other major units in Wattisham in Suffolk and Dishforth in North Yorkshire.

The 200-strong Brigade main headquarters is the nerve centre of its operations. It is broken down into a number of distinct teams that run specific activities. Supporting the commander and his staff is 216 Squadron of the Royal Signals, which provides the Brigade with its communications equipment and the specialists to operate it.

Heading up the Brigade is a brigadier, or one star general, and he has a very small tactical headquarters of half a dozen officers and radio operators, who follow him around the battlefield. This 'Tac HQ' can either move by Land Rover or helicopter and is fully parachute-trained.

The Brigade Main Headquarters is its core command centre and it is largely vehicle-borne. Here, the bulk of the staff monitors a number of radio networks or nets to control all aspects of the Brigade's operations. It also has communications links to other UK and allied headquarters to ensure the Brigade is co-ordinating its actions with the broader battle. Within this headquarters there are a number of specific cells or teams to co-ordinate intelligence, offensive air support, helicopters operations, air transport, artillery fire, reconnaissance and surveillance, logistic support and medical evacuation. All the cap badges of the British Army are represented in the headquarters, which usually contains more than 200 officers and soldiers, as well as the RAF, and on occasions, the Royal Marines and Royal Navy. The Brigade headquarters is almost twice the size of a British armoured or mechanised brigade headquarters.

At the heart of the main headquarters is a 'bird table' map, which plots all the friendly and enemy forces and allows all the staff officers to see at a glance how the battle is progressing. Until recently this was just a large paper map but the Brigade is starting to receive electronic systems with plasma screens to replace it. The Brigade had a RAF-led Air Manoeuvre Recognised Air Picture Flight attached in 2003 that allowed a real-time graphical map of all aircraft flying in a theatre of operation to be projected onto a large computer screen in the headquarters. The Brigade is in the process of being equipped with the Bowman digital communications system to replace its 1960s vintage Clansman radios. One importance feature of Bowman is that each radio contains a tracking device that feeds back positional data to the Brigade headquarters to allow an electronic map showing where all its ground units are to be created. When combined with the air picture, this capability gives the headquarters staff an unprecedented view of what is happening on the battlefield to allow them to plan missions and organise air and fire support, as well as track the location of friendly air and land forces.

On operations the main headquarters is run by the Brigade deputy commander and the Brigade chief of staff, to allow the commander to spend most of his time out on the ground with the frontline troops. At the heart of the smooth running of the main headquarters is its ability to split itself into two echelons when it has to move. Known as 'Step-up', the advance element is able to move first and then set up a second headquarters to start running the Brigade to allow the rest of the main headquarters to begin moving. This procedure ensures that the Brigade is never out of communications. The ability to do this while major units are moving by aircraft or helicopter is a key capability for 16 Brigade and ensures it can maintain a tempo of operations.

16 Air Assault Brigade Order of Battle, January 2008

Brigade Headquarters
216 Signal Squadron
Pathfinder Platoon (Wattisham airfield)
1st Battalion, The Royal Irish Regiment (Ternhill)
5th Battalion, The Royal Regiment of Scotland (Argyll & Sutherland Highlanders) (Canterbury)
2nd Battalion, The Parachute Regiment (Colchester)
3rd Battalion, The Parachute Regiment (Colchester)
D Squadron, Household Cavalry Regiment (Windsor)
7 Parachute Regiment Royal Horse Artillery (Colchester)
23 Engineer Regiment (Air Assault) (Woodbridge)
13 Air Assault Regiment, Royal Logistic Corps (Colchester)
7 Air Assault Battalion, Royal Mechanical and Electrical Engineers (Wattisham Airfield)
16 Close Support Medical Regiment (Colchester)
156 Provost Company, Royal Military Police (Colchester)

3 Regiment Army Air Corps (Wattisham Airfield)

653 Squadron – Apache AH.1 (converting from Lynx)
662 Squadron – Apache AH.1
663 Squadron – Apache AH.1

4 Regiment Army Air Corps (Wattisham Airfield)

654 Squadron – Apache AH.1 (converting from Lynx)
656 Squadron – Apache AH.1 (ex 9 Regt)
664 Squadron – Apache AH.1 (ex 9 Regt)

9 Regiment Army Air Corps (Dishforth Airfield)

659 Squadron – Lynx AH.7/9 (ex 4 Regt)
669 Squadron – Lynx AH.7/9 (ex 4 Regt)
672 Squadron – Lynx AH.7

RAF Units earmarked to support 16 Brigade include:

18 Squadron – Chinook HC.2 (RAF Odiham)
27 Squadron – Chinook HC.2 (RAF Odiham)
33 Squadron – Puma HC.1 (RAF Benson)
230 Squadron – Puma HC.1 (RAF Aldergrove)
28 Squadron – Merlin HC.3 (RAF Benson)

85 Expeditionary Logistics Wing (RAF Wittering)

No. 1 Expeditionary Logistics Squadron (RAF Wittering)
No. 2 Mechanical Transport (MT) Squadron (RAF Wittering)
No. 5001 (Expeditionary Infrastructure) Squadron and No. 3 Mobile
   Catering Squadron (RAF Wittering)
Tactical Communications Wing (RAF Brize Norton)
Tactical Medical Wing (RAF Lyneham)
1 Air Mobility Wing (RAF Lyneham)

Lyneham Transport Wing

24 Squadron – C-130J
30 Squadron – C-130J
47 Squadron – C-130K
LXX Squadron – C-130K
47 Air Despatch Squadron, Royal Logistic Corps

A sniper team from the 2nd Battalion, The Parachute Regiment's reconnaissance platoon. (*Tim Ripley*)

AgustaWestland AH.1 Apache

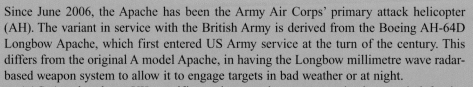

Crew: 2

Engine: 2 x 850 shp Rolls-Royce RTM-322

Length: 9.53 m

Height: 3.8 m (without radar)

Max speed: 330 kph

Cruise speed: 272 kph

Range: 462 km

Armament: 16 x Hellfire missiles,
76 x 2.75" CRV-7 rockets,
1200 x 30-mm cannon rounds,
4 x Air to Air Missiles

**Surveillance/target
acquisition:**
TV (127 x mag), thermal
imaging (36 x mag),
direct view optics (18
x mag)

AgustaWestland Apache
AH.1 attack helicopter.
(AgustaWestland)

Since June 2006, the Apache has been the Army Air Corps' primary attack helicopter (AH). The variant in service with the British Army is derived from the Boeing AH-64D Longbow Apache, which first entered US Army service at the turn of the century. This differs from the original A model Apache, in having the Longbow millimetre wave radar-based weapon system to allow it to engage targets in bad weather or at night.

AAC Apaches have UK-specific engines, rockets, communications and defensive systems.

By late 2007, four AH squadrons, each of eight helicopters, had converted to the Apache and all of these units had been concentrated at Wattisham Airfield in Suffolk.

Since May 2005, the main strike power of 16 Brigade has been its Apache-equipped attack helicopter (AH) regiments. The US-designed Apache is armed with up to sixteen AGM-114 Hellfire missiles, 30-mm chain gun, advanced night vision systems and a Longbow millimetric radar. This latter system allows it to monitor enemy vehicle and troop movements in bad weather and at night. The radar can sweep an arc of 50 square kilometres in front of the aircraft. The radar can detect moving targets at ranges up to eight kilometres while the detection range for static targets is reduced, at six kilometres. At this time, the Longbow system can display, classify and track up to 128 targets simultaneously. All the helicopter's weapon systems are slaved to the pilot's helmet so the weapons are aimed wherever he moves his head. The two aircrew sit in armoured seats so they are protected against enemy fire. Each helicopter also has a set of electronic defensive systems to detect and defeat enemy heat-seeking missiles being fired at it.

The Apache was designed in the 1970s and 1980s to operate at night, deep behind enemy lines to stage mass attacks on Soviet armoured divisions.

The US, Israeli and Dutch armies have used the Apache extensively in action since 1989 and it has an awesome reputation for reliability and ruggedness in combat. 16 Brigade used the Apache for the first time in Afghanistan in the summer of 2006, where it lived up to its reputation.

In the Army Air Corps, the basic unit AH unit is the squadron, which has eight Apaches and sixteen aircrew. The squadron is trained to either operate *en masse* or to conduct smaller operations involving pairs of helicopters. The latter is particularly applicable when a sustained presence is required over a particular objective. As well as the aircrew and helicopters, each AAC squadron also includes refuelling, arming and maintenance teams. These teams man and operate forward arms and refuelling points (FARPs) to allow AH units to operate from remote field locations.

Westland Lynx AH.7/9

The veteran Lynx was once the Army Air Corps' (AAC) main armed helicopter. It has now been replaced in the anti-tank role by the AgustaWestland AH.1 Apache and now is used primarily for manned airborne reconnaissance, small-scale troop transport, command and control and casualty evacuation.

The AH.7 variant was originally armed with eight TOW missiles but these were withdrawn from service at the end of 2004. These helicopters have skids. The wheeled AH.9 variant is the newest example of the Lynx in AAC service. This variant was never armed with TOW missiles.

Both variants are to be replaced from 2014 by the Future Lynx.

Crew: 2 (3 with door gunner) + 10 troops

Engines: 2 x 850 shp Rolls-Royce Gem 41

Length: 12.06 m

Height: 3.4 m

Max speed: 330 kph

Cruise speed: 232 kph

Range: 885 km

Combat radius: Approx 100 km
with 2 hour loiter

Armament: 2 x 7.62-mm GPMG
machine-guns

Westland Lynx AH.7
utility helicopter.
(Tim Ripley)

Three squadrons of Apaches are grouped into a regiment and they also include a larger ground support element as well as a fully equipped command post. The Brigade currently has two AH regiments, 3 and 4 Regiments, which are both based at Wattisham Airfield in Suffolk. This is the AAC's only operational Apache base and it is also the site of the main

Westland Gazelle AH.1

Like the Lynx, the Gazelle was the result of a Anglo-French helicopter collaboration in the late 1960s and early 1970s. In its time the Gazelle was a very advanced design.

The age of the light observation and liaison helicopter and its limited performance in 'hot and high' environments means the Gazelle is increasingly relegated to non-combat roles. When its attack helicopter regiment completes its conversion to the AgustaWestland AH.1 Apache by 2009, the Gazelle will be formally retired from service with 16 Air Assault Brigade. The veteran helicopter is not expected to deploy on operations with the Brigade again.

Crew: 2+3 passengers
Engine: 592 shp Turbomeca/Rolls-Royce Astazou 111N2
Length: 9.53 m
Height: 3.18 m
Max speed: 265 kph
Cruise speed: 233 kph
Range: 670 km
Combat radius: Approx 100 km with 2 hour loiter
Armament: 2 x 7.62-mm machine guns (not standard)

Westland Gazelle AH.1 observation helicopter. *(Tim Ripley)*

Apache logistic support facility in the UK where the helicopters are overhauled and repaired by teams from the Royal Electrical and Mechanical Engineers (REME) and contractors from Boeing, Lockheed Martin, AgustaWestland and Serco.

AH regimental headquarters can command what are termed aviation battlegroups. These are all arms units, which can also include infantry, artillery and ground-based reconnaissance units to provide a range of combat power to the battlegroup commander to enhance the effectiveness of his helicopters. They, for example, could use the infantry to seize and hold a FARP deep behind enemy lines, from where Apaches would strike at strategic enemy targets.

The two AH regiments take it in turns to provide what is termed the Lead Aviation Task Force to the JRRF. This means they have to have up to a squadron's worth of helicopters at ten days' notice to move in response to an international crisis. Three Apaches can be carried in a RAF C-17 Globemaster II airlifter.

16 Brigade also contains one of the AAC's battlefield utility helicopter regiments, equipped with Westland Lynx AH.7 and AH.9 light utility helicopters. The Lynx AH.7 used to be armed with the TOW wire-guided anti-tank missile until early 2005 but this was withdrawn from use after the arrival of the Apache. These helicopters have now been stripped of their missiles and are used for general utility tasks, such as flying senior commanders and other high-value passengers, as well as small-scale casualty evacuation tasks and carrying airborne command posts. They can be armed with 7.62-mm door-mounted machine-guns. Until the summer of 2007, 16 Brigade used to have three AH regiments, each with two AH squadrons and one Lynx squadron. To reduce operating and training costs, 16 Brigade has now concentrated all its Apaches at Wattisham and its three Lynx squadrons in 9 Regiment at Dishforth. This latter regiment, however, still retains the capability to act as an aviation battlegroup headquarters.

The famous Paras or 'Red Berets' have a fearsome reputation for being the British Army's toughest fighting unit. Despite being the British Army's 'youngest' infantry regiment, the Parachute Regiment has a legendary collection of battle honours dating back to the Bruneval raid in 1942, to North Africa, Sicily and Normandy in World War Two. Its most famous airborne operation is the Battle for Arnhem when 10,000 British paratroopers dropped into Holland to capture strategic bridges over the Rhine only to be surprised and massacred by two German Waffen SS panzer divisions. Immortalised in the film *A Bridge too Far*, the Arnhem campaign saw 10,000 British paratroopers

Pegasus Company (P Coy)

Any British soldier aspiring to become a member of the Parachute Regiment must pass the Pre-Parachute Selection (PPS) course run by Pegasus Company or as it is more commonly known 'P Coy' at the Infantry Training Centre in Catterick, North Yorkshire. All officers and soldiers who wish to serve with Airborne Forces, must attend the Pre-Parachute Selection course with P Coy. The Pegasus Company tests the physical fitness, determination and mental robustness (under conditions of stress) of potential paratroopers to determine whether or not an individual has the self discipline and motivation required for service with Airborne Forces.

Known as 'Test Week', the course comprises eight separate events over a four and a half day period. They are as follows:

1. The ten-mile march is conducted as a squad, over undulating terrain with each candidate carrying a bergen rucksack weighing 35 pounds and an SA-80 rifle.
2. The Trainasium is an 'Aerial Confidence Course', which is unique to P Coy. It tests a candidate's ability to overcome fear and carry out simple activities and instructions at a height above ground level.
3. A team event with eight soldiers working together to carry a 60 kg log over a distance of 1.9 miles over undulating terrain.
4. The two-mile march is conducted over undulating terrain with each individual carrying a bergen rucksack weighing 35 pounds and an SA-80 rifle.
5. An individual test with candidates running against the clock over a 1.8 mile cross-country course.
6. The Milling phase comprises sixty seconds of boxing or 'controlled physical aggression' against an opponent of similar height and weight.
7. A squadded endurance march conducted over twenty miles of severe terrain. Each individual carries a bergen rucksack weighing 35 pounds and an SA-80 rifle.
8. In the final event of Test Week teams of sixteen men carry a 175-pound stretcher over a distance of five miles. No more than four men carry the stretcher at any given time. Individuals wear webbing and carry an SA-80 rifle.

Those who are successful are awarded the coveted 'maroon beret' of the Airborne Forces and the opportunity to go on to conduct the Basic Parachute Course at RAF Brize Norton.

outnumbered, outgunned and surrounded. They put up days of determined resistance and only 3,000 returned to friendly territory. The operation was a disaster, but the paratroopers went down fighting.

The fighting spirit of those early paratroopers is still held in high esteem by the current generation of Airborne Soldiers, who value determination and perseverance in the face of adversity as core values and they say this is what makes them different from the soldiers of other infantry regiments. Ordinary paratroopers are nicknamed 'Toms' after the famous World War One soldier Tommy Atkins. In turn, they say they belong to the 'Para Reg'. To win the honour of wearing the Para wings of a modern Airborne Soldier, would-be Parachute Regiment soldiers and attached specialists have to pass one of three Pegasus or P Company courses. There is one for Regular Parachute Regiment soldiers, one for Territorial Parachute Regiment soldiers and another for soldiers of other regiments who hope to serve in the airborne or parachute role. These courses now take place at the Infantry Training Centre in Catterick but have lost none of their reputation for being some of the most physically and mentally demanding training courses in the British Army. Potential paratroopers first have to complete Infantry basic training before progressing to P Company or P Coy where they have to carry logs across gruelling assault courses,

Milan anti-tank missile. *(Tim Ripley)*

Milan Anti-tank Missile

The French-designed Milan wire-guided missile was originally purchased in the 1980s as the mainstay of the British Infantry's anti-tank forces.

It is a robust and reliable weapon and is often used in the direct fire role against snipers and other small targets because of its accuracy. The MIRA thermal imaging sight on the firing post is also used to augment night vision surveillance capabilities. The Milan is being replaced by the Lockheed Martin Javelin.

Missile: Max range 2,000 m
Min range: 400 m
Length: 918 mm
Weight: 6.73 kg
Rate of fire: 3–4 rpm
Warhead weight: 2.70 kg
Armour penetration: 352 mm
Missile speed: 720 kph
Guidance: Semi-automatic command to line of sight by means of wire
    guidance link

boxing (known as 'milling') and other tests of endurance. Only once they have passed these courses can they progress to the RAF-run No.1 Parachute Training School at RAF Brize Norton to conduct the parachuting phase of their training. The Parachute Regiment stresses that passing P Company is more about mental attitude than brute physical strength. Landing by parachute behind enemy lines requires Airborne Soldiers to overcome the fear of the unknown and to keep fighting when physically isolated from friendly forces, with limited medical evacuation and ammunition re-supply possible. Parachute Regiment officers and senior non-commissioned officers continue to insist this 'Airborne spirit' is still highly relevant today.

There are currently three battalions in the Parachute Regiment. The 1st Battalion is permanently assigned to the Special Forces Support Group (SFSG) and is based in South Wales. The 2nd and 3rd Battalions are based in Colchester as part of 16 Brigade. Each battalion has three infantry or rifle companies with around 120 men in each. A company is made up of three platoons of twenty-eight men each. The basic fighting unit of a platoon is the section, which contains eight men. Each section is heavily armed with a mix of SA-80 automatic rifles, Light Support Weapons, Minimi machine-guns, Light Anti-Tank Weapons (LAWs), grenade launchers and hand grenades. They also have night vision goggles and thermal night vision devices to allow them to fight around the clock. A parachute battalion has some 687 officers and soldiers in total.

Heavy firepower is provided by the support company, which has a number of specialist weapons platoons at its disposal. The weapons include 81-mm mortars, Milan wire-guided anti-tank missiles, high performance sniper rifles, 7.62-mm sustained fire general purpose machine-guns (GPMGs) and 0.50-cal machine-guns. These are in turn supported by the reconnaissance or patrols platoon, which is highly trained in operating covertly ahead of the battalion to find enemy positions. These specialist platoons all have Land Rovers or Pinzgauer light trucks to give them battlefield mobility.

The battalion is administered by a headquarters company, which contains specialist quartermaster (logistic) support, motor transport, medical and signals (radio) platoons. In addition to the main battalion headquarters or command post, each battalion's commanding officer also has his own small tactical headquarters team to allow him to control his troops while operating in the forward battle area. Leadership from the front is a quality that is in demand in the Parachute Regiment.

The two parachute battalions of 16 Brigade take turns to provide what is termed the Lead Airborne Task Force (LATF), which is held at five days' notice to conduct a parachute assault anywhere in the world. This is the UK's elite high readiness combat force, which would be called into action if any kind of short-notice combat operation is required.

A formal process of training and certification has to be followed before a battalion can take on the LATF role and once in this role the unit is usually held at high readiness for six months to a year. In addition to its own troops, the LATF also includes a 'slice' of airborne capabilities and qualified personnel drawn from across 16 Brigade, including a parachute-droppable artillery battery, engineers, intelligence, medical, logistic and communications specialists.

L188 105-mm Light Gun

The famous 105-mm Light Gun has been in use with the British Army since the 1970s and played a key role in the 1982 Falklands conflict. It has since been used in action by the British Army in Bosnia in 1995, Iraq in 2003 and in Afghanistan since 2006. Parachute and Commando trained regiments of the Royal Artillery use the weapon exclusively for expeditionary operations.

The weapon is simple, robust and can easily be under-slung beneath a Chinook, Puma or Sea King helicopter and can be parachute dropped from a C-130 Hercules aircraft.

Originally designed by Royal Ordnance, the weapon is still offered for sale by BAE Systems and has been exported to eighteen countries.

Crew: 6
Length: Gun forward 8.8 m
Height: 2.13 m
Width: 1.78 m
Combat weight: 1,858 kg
Ammunition: HE, Smoke, Illuminating, Target Marketing
Max range: (HE) 17.2 km
Shell weight: (HE) 15.1 kg

105-mm Light Gun. *(BAE Systems)*

16 Air Assault Brigade Pathfinder Platoon prepares for a high-altitude, low-opening parachute drop. *(Bob Morrison)*

The formal LATF requirement is very expensive to maintain in terms of making RAF C-130 Hercules aircraft available for qualification training and exercises, so in recent years the force has not been properly constituted on several occasions. When a large part of 16 Brigade is committed to operations, it is also very difficult to maintain the LATF.

The UK has not conducted a combat parachute drop since Suez in 1956 and the LATF capability is often targeted for budget cuts, but to date the British Army has fought off attempts to downscale its size or scope. The role of the airborne battalions in nurturing future Special Forces soldiers is now seen as very important and is emerging as an important argument to keep the LATF.

Combat landing by helicopter or air transport aircraft is dubbed an air assault operation by the British Army. The main role of 16 Brigade's three non-parachute-roled infantry battalions is air assault operations. In addition to the non-LATF Parachute Regiment battalion, 16 Brigade currently has the 1st Battalion, The Royal Irish Regiment and the 5th Battalion, The Royal Regiment of Scotland (Argyll and Sutherland Highlanders). The latter two regiments take turns to serve in 16 Brigade with the 2nd Battalion, The Royal Gurkha Rifles. The Royal Irish are based at Ternhill in Shropshire, the Argylls are at Canterbury and the Gurkhas are at Folkstone.

The air assault-roled infantry battalions each have 530 officers and soldiers. They are similar in organisation to the two Parachute Regiment battalions of the Brigade but are, of course, not required to be trained to parachute, although it is common for a high percentage of their personnel to undergo some parachute training.

Like the LATF, the air assault battalions have to undergo a formal training process to qualify for the role. This is to ensure its personnel are fully familiar with the safety procedures for flying in helicopters and C-130s. It also ensures that commanders at all levels are trained in how to control their troops as they move around the battlefield by air.

The battalion or battlegroup headquarters of the LATF and the air assault units are all provided with the communications equipment to allow them to take command of a variety of different types of units to become all-arms battlegroups. Uniquely for 16 Brigade, its battlegroup regularly includes army aviation units.

All the parachute and air assault battalions take turns to provide the UK spearhead lead elements (SLE) or battalion, which is a national emergency infantry force that is held at seventy-two-hour notice to move.

Next to its Apache, the 105-mm Light Guns of 7th Parachute Regiment Royal Horse Artillery (7 RHA) are 16 Brigade's main long-range firepower. The veteran 105-mm gun has been a stalwart of the airborne artillery role since the 1970s and played a vital role in the Falklands war. It is simple, robust and can easily lifted by all the RAF's support helicopters.

These guns can be bought into action in less than a minute of arriving at their firing locations. Although they have a modern computerised aiming system, they still retain their basic dial sights in case they are damaged. The 17.2-kilometre range of the guns is considered a bit short by modern standards.

The Royal Horse Artillery is considered the elite of the Royal Artillery and has had the airborne artillery role since the mid-1980s after the formation of 5 Airborne Brigade. It has three batteries of guns, each with six weapons.

Finding targets for the guns and calling down fire is the job of the regiment's forward observation battery. This has three four- to six-man forward observation officer or FOO teams who are each usually assigned to each of 16 Brigade's airborne and air assault infantry battalions. They move with the forward infantry companies to call for and adjust artillery fire onto targets. The FOOs are supported by what are called 'Tac Groups' led by a Royal Artillery major who is assigned to each infantry battlegroup headquarters to co-ordinate fire support plans with infantry commanders. In 16 Brigade, all its FOOs and Tac Groups are qualified to operate from airborne helicopters. Many of the FOO teams are parachute qualified. An additional Tac Group works within the AH regiment's headquarters.

The FOOs and Tac Groups in turn report back to the fire support co-ordination centre inside Brigade headquarters. This is the nerve centre of fire support operations and also co-ordinates all artillery fire missions with air operations to ensure aircraft and shells do not share the same airspace.

16 Brigade is unique because it has three RAF Regiment Tactical Air Control Parties (TACPs) attached to direct air strikes by fast jets and attack helicopters. These six-man teams contain qualified forward air controllers (FACs) and they are all parachute trained.

To enhance the number of FOOs and FACs available to 16 Brigade a significant number of AAC aircrew are also qualified to call in artillery fire and air strikes. The British Army is in the process of modernising its fire support procedures to dramatically increase the numbers of qualified personnel who can call down artillery and air support. On operations it is currently merging its FOOs and FACs into multi-skilled Fire Support Teams (FSTs).

The ability to bringing offensive air (both fixed wing and attack helicopters) and land-based firepower together in so-called Composite Air Operations (COMAO) is at the heart of being a FST member. They have to be able to understand the ground battle, air weapon effects and at the same time use multiple radios to choreograph aircraft and helicopters to bring them into action at exactly the time required by frontline troops. While the misnamed 'friendly fire' – when aircraft bomb their own troops – is the biggest fear of FST personnel, they also have to balance this with the need to take risks to bring firepower to bear to help frontline troops in close combat with the enemy. For lightly equipped airborne and air assault troops, air power and artillery are often the only means to compensate for their lack of armoured vehicles and other heavy support.

Scimitar Combat Vehicle Reconnaissance (Tracked) (CVR(T))

The CVR(T) is the workhorse of 16 Air Assault Brigade's Formation Reconnaissance Squadron, which is normally provided by the Household Cavalry Regiment (HCR) at Windsor.

It has been in service since the early 1970s but was upgraded during the 2003 Iraq conflict with enhanced armoured protection.

Four basic CVR(T) vehicles are assigned to each troop and each squadron comprises four troops. Recovery, troop carrying, ambulance, command post and repair variants are also used by the HCR. CVR(T) family vehicles can be para-dropped from a C-130 Hercules aircraft or under-slung beneath a Chinook heavy lift helicopter.

Crew: 3
Length: 4.9 m
Height: 2.1 m
Width: 2.24 m
Combat weight: 8,070 kg
Main armament 1 x 30-mm L21 Rarden cannon
Secondary armament: Coaxial 7.62-mm GPMG, smoke grenades
Ammunition carried: 160 rounds of 30 mm, 3,000 rounds of 7.62 mm
Engine: Cummins BTA 5.9 diesel engine developing 190 hp
Max speed: 80 kph

Scimitar Combat Vehicle Reconnaissance (Tracked).
(Tim Ripley)

Boeing Chinook HC.2/2A

The Chinook has been the workhorse of the RAF transport or support helicopter (SH) fleet since the early 1980s. Although the design dates from the late 1950s, the Chinook has been progressively updated and modified.

The RAF updated its aircraft to HC.2/2A standard in the early 1990s and has since installed a number of self-defence systems. Further improvements are planned to allow the helicopter to remain in service for up to thirty years.

The RAF ordered its first Chinooks in 1978 and then topped up its fleet with nine extra aircraft in 1995. It also bought eight HC.3 special forces variants in 1995 but these have yet to enter service.

Engines: Two Textron Lycoming T55-L712F turboshafts
Thrust: 3,148 lb
Max speed: 160 kt
Range: 1,136 km
Max altitude: 15,000 ft
Length: 30.18 m
Span: 18.29 m
Aircrew: 4 + 50 fully armed troops

Boeing Chinook HC.2 heavy-lift helicopter.
(Tim Ripley)

The commanding officer of 7 RHA is known within the Brigade as 'CO Guns'. He controls any fire support from outside the Brigade that might be attached for specific operations. All long-range firepower is grouped within what is known as the Offensive Support Group (OSG) and this is also given control of intelligence, surveillance, targeting and reconnaissance (ISTAR) assets needed to find the enemy. The OSG works closely with RAF air planners inside 16 Brigade's main headquarters to ensure that all types of long-range firepower can rapidly be brought to bear on targets as they emerge.

Within the Brigade there are three main ISTAR units. First is the 16 Brigade Pathfinder Platoon, which is a highly trained 'deep reconnaissance' unit. It is trained and equipped to penetrate deep behind enemy lines to find targets for the Brigade's OSG. It has its origins in 5 Airborne Brigade's Pathfinder Platoon, which was tasked with the marking of drop zones for parachute drops. Today's Pathfinders retain the ability to conduct covert High Altitude Low Opening (HALO) parachute drops *en route*, setting up observation posts far behind enemy lines. Now they also have a fleet of heavily armed WIMK Land Rovers to give them manoeuvrability and range when on the ground. This combination of high speed and heavy firepower means they are often used as the Brigade Commander's reserve, ready to intervene in crisis situations when no other troops are available.

The other specialist reconnaissance unit permanently assigned to 16 Brigade is D Squadron of the Household Cavalry Regiment (HCR). It has the Brigade's only armoured vehicles, in the shape of twenty Scimitar Combat Vehicles Reconnaissance (Tracked) (CVR(T)). These look like tanks and have a turret-mounted 30-mm Rarden cannon. Recently the vehicles have had new thermal imaging night vision cameras fitted, as well as an enhanced armoured package. The Squadron's main task is long-range reconnaissance operating far ahead of the infantry units of the Brigade.

Both the Pathfinders and D Squadron contain a high percentage of FOO and FAC trained personnel in their ranks, so every one of their vehicles is able to call for and direct artillery and air strikes onto targets.

The OSG is a powerful element of 16 Brigade and the fact that so many soldiers within the Brigade are trained and qualified as FOOs and FACs means it is uniquely placed to combine the firepower of land and air power to achieve decisive effect on the battlefield. Without heavy armoured vehicles at its disposal, the ability to rapidly bring firepower to bear is the main way the Brigade can protect its soldiers from the enemy. For this reason it has more than three times as many FAC qualified personnel as other armoured brigades.

The Light Electronic Warfare Team (LEWT) of 237 Signal Squadron (Electronic Warfare) provides EW support for 16 Air Assault Brigade. It is designed to be inserted by parachute very close to the frontline in any operational situation. The Squadron operates advanced equipment to allow it to monitor enemy radio communications. This small and highly mobile team has proved itself time and again on recent operations as one of the best intelligence sources available to Brigade about enemy activity.

The final Royal Artillery element of the Brigade is 21 Battery of 47 Regiment, which is equipped with the Thales High Velocity Missile (HVM) to provide point air defence of key locations. The battery is often re-roled for non-air defence tasks during peacekeeping missions.

The RAF's transport or support helicopters (SH) are an integral part of 16 Brigade,

AgustaWestland Merlin HC.3/3+

The RAF's newest transport or support helicopter (SH) entered service in 2000 and has since seen action in Iraq.

The Merlin was originally developed for use by the UK and Italian navies and has since been been adapted for battlefield use. Its three engines give the Merlin an impressive performance in 'hot and high' conditions.

The Merlin Force is being augmented by six ex-Royal Danish Air Force helicopters.

Engines: Three Rolls-Royce Turbomeca RTM 322 turbines
Thrust: 5,172 kW
Max speed: 167 kt
Max altitude: 15,000 ft
Range: 1,158 km
Length: 22.8 m
Span: 18.6 m
Aircrew: 4 + 30 fully armed troops

AgustaWestland Merlin HC.3. *(Tim Ripley)*

even though they are not formally under its command. Up to 1999, the lack of formal control over RAF support helicopters was also a great bone of contention between the Army and the junior service. The creation of the Joint Helicopter Command (JHC) has largely resolved this problem because it is in charge of both the RAF SH and 16 Brigade. So during routine training, JHC can ensure that the Brigade has its required helicopter support. It is also involved in the force generation process for operations, although tactical employment is up to the joint force commander in theatre.

There are currently three main types of SH in RAF service. The most important is the big Boeing Chinook HC.2. Nicknamed the 'Whooka, Whooka' after its distinctive sound, the tandem rotor Chinook usually carries up to fifty-five fully equipped combat troops or 10 tonnes of cargo but in extreme cases has carried around eighty troops.

Westland Puma HC.1

Known as the 'sports car' of the support helicopter force because of its speed and manoeuvrability, the Puma has been in service since the early 1970s.

Its twin doors mean it is easy for troops and cargo to be quickly loaded and off-loaded in combat situations.

The RAF expects to keep the Puma in service for at least another decade, although it is increasingly rare for the helicopter to be used to support 16 Air Assault Brigade on operations because of the availability of the bigger Chinook and Merlin.

Engines: Two Turbomeca Turmo 3-C4 turbines
Thrust: 2,350 kW
Max speed: 147 kt
Max altitude: 17,000 ft
Range: 572 km
Span: 15.09 ft
Length: 14.08 m
Aircrew: 3 + 16

Westland Puma HC.1. *(Tim Ripley)*

Large loads, such as Land Rovers and trailers, 105-mm Light Guns or pallets of ammunition can be under-slung or the seats can be removed and bulky cargo loaded inside. Although under-slinging limits the performance of the helicopter, it has the advantage of rapid unhooking in combat situations.

For self protection 7.62-mm door mini-guns can be fitted to the fuselage doors and a M60 single machine-gun mounted on the rear ramp. The usual crew is two pilots and two load masters. Most RAF Chinooks have armoured floors and seats, as well as missile defence systems fitted.

The Chinook Force is based at RAF Odiham in Hampshire. Two squadrons, 18 (Bomber) and 27 Squadron, are the main Chinook units assigned to support 16 Brigade. They are in turn each divided into two flights, which are intended to be able to operate eight to ten helicopters for up to four months away from home base. This allows the Chinook Force to sustain a training cycle over extended periods. So at any one time, one

Lockheed Martin Hercules

The Hercules Force operates two variants of the best-selling airlifter. It has nineteen Lockheed (C-130K) Hercules C.1/3 variants, which were purchased in the mid-1960s. An additional twenty-five Lockheed Martin (C-130J) Hercules C.4/5 aircraft were purchased in the late 1990s to replace some of the older K-model aircraft. One was lost in Iraq during 2007. Until a few years ago the bulk of the tactical support work for 16 Brigade was undertaken by the K-model aircraft of 47 and 70 Squadrons. These two squadrons' crews were highly trained to tactical standards to conduct military parachuting of personnel or cargo at low level and at night, as well as to land on unprepared airstrips.

Until 2004, the J-model fleet was not cleared to conduct a full range of tactical missions by flight safety experts at the Ministry of Defence's aviation test centre at Boscombe Down. This process has now been completed and the J-model crews from 24 and 30 Squadrons are taking on the majority of the tactical support work in operational theatres.

(data for C-130J)
Engines: Four Allison AE 2100D3 turboprops
Thrust: 4,700 shp
Max speed: 340 kt
Length: 34.34 m
Max altitude: 32,000 ft
Span: 40.38 m
Aircrew: 3 + up to 128 passengers
Cargo: 20 tons

Lockheed Martin C-130K Hercules. *(Tim Ripley)*

flight will be on operations, one will be preparing to deploy, one recovering after returning home and the fourth is able to support routine training exercises and other commitments in the UK. At any one time twenty-seven Chinooks out of the fleet of forty airframes are available to support UK operations around the world. Up to half a dozen of these are usually dedicated to Special Forces tasks with 7 Squadron.

The AgustaWestland Merlin HC.3 Force has its main base at nearby RAF Benson in Oxfordshire. The twenty-two Merlins are the next largest support helicopter in the UK inventory and one can carry around thirty combat troops. The three-engined Merlin is fast and has good performance in hot-high conditions. The Merlin has been used extensively by 16 Brigade on exercises in the UK but the Brigade has not yet used it on a major operation. The Merlin Force has been committed to operations in Iraq since early 2005.

The Westland Puma HC.1 Force is the smallest RAF support helicopter and it now rarely works with 16 Brigade because of its small size compared with the Merlin and Chinook. The two squadrons, 33 at RAF Benson and 230 at RAF Aldergrove, currently take turns to supply a detachment to support the UK forces conducting combat operations in the Baghdad region.

RAF Odiham and RAF Benson are also home to rapidly deployable command post teams, which are activated when an overseas operation is launched. The two station headquarters both have personnel earmarked to support any deployment by their flying squadrons, depending on the nature of the operation. So, for example, any Chinook 'heavy' operation would most likely be led by the station commander of Odiham. Each station also has a number of mobile air operations teams (MOATs) who are highly trained at running helicopter landing sites and organising helicopter cargo or passengers.

The Hercules Force at RAF Lyneham in Wiltshire provides a vital element of 16 Brigade's air manoeuvre capability. The forty-three C-130 Hercules in RAF service give 16 Brigade its combat theatre entry capability either by parachuting or by *coup de main* operations to seize airfields for use by follow-on forces, known as Tactical Air Land Operations (TALO). They also provide what is known as 'intra-theatre airlift', moving personnel and cargo around operational theatres after they have been delivered to a forward airbase by strategic airlift.

The Hercules Force plays a key part in the LATF concept and, to support it, it has to have fifteen aircraft available at five days' notice. Heavy tasking in the Middle East to support operations in Iraq and Afghanistan since 2006 has meant this has been increasingly difficult to maintain.

To allow the Hercules Force to fly into forward airstrips, the RAF has a parachute-trained element of its Tactical Air Traffic Control Squadron that works closely with 16 Brigade on exercises and operations.

Some 160 RAF Parachute Jump Instructors who run the parachute courses at RAF Brize Norton also have a war role to fly with the LATF, acting as jump masters on Hercules aircraft.

The rigging and dispatch of cargo pallets to be parachuted from C-130s is the job of 47 Air Dispatch Squadron, Royal Logistic Corps, which is forward based at RAF Lyneham.

RAF Boeing C-17 Globemaster II, Lockheed TriStar and Vickers VC-10 aircraft provide the UK's strategic airlift capability. The first aircraft is new to the fleet and can carry outsized cargo into unprepared airfields. It has a drive on-off ramp to allow vehicles and helicopters to be easily loaded. The veteran TriStars and VC-10s are converted airliners and are used predominately to carry passengers, although they can carry cargo pallets if specialist loading equipment is available.

Like other British Army formations, 16 Brigade has its own combat support elements. They, however, have a significant 'slice' that is parachute-trained so the men can jump into action to support the LATF.

The Brigade's Royal Engineer unit, 23 Air Assault Regiment, has combat engineer units. They are trained and equipped to clear battlefield obstacles, such as minefields, and help build force protection bunkers, life support infrastructure such as showers and sewerage, and helicopter fuel storage tanks.

13 Air Assault Logistic Regiment, Royal Logistic Corps, is specially configured to provide all the supplies 16 Brigade needs to operate. This not only includes the usual supplies needed for land operations, such as food, water and ammunition, but the specialist aviation supplies, including fuel, weapons and spare parts, for all the Brigade's helicopters and aircraft. Ensuring all the Brigade's helicopters have enough fuel to fly when and where they are needed is a 'total show stopper'. 13 Regiment has tankers to move fuel up to FARPs or can use rubber fuel bladders that can be under-slung below a Chinook to move fuel to FARPs that cannot be reached by road for terrain or tactical reasons. Likewise, helicopter weapons also need specialist handling to ensure they are moved safely to where they are needed.

The specialist fuel tanker crews of RAF Expeditionary Logistic Wing although not formally part of 16 Brigade, are regularly used to support its operations. Also, the Joint Helicopter Support Unit (JHSU) at RAF Benson regularly works with 13 Regiment to pack and prepare under-slung loads for helicopter movement.

REME's 7 Battalion is a key element of the Brigade during long deployments, repairing all its weapons, vehicles and helicopters in the field.

Medical support for 16 Brigade is provided by Regimental Aid Posts (RAPs) attached to each battlegroup and 16 Close Support Medical Regiment of the Royal Army Medical Corps (RAMC). The task of 16 Regiment is medical evacuation to field hospitals after casualties have been stabilised in RAPs.

The final specialist unit permanently attached to 16 Brigade is 156 Provost Company of the Royal Military Police. This unit's war role is to maintain lines of communications for 16 Brigade, marking routes, organising traffic control around key points and controlling prisoners of war. Like all other elements of the Brigade it has a cadre of parachute-trained personnel. In peacekeeping operations they are often given the task of working with locally recruited law enforcement agencies.

When 16 Air Assault Brigade was formed in 1999 it was configured to what the British Army calls a 'capability golf bag'. Only in very exceptional circumstances was it envisaged that all the Brigade's major units and personnel would deploy *en masse*. The idea was that Permanent Joint Headquarters (PJHQ) and other senior commanders would be able to pick and choose units or specific capabilities to deploy on operations at any given time.

This was to allow some units and capabilities to remain available for unforeseen eventualities. So, for example, when the LATF or Spearhead battalion is deployed, another

The Boeing C-17A Globemaster II is the RAF's primary strategic airlifter. *(Tim Ripley)*

unit is immediately alerted to take its place.

The other important reason was to allow for operations to be sustained over an extended period and allow replacements units and personnel to be rotated out to operational theatres.

CHAPTER 2

British Army and Air Mobility

At dawn on 6 November 1956 the launching of twenty-two Westland Sycamore and Whirlwind helicopters loaded with Royal Marines from the decks of the aircraft carriers HMS *Ocean* and *Theseus* lying off the Egyptian coastline made British military history. The Sycamores were far from ideal machines for troop transport and could only carry three passengers, but the Royal Marines used the helicopters aggressively during the assault on Port Said. One Sycamore took thirty-one bullets and kept flying, proving that helicopters could survive on the battlefield. This was the first ever helicopter-borne air assault operation by British troops and it even pre-dated more famous US air mobility operations in Vietnam by almost a decade.

However, it would be nearly thirty years before the British Army formed its first dedicated air mobile brigade. In the autumn of 2004 the British Army's air mobile or air manoeuvre capability was transformed when its first attack helicopter squadron entered frontline service after achieving initial operating capability. The British Army and RAF's experience of using helicopters to move troops into battle has been long and tortuous. Until the late 1990s it was not even clear if the UK Armed Forces were really serious about fielding a major force capable of using helicopters to bring about a decisive effect on the battlefield.

The 1956 Suez crisis saw the first combat use of helicopters by the UK armed forces. (*Cody Images*)

The Bristol Belvedere was the first heavy-lift helicopter used by the RAF and it saw extensive service in Aden and Borneo during the 1960s. *(Cody Images)*

The British Army and the RAF gained plenty of experience using helicopters to support their colonial counter-insurgency and peacekeeping operations during the 1960s. During the so-called 'End of Empire' conflicts in South Arabia (now Yemen) and Borneo, helicopters played prominent roles, particularly the twin-rotor Bristol Belvedere heavy lift helicopter, the veteran Westland Wessex medium transport helicopter and the small Westland Scout liaison helicopter. During bitter fighting in the Radfan mountains of South Arabia and the trials of Borneo, the RAF's Belvederes played important roles flying supplies and howitzers to remote fire bases. RAF and Royal Navy Wessex helicopters were used to move small groups of troops out on patrol, while the Scouts looked for insurgents and carried commanders to important planning meetings. These helicopters were very advanced for the era. The Belvedere, for example, was one of the first tandem rotor helicopters and could lift 6,000 lb (2,700 kg) of cargo. Like all helicopters of this era, the Belvedere was technically temperamental and required considerable maintenance support. The Wessex and Scout were more robust machines and eventually served through until the early 1990s in the case of the Scout and it was 2002 when the last Wessex was retired.

A major operation in the Radfan mountains in 1964 brought together paratroopers, RAF Belvederes, Royal Navy Wessex helicopters and RAF transport aircraft in a joint mission to defeat rebel tribesman. The operation saw plans for air drops of paratroopers, Special Forces' deep reconnaissance patrols, extensive use of close air support and movement of army units by helicopter.

Although helicopters proved useful in difficult terrain to set up fire bases on high mountain peaks and allowed British forces to out-fight the rebels on numerous occasions, they were not used aggressively to fly large formations of troops into battle. This was the

British Armed Forces' first large-scale air mobile operation and the battlefield use of helicopters showed much potential. It occurred only a few months before the US Army's air cavalry division deployed with hundreds of helicopters to fight in the Vietnam War. The key lesson of these early air mobile operations was that helicopter squadrons need to work closely with ground units on a regular basis to allow both the air and land elements to exploit the unique capabilities of helicopters to maximum effect.

While the Americans persevered with air mobile forces and incorporated them into the US Army permanently after the Vietnam War, the British Armed Forces failed to follow this example. In the aftermath of the withdrawal from east of Suez in the late 1960s, the British began to wind down their battlefield helicopter forces. Problems finding the money needed to buy significant numbers of helicopters and inter-Service rivalry between the Army and the RAF meant that until the 1980s there was little progress forming a specialised air mobile brigade along the lines of the US Army 'air cavalry' forces that proved themselves in the Vietnam War.

At the end of the 1960s the RAF Belvedere squadrons were disbanded and not replaced, while the RAF Wessex squadrons returned to UK and Germany to work only on an ad hoc basis with army units. Only the Royal Navy and Royal Marines learnt the lesson of regular teaming of helicopter and ground units. The Fleet Air Arm's Commando or 'Junglie' helicopter squadrons worked almost exclusively with the Royal Marines' 3 Commando Brigade during the 1960s and 1970s. In the late 1970s the Fleet Air Arm began replacing the Wessex in its Commando squadrons with the more powerful HC.4 variant of the Westland Sea King helicopter. The RAF, however, could not afford to replace all its Wessex with the new Anglo-French designed Westland Puma HC.1 helicopters, and the veteran Wessex served until 2002.

During this period the UK's interest in global intervention operations was minimal. The British Army's only airborne brigade – 16 Independent Parachute Brigade – – was disbanded and the UK's airborne forces were grouped around a single parachute-trained battalion.

There were a number of major exercises in the 1970s, including Sky Warrior in 1972 and Nap Archer in 1975, to develop air mobile concepts. These saw the RAF, Royal Navy and Army Air Corps (AAC) bring together almost every helicopter they could muster to try to come up with some sort of realistic operational concept of operations for using helicopters in combat. The real focus of these efforts were wartime scenarios involving a major conflict between NATO and the Warsaw Pact in central Europe.

This was at the height of the Cold War and the British Army was desperate to find some way to counteract the huge Soviet tank force based in Eastern Germany. Armed helicopters offered a way to bring the large numbers of the new generation of wire-guided anti-tank missiles to bear against the Red Army's tank divisions. These efforts led the British Army Air Corps to buy TOW missile-armed versions of the Westland Lynx AH.7 battlefield helicopter and the British Army was keen to find ways to make the helicopters more effective on future Cold War battlefields.

In 1978, the RAF bought its first Boeing Chinook HC.1 heavy lift or support helicopters to the fill the gap left by the retirement of the Belvedere a decade earlier. The British Army launched a four-year long experiment to trial an air mobile formation, dubbed 6 Airmobile Brigade, in 1983. The troops were only made available for this trial because a major re-organisation of BAOR (British Army of the Rhine) left one brigade without armoured vehicles for a five-year period. Before the brigade could be formed

Britain found itself at war in the South Atlantic.

Although the bulk of the British Army was primarily focused on the Cold War during the 1970s and 1980s, the on-going conflict in Northern Ireland, and the brief war with Argentina over the Falklands in 1982, gave the British Armed Forces' unprecedented exposure to using helicopters in combat operations. At the time, these conflicts were seen largely by the British Army's senior leadership as aberrations that did not inform combat doctrine development or equipment procurement.

The Northern Ireland campaign had a mixed influence on British helicopter operations and procurement during the 1980s. Provisional IRA attacks on road convoys in the so-called 'bandit country' of South Armagh forced the British Army to rely on helicopters to move its troops and supplies around the region. This requirement soaked up several squadrons of RAF and RN helicopters continuously through the 1980s, cutting down considerably the number of rotorcraft available for mainstream air mobility operations and training in Germany. Northern Ireland did, however, expose a large number of army personnel to the giant Chinook, a couple of which were regularly detached for service in the Province. Although there was a number of large battalion-sized operations involving helicopters in Northern Ireland, most helicopter work involved moving only a half a dozen soldiers at a time, on small patrol or vehicle checkpoint tasks, so had limited application to general war scenarios.

One major area where Northern Ireland did influence British helicopter operations was in the development of defensive equipment to counter small arms and manportable surface-to-air missile (MANPAD) systems, which the IRA tried to use against security force helicopters. This led to the development of defensive aid suites and their installation across all the main UK types of battlefield helicopters. This development work meant that during the 1990s, when British helicopters needed such systems for expeditionary operations, there was a significant team of expertise in the UK defence industry to provide them relatively quickly. Perhaps more importantly, it led to a generation of UK military helicopter aircrews gaining invaluable experience of the tactics needed to operate in high threat environments. Year after year, they dodged IRA machine-gun crews and MANPAD teams in South Armagh as they landed their helicopters in Bessbrook Mill and other remote security force bases in South Armagh.

The influence of the Falklands campaign was more mixed. The brief war to eject the Argentine garrison from the South Atlantic islands saw the deployment of around 100 British battlefield helicopters at a time – including eventually one Chinook, around thirty troop-carrying Sea Kings, some fifty Wessex and thirty Scouts and Gazelles. The helicopters played a part in every aspect of the campaign, including inserting Special Forces' teams, logistic support, positioning artillery batteries and air defence weapons, as well as on a handful of occasions direct fire missions with wire-guided missiles. On two occasions helicopters, including the sole Chinook, were used in daring *coup de main* operations to land assault troops directly onto objectives. These were classic air assault missions and were unprecedented in British military experience. The first occasions involved the Special Air Service (SAS) troops during the operation to seize Mount Kent, which dominated the Argentine defensive position outside the capital of the Falklands, Port Stanley. On the second occasion, eighty-one paratroopers were flown by Chinook and Scout helicopters to seize a key bridge on the southern route to Port Stanley. The paratroopers of 5 Infantry Brigade had to 'hijack' Chinook Bravo November from a routine re-supply mission to divert it on a surprise raid to capture Bluff Cove and to open up a new route to Port Stanley. These operations were literally planned on the 'back of a fag packet', to exploit fleeting advantages and 'holes' in the terrible Falklands weather.

To Mount Kent

Chinook Bravo November was immediately put to use moving huge loads of ammunition from the British bridgehead to frontline artillery batteries. Special Air Service (SAS) patrols had occupied Mount Kent, which overlooked the Argentine-occupied capital of the Falklands, Port Stanley. The SAS men were coming under artillery fire and needed reinforcement quickly. Bravo November's co-pilot, Flight Lieutenant Andy Lawless, was called to a briefing with the SAS commander, the famous Lieutenant Colonel Michael Rose, who wanted to make maximum use of the Chinook's lifting power. It was an eye-opener for Lawless, who had never worked with the SAS before. Lawless recalled, 'Rose started asking if we could drop bombs off the rear ramp of the Chinook. "Yes or no?" he asked. The briefing quickly moved from the ridiculous to the sensible.'

> We knew the SAS were outgunned. Our job was to land 105-mm [howitzers] of 29 Regiment Royal Artillery. Rose told me the landing site was flat and secure. The mission was to be flown all at night with night-vision goggles. We had three 105-mm guns inside and ammunition pallets under-slung.
>
> Then the fog of war intervened. The ground was not flat and covered in boulders. We could not find anywhere to land and we spent time manoeuvring to drop off the under-slung loads. We had to put them exactly where the gunners wanted because they could not roll the guns very far across the terrible terrain. I can distinctly remember troops moving under the rotor disking firing their guns – this was not part of the plan. There were incoming artillery rounds. Once we dropped off the guns we went straight back to San Carlos to bring in more guns and ammo.

The surviving Chinook, call sign Bravo November, played a vital role moving British troops up to the frontlines outside Port Stanley.
(Andy Lawless)

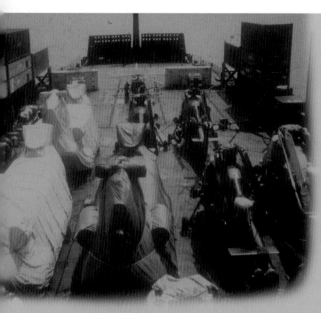

Only one RAF Chinook helicopter survived the loss of the SS *Atlantic Conveyer* in May 1982 during the height of the Falklands war. *(Andy Lawless)*

If that was not eventful enough, Lawless and his pilot, Dick Langworthy, soon found themselves flying into a snowstorm and then their night-vision goggles began to fail. Lawless recalled:

Then we hit water. We were lucky because if we had hit solid ground we would have been dead. We hit at 100 knots. The bow wave came over the cockpit window as we settled and the engines partially flamed out. I knew we had ditched but I was not sure if we had been hit. Dick said he thought we had been hit by ground fire. As the helicopter settled the bow wave reduced. We had the collective still up and the engine wound up as we came out of the water like a cork out of a bottle. We were climbing.

Bravo November held together and managed to get back to base. Its radio antenna had been ripped off, the autopilot had long failed, there were holes in the fuselage and the cockpit door was missing. Lawless recalled that the helicopter was gradually falling to bits and the lack of specialist lubricants meant its engine and gearbox were always in danger of failing. 'We used and abused it – peacetime constraints went out the window.'

In the aftermath of the Falklands, the British Army and RAF hierarchies did not rush to form additional air mobile forces. The newly introduced Chinook fleet was still split between supporting the RAF Harrier Force, Northern Ireland tasks, general army logistic support and supporting the new air mobile brigade. In 1983 the capabilities of the Chinook Force were demonstrated when three helicopters successfully airlifted an army armoured reconnaissance squadron from Lebanon to Cyprus, when the squadron in Beirut was threatened by Islamic suicide bombers.

The British Army did reform 5 Infantry Brigade as 5 Airborne Brigade as the UK's strategic intervention force, with responsibility for planning operations outside the main NATO area in central Europe. It contained one of the Parachute Regiment's three regular battalions but was focused on airborne operations by parachute rather than air mobility using helicopters.

For the Royal Marines, the Falklands confirmed their policy of dedicating the Fleet Air Arm's commando helicopter squadrons to support 3 Commando Brigade. One area where the RAF did make a move towards dedicating helicopters to support specific grounds units was in the world of special forces, with the formation of a dedicated flight-sized unit within the RAF's 7 Squadron to fly Chinooks in support the SAS. This small elite Chinook aircrew had a disproportionate impact on the development of air mobility in the UK

The Lynx was the AAC's primary anti-tank helicopter when armed with TOW wire-guided anti-tank missiles. *(Tim Ripley)*

Armed Forces. Throughout the 1980s, it pioneered the development of long-range night flying tactics in the Chinook and honed air assault tactics with the UK Special Forces community. Later in their careers, the RAF Chinook aircrew from this small team would rise to prominence in the Joint Helicopter Command from 1999 and in 16 Air Assault Brigade. Also, many of the young SAS officers who worked with 7 Squadron's Special Forces Chinook Flight would also eventually help found 16 Brigade and then play important roles in its combat operations. During this time the value of working on a regular basis with the same helicopter crews was learnt in spades by the young SAS officers. Only by building a bond of trust with their supporting aircrew could the SAS officers and troops come to rely on them to provide support during daring helicopter-borne missions behind enemy lines.

During the mid-1980s, the newly formed 6 Airmobile Brigade took part in a series of major BAOR exercises in Germany. At the heart of British Army air mobile thinking at the time was using RAF Chinook helicopters to react to Soviet armoured thrusts by rapidly deploying anti-tank missile teams to set up blocking positions. The 6 Airmobile Brigade was in effect the anti-tank reserve of the BAOR. In a series of exercises it tested the concept of setting up 'killing zones' of helicopter-borne infantry missile teams and TOW missile-armed Lynx helicopters to blunt Soviet tank spearheads. Unlike the Americans, the British at this point did not envisage using their helicopters to 'fight through' enemy air defences to strike high value targets behind enemy lines. At this time the bulk of British military helicopters was not equipped with defensive systems or the long-range radios to allow them to fly beyond what was termed the 'forward line of troops' or FLOT into enemy-controlled airspace, let alone conduct deep strike missions.

6 Airmobile Brigade on Exercise

6 Airmobile Brigade's concept of operations involved it deploying to a reserve position behind the main BAOR defensive line. Once the Soviet main effort of attack had been identified, reconnaissance teams would deploy by helicopter to scout out the best place to set up the main 6 Brigade blocking position. Then RAF Chinooks and Pumas would fly in the main infantry battalions, each of which had forty-two Milan wire-guided missile teams assigned to them, to prepare defensive positions. To stand any chance of survival from Soviet artillery fire, the air mobile infantry battalions needed at least twenty-four hours in their positions to allow them to dig firing trenches with overhead protection. One participant described how 6 Brigade exercises during this period did not involve much flying in helicopters, but long periods of digging trenches. The Brigade's main infantry fighting position was usually sited on ridge lines to give the Milan teams good fields of fire. It also meant the Lynx helicopter crews could use the high ground to shield them from view. They could then pop-up from behind cover to join the missile barrage against the Soviet tank armada. Not surprisingly, the employment of 6 Brigade was considered a 'one-shot' weapon. Once it was in position on the battlefield, its missile teams had limited mobility and when battle was joined by a Soviet tank force, British Army commanders clearly expected the Brigade to go down fighting to buy time for heavy armoured forces to mass and mount an effective counter-attack and drive back the Soviets. The Brigade was jokingly called a 'speed bump' for Red Army tanks.

RAF Westland Puma HC.1 helicopters provided troop lift for the anti-tank teams of 6 Airmobile Brigade during the mid-1980s. *(Private Collection)*

Even with its obvious limitations, the air mobile experiment was judged a success and in 1988 a brigade based at Catterick in North Yorkshire was converted as a permanent air mobile formation. Crucially, 6 Brigade and its successor, 24 Brigade, had no direct 'day-to-day' command of the RAF support helicopters, which were needed to move its troops around the battlefield. The RAF had resisted every move to place its support helicopters under direct day-to-day command of 6 Brigade, fearing that they would not be available to support the field operations of the RAF Harrier Force in Germany or general logistic tasks. Under RAF war plans, its Harrier jump jet squadrons in Germany were to move into hide locations in forests and farms close to the Iron Curtain to allow the Harriers to provide close air support for frontline troops. The Chinook Force was earmarked to move much of the fuel and arms needed to keep the Harriers fighting from the field locations. The army logistic support mission was considered very important by senior army commanders, who said helicopters were needed to rapidly move vital war stocks of ammunition, nuclear warheads and air defence missile batteries into position in case of a surprise Soviet assault across the Iron Curtain. RAF helicopters were also a vital part of the casualty evacuation chain to rapidly move wounded soldiers from the frontline to field hospitals. The RAF did form a special field command post, dubbed the Support Helicopter Force (SHF) Headquarters, in 1988 at RAF Gutersloh. This would provide an important link between the RAF helicopter crews and army commanders, but it was very much a tactical headquarters to work with 6 Brigade and did not have input into operational or strategic level planning in army divisional or corps headquarters.

Also, the British Army's arms plot policy of moving infantry battalions around every two or three years meant the infantry units assigned to 6 Brigade, and later 24 Brigade, had to be continuously retrained every time they joined the formation, so it was difficult to build up a pool of expertise and experience of working with helicopters. The need to draft infantry units to Northern Ireland for six-month emergency tours drew heavily on 6 and 24 Brigade's infantry battalions and meant there were long periods when it could not train for its air mobile role. This fuelled the view of senior RAF officers that it was a waste of resources to assign helicopters to work with the Brigade on a permanent basis.

The Iraqi invasion of Kuwait in August 1990 and the subsequent massing of Coalition forces in Saudi Arabia, led to the largest deployment of British military helicopters to date. The Army Air Corps sent a full anti-tank regiment to be an offensive element of 1 (UK) Armoured Division to Saudi Arabia. 4 Regiment AAC, with 654, 659 and 661 Squadrons attached, took twenty-four Lynx AH.7 TOW missile-armed helicopters and twenty-four Westland Gazelle AH.1 reconnaissance helicopters. A large support helicopter force was formed under the command of the RAF SHF Headquarters to provide logistic support to the British division. It boasted fifteen Chinooks, nineteen Pumas and eighteen Royal Navy Sea King HC.4s.

The British deployment to Saudi Arabia was predominately a tank-heavy operation, and little consideration was given to airborne or air mobile operations. 5 Airborne Brigade's paratroopers had to kick their heels in Aldershot as the US 82 Airborne and 101st Air Assault Divisions spearheaded the US rapid deployment to Saudi Arabia in August and September 1990. As war planning for the operation to liberate Kuwait ramped up in late 1990, the British Army high command concentrated on building up its tank forces for a head-on clash with Saddam Hussein's Republican Guard armoured divisions. The daring moves out into the desert to cut off Iraqi forces in Kuwait were left to the

The veteran Westland Scout AH.1 served in the AAC through to the early 1990s. *(Tim Ripley*

American and French air mobile forces. The British helicopter forces were almost totally dedicated to providing logistic support for the British ground force. They spent the brief '100 hour land war' flying supplies forward and evacuating casualties. This was a very conservative employment for the largest ever concentration of British battlefield helicopters.

The first combat operations by British helicopters were conducted by Special Forces Chinooks of 7 Squadron who flew SAS teams behind Iraqi lines as part of the famous 'Scud Hunt' in the first days of the air campaign in January 1991. A handful of anti-tank engagements were conducted by 4 Regiment AAC in support of 1 (UK) Division's advance into southern Iraq, but heavy rain and low cloud severely hindered its operations. The first ever engagement by a British TOW-armed helicopter occurred on 26 February 1991 when a Lynx of 654 Squadron AAC, supporting 7 Armoured Brigade's attack on Objective Platinum, destroyed two MTLB-armoured personnel carriers and four T-55 tanks with TOW missiles.

The finale of the war as far as the UK helicopter force was concerned took place in the UK Embassy in Kuwait City when Special Boat Service (SBS) troops fast-roped into the building to raise the Union flag over the liberated city.

Only a few weeks later, the RAF and Royal Navy's support helicopter units found themselves at the centre of a more dramatic operation in the mountains of northern Iraq. In response to Iraqi attacks on Kurdish civilians, hundreds of thousands of refugees fled to the mountains astride the Iraq–Turkish border. This inhospitable terrain meant helicopters were the only way US-led coalition forces could move rapidly to set up a 'safe haven' to protect the Kurds from Saddam Hussein's troops. At the heart of Operation Haven was 3 Commando Brigade, supported by its commando Sea King squadrons and a contingent of RAF Chinooks, with crews drawn from the training organisation at RAF Odiham. The helicopters flew British troops into the hills to set up defensive positions and establish drop zones for humanitarian aid. The operation was a dramatic success and soon the Kurds were heading home. Thousands of lives had been saved and not a single shot had been fired by British or US troops. More importantly, it was perhaps the first military operation of the 'new world order' in the aftermath of the fall of the Berlin war. The next decade would see a series of similar operations to deliver humanitarian aid and impose peace.

The end of the Cold War and the dramatic performance of US Army McDonnell Douglas (now Boeing) AH-64A Apache attack helicopters during deep attack missions during the 1991 Gulf War set in train a revolution in British Army thinking about air mobile operations.

US Army Apache helicopters destroyed approximately 500 Iraq tanks, 120 artillery pieces, 120 armoured personnel carriers, 300 trucks and thirty air defence sites during Operation Desert Storm, which convinced the British Army that it needed a similar capability. In the early summer of 1991, the United Kingdom Ministry of Defence formally endorsed Staff Target (Air) 428 for an attack helicopter, which set in train the procurement process that eventually led to the purchasing of Britain's Apaches.

Troop transport remained a task of the RAF Westland Wessex HC.2 until the late 1990s. *(Tim Ripley*

These were still primarily seen as anti-tank weapons and a major element of the case for buying the helicopters was a study in the late 1980s into the British Army's anti-tank weapon mix. The British had first been exposed to the US Army Apache during the late 1980s during NATO exercises and were hugely impressed by its night attack capabilities with the laser-guided Hellfire missile. However, at the time, this was not enough to shift spending priorities in the British Army during the mid-1980s. During this period, the British Army placed major orders for new tanks, armoured vehicles and self-propelled artillery. There were no major orders for new battlefield helicopters in the 1980s except for the purchase of twenty-four unarmed utility Lynx AH.9s for 24 Brigade.

Two years later an invitation to tender was issued, sparking a competition between the world's helicopter manufacturers for the prize of supplying some ninety-one advanced attack helicopters to the British Army. For budgetary reasons the size of the purchase was later reduced to sixty-seven helicopters.

McDonnell Douglas offered its AH-64D version helicopter fitted with the Martin-Marietta (now Lockheed Martin's Orlando business unit) Longbow millimetre wave radar that allowed it to detect targets in rain and bad weather. The helicopters were to be assembled by Britain's only helicopter company, the then GKN subsidiary GKN-Westland Helicopters Ltd of Yeovil (now Italian-owned AgustaWestland). Bell Helicopters Textron teamed with GEC-Marconi to propose a British-built version of the AH-1W Cobra gunship then in service with the US Marine Corps, with the UK-assembled version dubbed the Cobra Venom. British Aerospace (now BAE Systems) and Eurocopter joined forces to offer the Tiger gunship. South Africa's Denel entered the fray teamed with Marshall's of Cambridge to offer the Kestrel/Rooivalk gunship. Italy's Agusta offered its A129 Mengusta and the Boeing/Sikorsky team put their RAH-66 Comanche into the fray. An outsider that never got formally into the contest was the Russian Kamov Ka-50.

The Chinook became the workhorse of the RAF's battlefield helicopters force during the 1980s. *(Tim Ripley)*

An additional twenty-four Westland Lynx AH.9s were purchased in the late 1980s to provide additional mobility for 24 Airmobile Brigade's anti-tank missile teams. *(Westland Helicopters)*

The contest was noted for high-profile sales stunts and over-the-top lobbying but it was clear that the British Army only wanted Apaches and some observers suggested that the staff requirement was actually written in such a way that the Apache was bound to win. For example, only the Apache boasted the adverse weather attack capability offered by its millimetre wave radar. The inclusion of Rolls-Royce in the Westland-McDonnell Douglas team was also an astute move because the company's lobbying power is renowned in Whitehall, particularly within both the Ministry of Defence and the then Department for Trade and Industry.

In one of his first acts after being appointed UK Defence Secretary, Michael Portillo oversaw the selection of the Apache in July 1995 and contracting of the deal in April 1996. Westland Helicopters won the prime contractorship to deliver sixty-seven helicopters, and Rolls-Royce was selected to supply the engines, giving the deal a high 'made in Britain' content. The programme was now no longer an 'off the shelf' purchase and this would impact at a later date as the contractors ran into problems developing and delivering many of the complex 'UK only' elements.

The early 1990s was a period of major upheaval in the British Army as it coped with the aftermath of the collapse of the Berlin Wall and the end of the Cold War. UK defence spending was cut back, while the defence budget and the size of the army were both cut by a third. This culminated in the 1992 Options for Change defence spending cuts programme, which envisaged a major withdrawal of British forces from Germany and the establishment of what was termed 'capability-based' armed forces. No longer would the

RAF Chinooks were relegated to logistic support tasks during the 1991 Gulf war. *Andy Lawless)*

The US Army's aggressive use of McDonnell Douglas AH-64As in the 1991 Gulf war convinced the British Army that it needed a modern attack helicopter force. *(US DoD)*

British military be specifically tailored to solely fight the Red Army but would have to field a range of generic capabilities to enable it to deal with a variety of potential opponents and scenarios, known as 'contingent operations'. Direct threats to the UK homeland or our major NATO allies were declared to be minimal and future operations would have to deal with incidents far from home.

For the British Army's air mobile brigade it brought mixed news. Its place in the British Army's order of battle was confirmed and it was envisaged that it would eventually take control of the bulk of the new Apache Force. This good news was balanced with the fact that the Brigade was to relocate from Catterick to Colchester and a handful of the Brigade's staff or major units would move with it. The army's redundancy programme also meant many experienced officers and senior non-commissioned officers were lost, creating a period of great disruption throughout the army – not just in 24 Brigade. Many of its infantry units would continue to have to provide manpower for Northern Ireland tours. This was also the case with the Brigade's Army Air Corps squadrons and for its RAF support helicopter units.

At the same time, 24 Brigade's role was for it to be transformed into a more wide-ranging formation capable of projecting its fighting troops by air over some 120 kilometres at short notice. The anti-tank 'speed bump' concept was history and the British Army's air mobile force was now considered as an offensive capability. The Kurdish relief operation was seen as the kind of mission the British Armed Forces needed to be prepared for in the coming decade, rather than the tank battles of the 1991 Gulf war. Unfortunately, the British Army's ambitious plans for 24 Brigade were not matched by the required level of funding. Although an upgrade was ordered for the RAF's Chinooks in the 1990s, the Apaches were not actually ordered until 1996 and they would not be scheduled to enter service for another five years. New Westland Merlin HC.3 support helicopters and additional Chinooks were not ordered until 1995.

All this meant that during the first half of the 1990s, 24 Brigade was struggling to move to Colchester, re-organise and re-train itself for its new role, whilst at the same time continuing to provide manpower and helicopters for the ongoing conflict in Northern Ireland.

After a good start in the 1960s, the British Armed Forces failed to capitalise on the battlefield potential of the helicopter to the same degree as the US and other armies. The exceptions were the Special Forces and the amphibious forces of the Royal Navy and Royal Marines, which continued to closely integrate their helicopters and ground units. However, the British Army and RAF had other priorities during the 1970s and 1980s. For the army, its primary focus was building up its armoured forces in central Europe to confront the tank divisions of the Warsaw Pact. Its secondary effort was the on-going conflict in Northern Ireland. The Army Air Corps was pre-occupied with its anti-tank mission. Even though the British Army said anti-tank operations were its primary procurement priority in the 1980s, purchases of new tanks took place ahead of the replacement of the Lynx helicopters with more modern Apaches. The Parachute Regiment and 5 Airborne Brigade were given an 'out-of-area' rapid reaction role but this had little to do with the army and RAF's helicopter forces, concentrating instead on honing their parachuting tactics and skills.

In the RAF, budget pressures in the 1970s and 1980s meant there was little money to spare to buy large quantities of modern helicopters and the veteran Wessex soldiered on until the early 2000s. The purchase of the Chinook fleet in 1978 was a major boost but this was not matched by any major innovation in the way the helicopters were used on the battlefield, outside the small Special Forces' community during the mid and late 1980s.

At the heart of these problems was the lack of a high-level champion for battlefield helicopters to pull together all the divergent tactics, procedures, budget and procurement plans, logistic support, command and control, training and readiness standards for the British Army, RAF, Royal Navy, Royal Marines and Special Forces. While some parts of the British Armed Forces were very advanced and innovative in their use of helicopters, the British Army and the RAF had very conservative attitudes to the employment of helicopters on the battlefield. The 1980s was a period of three steps forward, two steps back in terms of the British use of battlefield helicopters. The late 1990s would see a revolution.

CHAPTER 3

24 Airmobile Brigade to Bosnia

The media called it the 'United Nation's Apocalypse Now Moment', after the famous Vietnam war movie. Along the Adriatic Coast the swarm of helicopters could be seen far in the distance. The rows of television crews and news photographers swung to catch the helicopters of 3 Regiment Army Air Corps approaching their landing spots.

As the first Lynx helicopter landed a huge dust cloud enveloped the landing zone. One by one, marshallers directed the helicopters around the large landing zone to their individual positions. Refuelling teams then moved into action. It seemed as if the whole camp of more than 4,000 soldiers had turned out to watch the arrival of the helicopters. Senior officers stood by to meet the commanders of 3 Regiment, as they emerged from their cramped helicopters. 24 Airmobile Brigade was now ready for action.

THE FORMER YUGOSLAVIA THEATRE OF OPERATIONS 1995

British Army Westland Lynx AH.9 light utility helicopters arrive at Ploce in Croatia at the height of the Bosnian war in August 1995. (*Tim Ripley*)

AAC Lynx AH.7s flew into the heart of the Bosnian conflict in early 1995 in support of the UN Protection Force. *(Tim Ripley)*

Britain's military involvement in the Bosnian conflict from 1992 was the first major test of the UK's post-Cold War defence strategy. Even as the first troops of the Cheshire Regiment, under the command of the redoubtable Lieutenant Colonel Bob Stewart, were pushing into central Bosnia in October 1992 to try to deliver humanitarian aid, the limits of Britain's military capabilities were becoming apparent. When the Bosnian conflict escalated in the summer of 1995, the shortcomings in Britain's power projection and air mobile capabilities became all too apparent. The RAF lacked the necessary heavy lift aircraft to move 24 Airmobile Brigade to the Balkans, so it took almost three months for the Brigade to deploy to Croatia as part of the UN Rapid Reaction Force by American ships and aircraft. Once in theatre, the Brigade found it lacked vital communications and logistic support to operate across the ethnic frontlines and protect UN peacekeepers trapped in so-called 'safe areas' behind Serb lines. The Army Air Corps and RAF also found themselves desperately short of defensive aid suites (DAS) to protect all their helicopters from manportable surface to air missiles or MANPADs.

Since 1991 Serb, Muslin and Croat forces had been waging a brutal war across much of the former Yugoslavia, which led to the coining of the phrase 'ethnic cleansing' to describe their tactic of murdering or evicting members of rival ethnic groups. UN troops

USAF Lockheed C-141 Starlifter aircraft carried 24 Airmobile Brigade's personnel to Bosnia in the summer of 1995. *(Tim Ripley)*

attempted to deliver humanitarian supplies during this mayhem with varying degrees of success but their weak mandate and lack of heavy weapons meant they were often reduced to bystanders to cold-blooded murder.

How to rescue the Cheshire Regiment if it was threatened with being overwhelmed by troops of the three warring factions was a continuous concern of the Ministry of Defence in London. An amphibious force with pre-positioned equipment, including a 105-mm Light Gun artillery battery, was dispatched to the Adriatic in the spring of 1993. Over the next two years Britain's involvement in UN-led peacekeeping and humanitarian operations in Bosnia escalated and by May 1995, the British Army had a brigade of some 5,000 troops in the war-ravaged country. The UK was leading the United Nations Protection Force (UNPROFOR) from its headquarters in Sarajevo.

In May 1995, the 400-strong British garrison in the so-called 'safe area' of Gorazde, 30 miles to the east of Sarajevo, was isolated behind the Serb frontlines. It had the impossible task of protecting the largely Muslim population of the enclave but lacked heavy armour or artillery. Crucially, the supply lines of the 1st Battalion, The Royal Welch Fusiliers, ran through Serb territory making them very vulnerable to the whims of the Serb military strong man General Ratko Mladic. His troops regularly delayed British convoys and during searches for prohibited material seized any items that took their fancy. Helicopter flights into the enclave were also controlled closely by the Serbs and UN helicopters had to land in Serb territory to be searched before they could proceed into Gorazde. The enclave could be easily targeted by Serb artillery so unauthorised flights were not really an option unless the UN was prepared to ask NATO to provide a huge armada of escort strike aircraft to suppress any opposition. Up to the summer of 1995 the UN's policy was to stay neutral in the conflict and work with both sides to try to deliver humanitarian aid.

The Serbs were not the only problem for the UN force in the enclave. Gorazde's Muslim garrison was prone to try to provoke the Serbs and had also threatened to use the UN troops as human shields if they tried to withdraw and leave them to the mercy of the Serbs.

When the war dramatically escalated after a NATO air strike on a Serbian ammunition dump near the Bosnian capital Sarajevo, at the end of May 1995, hundreds of UN troops were taken hostage by the Bosnia Serb Army (BSA). This included thirty-three Welch Fusiliers from the Gorazde garrison.

The British Government of Prime Minister John Major reacted angrily to this incident and ordered the reinforcement of its UN contingent in Bosnia. Some 5,500 extra troops would be sent, including the bulk of 24 Airmobile Brigade. It was envisaged that the Brigade could rapidly move to reinforce or withdraw isolated UN garrisons in the 'safe areas', with its complement of around forty helicopters.

After talks with the French and the UN, it was decided to group the extra British reinforcement into what became known as the UN Rapid Reaction Force or RRF. This was to be mandated to use force to go to the rescue or assistance of UN troops under attack in

The arrival of AAC Lynx helicopters at Ploce provided 24 Brigade with its main combat power. *(Tim Ripley)*

Lynx utility helicopters of 3 Regiment AAC flew across Europe to join the UN Rapid Reaction Force at Ploce in Croatia. *(Tim Ripley)*

Bosnia. The RRF would eventually have two brigades. One French-led formation was dubbed the Multi-National Brigade (MNB). It was an armoured unit with heavy infantry fighting vehicles and self-propelled artillery. The other element of the RRF was to be the UK's 24 Brigade. To emphasise the combat nature of the RRF its vehicles and helicopters were not to be painted in traditional UN white but were to remain camouflaged. The 'green' or combat RRF elements of the UN tried to separate themselves from the peacekeeping or 'white' elements of UNPROFOR because the French and British governments had yet to commit themselves to military action in Bosnia.

The MNB was quickly formed from British troops of the Devonshire & Dorset Regiment already in Bosnia and newly arrived French Foreign Legion units. The RRF would be commanded from UN headquarters in the Croat capital, Zagreb, until it was ready to move into action inside Bosnia.

While the MNB was slowly getting its act together in central Bosnia during June and early July, the major British contribution to the RRF, 24 Airmobile Brigade, was still kicking its heels back at Colchester, Essex. It had been involved in early 1995 in various contingency planning exercises to take part in the NATO withdrawal plan or support the former UN President Jimmy Carter Cessation of Hostilities Agreement but actually getting to Bosnia was to prove its most difficult task.

As June progressed, it became increasingly obvious that the deployment of 24 Brigade was running into serious problems. The Croats were being very obstructive in retaliation for the behaviour of the French Foreign Legion at Ploce on the Adriatic coast, where the Brigade was to establish its main operating base. Their hosts demanded at least three weeks' notice of troop arrivals, either by plane or ship, and only a couple of flights were allowed to land at Split airport each day. The Croats claimed they did not want to interrupt their tourist traffic. UN and British engineers soon found themselves locked in hours of fruitless negotiations with the port authorities at Ploce over plans to turn it into a base for 24 Brigade's thirty-nine helicopters, 1,718 vehicles and 4,700 troops. Large amounts of money were involved and the Croats wanted to maximise their profit. 'The Croats were bloody awful and wanted to make a lot of money,' commented UK Chief of Defence Staff, Field Marshal Sir Peter Inge.

According to RRF planners in Zagreb, the Croats were also trying to delay the arrival of 24 Brigade until after the conclusion of their own impending offensive against the Serb-controlled Krajina region. 'The Croats were happy with the MNB going to Sarajevo because it suited their purposes, but the ability of 24 Brigade to jump around really worried them,' said RRF planner, Parachute Regiment Lieutenant Colonel Simon Barry.

'I was aware of the Machiavellian accusations being made against the Croats,' recalled Brigadier Robin Brims, 24 Brigade's commander. 'My job as tactical commander was not to get involved [in the discussions with the Croats] on "white" 1st Echelon issues.' It is also clear that the imminent arrival of the Brigade was not generating excitement in UNPROFOR in Bosnia. After requesting armoured reinforcements at the height of the hostage crisis in late May, the commander of British Forces in Bosnia, Brigadier Andrew Pringle, was surprised to hear that 24 Brigade had been selected to go to Bosnia. 'I asked why it was being sent and all they could tell me was "because the Prime Minister said it is going". Once it had been announced there was no going back.'

However, the Brigade's infantry lacked armoured vehicles for protection against mines or artillery fire. Once landed, they would be very vulnerable and could have suffered heavy casualties. Sustaining the Brigade's helicopters would also be very difficult if forward refuelling bases could not be established inside Bosnia. Its helicopters lacked many of the defensive systems needed to operate in high-threat environments and it took time to get them fitted. There was a shortage of satellite communications equipment to allow the Brigade's troops to operate in Bosnia's mountainous interior. Perhaps most crucially, the Brigade fuel tankers were not four-wheel drive vehicles so they could not operate off road. This potentially limited where forward arming and refuelling points (FARPS) could be established to support long-range missions.

The British commander of UNPROFOR, Lieutenant General Rupert Smith, could only see limited use for the Brigade in a withdrawal of troops from the enclaves. At the same time in Britain, planners at the Joint Headquarters at Wilton and the Directorate of Special Forces in London were developing rival plans that utilised paratroopers and the SAS to extract the Gorazde garrison from its precarious position. Brims and Pringle toured Bosnia on a reconnaissance in June and reported back to the Commander-in-Chief of the British Army's Land Command, General Sir John Wilsey, that the air mobile force would have little use as part of the RRF. Its helicopters might be useful to rescue the Gorazde garrison, but the other elements of the Brigade had little use in humanitarian operations. If there were no change to UNPROFOR's humanitarian mandate, then the Brigade would have no staying power or armour to protect itself. Pringle, however, reported that it would be an excellent warfighting force. In June 1995, this option was not on the agenda. Meanwhile, the RRF Planning Cell in Zagreb was also questioning the deployment of 24 Brigade. It was concerned that its personnel were not trained or equipped to operate in the extreme conditions of the coming Balkan winter and suggested that a smaller force of arctic-warfare trained Royal Marine Commandos and Royal Navy assault helicopters be sent. This small force could also be found a home in existing UN bases in Bosnia, unlike 24 Brigade, which would require huge new facilities. In June, there was still no certainty that the Muslims and Bosnian Croats would give up any more real estate to the UN to allow 24 Brigade to be based in Bosnia.

24 Airmobile Brigade, August 1995

Ploce Dockyard Camp
Brigade Headquarters and 210 Signal Squadron
 Det 2 Signals Regiment (Ptarmigan radio links)
 Det 30 Signals Regiment (Satellite Communications) (UK)
 Brigade Provost Unit, 156 Provost Unit, RMP
 19 Field Ambulance, RAMC

Force Artillery HQ
 19/5 Battery, RA (6 x 105-mm Light Gun)
 21 (Gibralter 1779-83) Battery, 47 Regiment, RA (HVM)

RAF Support Helicopter Force
 6 x Chinook HC.Mk 2, 6 x Puma HC.Mk 1 helicopters
 1 Field Squadron, RAF Regiment
 21 Signals Regiment (Air Support)
 244 Signals Squadron
 Mobile Air Operations Teams (MOATs)

1st Battalion, The Royal Anglian Regiment (Task Force Charlie)

3 Regiment, Army Air Corps (Task Force Delta)
 662, 663, 653 Squadrons, 9 x Lynx AH.Mk 7, 9 x Lynx AH.Mk 9,
 9 x Gazelle AH.Mk 1 helicopters
 72 Aircraft Workshop, REME

132 Aviation Support Workshop, REME

35 Engineer Regiment Group, RE
 44 Headquarters Squadron
 51, 37, 42 Field Squadrons
 45 Field Support Squadron
 522 STRE
 REME Workshop

24 Airmobile Combat Service Support Battalion, RLC
 HQ Squadron
 15 Logistic Support Squadron
 8 Field Workshop
 80 Postal and Courier Squadron, RLC

Total 4,700 personnel

Not surprisingly, Brims was enthusiastic about his Brigade's capabilities.

Our mission when we deployed was to be a contingency reaction force. We were ideal for the job because of the way we were developing air mobility. We could move into an area, do a job, and get out. It would not have involved holding ground for the sake of it. That job was better suited to the armoured forces. We had moved on from our Cold War 'speed bumps' concept of using air mobile forces. We were going to use air mobility to conduct raids, leap-frogging around supported by fire bases to give us the necessary range. This did not involve everything in the Brigade – you might just send two men.

In spite of the doubts coming from the men on the ground, the British Ministry of Defence stuck to its guns. No matter how long it took or how much it cost, 24 Brigade would be going to Croatia. The Americans were eventually persuaded to provide giant Lockheed C-5 Galaxy and C-141 Starlifter aircraft and Military Sealift Command ships, *Cape Race* and *Cape Diamond*, to move the Brigade to Croatia. The bad news was that the Brigade could not start arriving in Ploce until mid-July and would not be completely deployed for at least a month. Operation Quick Lift began on 3 July 1995, with USAF aircraft flying some sixty missions to move the Brigade to Split. The Pentagon picked up the $15 million bill. The first 24 Brigade helicopters were not flown out to Ploce until the first week of August.

General Smith was still unsure which way things would develop after the fall of the Srebrenica enclave in eastern Bosnia during the second week of July to Serb troops and the announcement at the subsequent London Conference that NATO air power would be used to defend Gorazde and the other 'safe areas' in the event of a Serb attack.

In the aftermath of Srebrenica and Zepa falling to the Serbs and the fall of Krajina to Croat forces, the UN 'white' forces were heavily pre-occupied coping with the massive movements of refugees, including 30,000 Muslims in Bosnia. More than 180,000 Serbs were on the move through north-western Bosnia and Croatia, heading for Serbia. An emergency aid airlift to Banja Luka was organised by the UN High Commissioner for Refugees (UNHCR) with chartered Ilyushin Il-76 transports from Ancona, in Italy, and RAF Chinook helicopters of 24 Brigade temporarily based in Zagreb. This was the first mission of the Brigade's helicopters and they were temporarily painted white for the mission.

The withdrawal of the UN garrison from Gorazde was to dominate the British agenda during August 1995. They were the last UN troops left behind Bosnian Serb lines, except for the Russians in Sarajevo, who were treated as 'fraternal allies' by the Serbs. The London Conference had put some backbone into the western position and perhaps made Mladic think twice about a direct attack. This did not, however, solve the problem of how to actually get the Royal Welch Fusiliers out in the face of opposition from the Muslims and Serbs who both might want to use the UN soldiers, respectively, as human shields or hostages. Air strikes might have kept Mladic's army at bay, but they would be of little use against crowds of women and children trying to pull British soldiers out of their vehicles.

On 8 August, Field Marshal Inge flew out to the UN base at Split on Croatia's Adriatic coast to meet British field commanders to find a way to get the Welch Fusiliers out of Gorazde. 'During my time as CDS [Chief of Defence Staff] my worst worry was that British soldiers in Gorazde would be put to the sword,' said Inge.

Brigadier Robin Brims, Commander of 24 Airmobile Brigade. *(Tim Ripley)*

'When I met Inge at Split airport, he was very relaxed and open to ideas,' recalled Pringle. 'He immediately broke the tension by telling me "we were in a bit of muddle".' The two officers then flew into Bosnia to allow Inge to see the Multi-National Brigade on Mount Igman, outside Sarajevo, and then to speak to General Smith at Kiseljak. Military planners in Britain were not convinced that the Welch Fusiliers could be safely extracted from Gorazde, without the committal of a huge rescue force of paratroopers, Special Forces and 24 Airmobile Brigade. It was a high-risk option, several helicopters could be shot down, there was little open terrain for paratroopers to land safely and Serb artillery could inflict heavy losses as troops tried to board evacuation helicopters. The loss of British life was potentially large and it was not certain what would happen once the Welch Fusiliers left. Serb troops might take the town and repeat the slaughter at Srebrenica, leaving the UK open to the accusation that it had left the population to be massacred. This nightmare scenario led the Joint Headquarters in Wilton to propose that the garrison actually be reinforced with the new British battalion just arriving in Croatia, the 1st Battalion, The Royal Regiment of Fusiliers, which was supposed to take over tasks in central Bosnia.

'Reinforcement was back on the agenda because we couldn't see how to get the troops out,' said Pringle. 'General Smith rubbished the plan and said it was ridiculous to reinforce the garrison – it was just reinforcing failure.' General Smith proposed talking

RAF Chinook helicopters of 24 Brigade had improvised UN markings but retained their camouflage paint. *(UNPROFOR)*

with General Ratko Mladic to get his approval for the UN garrison to leave.

Pringle said:

> It was intriguing to watch General Smith sow the seeds in the mind of Inge to negotiate with Mladic for a way out. He then went back to UK and sold the idea to the Secretary of State [Portillo], doing whatever Chiefs of the Defence Staff do. General Smith was then given authority to fix it. It was done over the head of [the Joint Commander] Wilsey. Inge was dealing directly with the UNPROFOR commander because General Smith was in some disagreement with Wilsey.

Inge recalled:

> The macho option had lots of disadvantages but talking to Mladic was a cleaner operation. In the end it was a question of whether I had faith in Rupert Smith's judgement when he said that he could get the Welch Fusiliers out – I did. I can put my hand on my heart and say I was proved right. The best option was to talk. It was less difficult and involved less loss of life.

After meeting General Smith, Inge and Pringle then went to Ploce to see 24 Airmobile Brigade. 'There were helicopters, French guns and ammunition everywhere but they were going nowhere, blocked from crossing into Bosnia,' said Pringle. 'He realised what a potential nightmare we were sitting on. The only task for 24 Brigade was Gorazde.'

On 17 August, the British Cabinet agreed to the negotiated withdrawal option and on 18 August the Ministry of Defence in London publicly announced that the Welch Fusiliers would be withdrawing by mid-September. Within a few days General Smith had concluded a deal with Mladic and by the end of the month the last Welch Fusiliers were out of the enclave. The indictment of Mladic by The Hague war crimes tribunal on 25 July was not a factor in British thinking. The safety of their troops was a top priority. 'Mladic's indictment was not a factor in my life,' said Inge. 'My aim was to get the Welch Fusiliers out of Gorazde. Who else was I supposed to talk too?'

For the soldiers and airmen of 24 Brigade, the summer 1995 deployment was a very frustrating experience. It took Herculean efforts to get themselves to Ploce on the Croatian coast. Apart from the UN aid mission to Banja Luka and some re-supply flights to the MNB on Mount Igman during the NATO bombing campaign in September 1995, 24 Brigade saw little action. Four of its AAC aviators were killed when a Lynx AH.7 crashed in the middle of August on a training mission over the Adriatic. Its main units never moved into Bosnia and during October as a cease-fire was agreed across the country ahead of the Dayton Peace talks, the Brigade began the withdrawal back to Colchester. The RAF Chinook Force remained and moved up the coast to Split to support the imminent arrival of the main British NATO peacekeeping force in December.

This three-month long delay in deploying 24 Brigade meant it was not in-theatre until a month after the fall of the Bosnian enclave of Srebrenica to General Mladic's troops and the subsequent killing spree that left more than 5,000 Srebrenican residents dead. The question must be raised whether or not this delay had any effect on Mladic's decision to attack the enclave. The British commander in Gorazde, Lieutenant Colonel Jonathan Riley, recounted that BSA officers in eastern Bosnia were very impressed when the Brigade's dispatch was announced. Riley recalled:

> The Serbs took notice big style. They recognised 24 Brigade as a demonstration of the UK government's intent to look after its people when John Major said our only national interest was the security of our soldiers. 24 Brigade was a supremely political act, which had the desired effect. The Serbs were much more careful in their dealing with me after the announcement to deploy 24 Brigade.

The 24 Brigade deployment may have persuaded the Serbs to leave the British alone in Gorazde, but they turned their attention elsewhere. Did Mladic attack Srebrenica in order to beat the arrival of 24 Brigade? Or could the Brigade and its helicopters have rescued the beleaguered enclave and its Dutch UN garrison? 'I don't know what would have happened if we had been there earlier,' said Brims. 'That is too far a "what if?"' As a signal of political intent, 24 Brigade's deployment had some effect. But as an exercise in practical power projection it left a lot to be desired. The deployment of 24 Brigade is still a subject of great controversy within the British Army and the actual deployment decision was put off limits in post-conflict debriefs and 'lesson learned' studies.

In the end the decision to negotiate the withdrawal of the Welch Fusiliers from Gorazde meant the Brigade had little to do. For the air mobilty enthusiasts in the British Army and RAF, 24 Brigade's deployment provided plenty of ammunition to use in battles in Whitehall to get the funding needed to enhance the ability of the UK's expeditionary forces to react quickly to the events of the new world disorder.

CHAPTER 4

16 Air Assault Brigade and JHC Formed

In the aftermath of the ill-fated 24 Airmobile Brigade deployment to Bosnia and the decision in 1995 to purchase sixty-seven AH-67 Apache attack helicopters, many in the UK Armed Forces were starting to think seriously about how to launch a root and branch overhaul of how the British Army, RAF and Royal Navy used their helicopters on the battlefield.

Not only were these forward-thinking officers considering how to mesh the three Services' helicopters in a coherent single fighting force, but they were keen to also make this united helicopter force relevant to future battlefields in the very fluid 'new world disorder'. Future British helicopter forces needed to be better organised and equipped, as well as configured to be able to move rapidly to operational theatres far from the UK homeland.

Once NATO troops deployed throughout Bosnia in December 1995 as part of the Implementation Force (IFOR), the UK significantly increased its helicopter forces in the Balkan country. RAF Boeing Chinook HC.2 and Royal Navy Westland Sea King HC.4 transport helicopters, along with an AAC aviation battlegroup with Westland Lynx AH.7 and Gazelle AH.1 armed and reconnaissance helicopters, transformed the capabilities of UK peacekeeping forces, allowing British troops to move freely across ethnic frontlines and over mountain ranges. Although the UK helicopters were not eventually involved in combat operations in Bosnia, commanders credited the mobility they provided with allowing them to conduct high tempo activity and retain the initiative over the local warring factions.

Tactical Air Landing Operations (TALO) are a core capability of 16 Air Assault Brigade. *(Tim Ripley)*

Westland Gazelle and Lynx helicopters were the mainstay of the Joint Helicopter
Command at its formation in 1999. *(Tim Ripley)*

British troops came to expect this level of mobility in future peacekeeping missions.

At the same time, the UK was experimenting with the Joint Rapid Deployment Force
(JRDF), which was formed in 1996 for expeditionary operations. For the first time this
envisaged the formal commitment of RAF Chinook and Westland Puma HC.1 support
helicopter forces to augment out of area operations by 5 Airborne Brigade and 3
Commando Brigade. This concept was tested during Exercise Purple Star in the United
States in the summer of 1996. It saw RAF Chinooks operating from Royal Navy
amphibious warfare ships and aircraft carriers to move Royal Marines ashore. The British
Army and RAF, as well as the Royal Marines, were now seriously looking at how to use
their helicopters in an aggressive manner during rapid reaction missions overseas.

In the mid-1990s, several papers and plans were prepared with the three armed
Services and UK Ministry of Defence to formalise this transformation of the battlefield
employment of helicopters by the British Armed Forces. The change of government in
1997 led to the launching by Prime Minister Tony Blair of his Strategic Defence Review
(SDR) that was reported in June 1998.

This enshrined expeditionary warfare at the heart of UK defence policy and also

RAF Odiham has been the home of the RAF Boeing Chinook Force since 1981. *(Tim Ripley)*

launched far-reaching overhauls of how Britain's Armed Forces were organised, equipped and trained. It appeared to be good news for the UK's helicopter forces. The SDR process, however, did not involve the firm commitment by the New Labour government of the financial resources to pay for this transformation.

As a result of the SDR on 25 January 1999, the then Defence Secretary, George Robertson, announced the formation of the new Joint Helicopter Command (JHC). The new headquarters was to be housed in the British Army's Land Command Headquarters (HQ LAND) at Erskine Barracks, at Wilton, with RAF Air Vice Marshal David Niven as its first commander. It became fully operational by 1 October 1999 and crucially had its £350 million annual operating budget established by April 2000. The JHC was placed under the control of Commander-in-Chief LAND, the army's main peacetime headquarters, with day-to-day command of all UK battlefield helicopters being exercised through AVM Niven.

The RAF's Lockheed Martin C-130 Hercules fleet provided 16 Brigade with tactical airlift across a spectrum of operations. *(Tim Ripley)*

By placing the RAF and Royal Navy transport or support helicopters within the British Army's formal chain of command and budgetary process, it was hoped that the inter-Service rivalry that had be-devilled UK battlefield helicopters operations would be a thing of the past. Although it did not place the RAF Chinooks and Pumas formally under the command of the army's newly formed air assault brigade, the fact that this brigade and the RAF support helicopters were both under the direct command of the new JHC was intended to place them inside a single chain of command. At a stroke it was hoped that UK battlefield helicopter operations would now be conducted to support land forces in a coherent and integrated way. For the British Armed Forces this was a revolution.

The formal role of this new command was to direct the training, planning and funding of battlefield helicopters across a range of missions and tasks, thereby making the most efficient use of available assets. It contained 12,000 servicemen and women and some 350 helicopters. The JHC also included the army's new 16 Air Assault Brigade, which initially operated Lynx AH.9 light utility, Lynx AH.7 anti-tank and Gazelle observation helicopters and was intended to be the sole operator of the Apache attack helicopter.

The SDR announced in 1998 that the UK government wanted to bring together all of the UK's battlefield helicopters, excluding those normally based on Royal Navy warships or used for search and rescue, in a single joint command. To put this vision into action, a study team drawn from all three Services was established, under AVM Niven, to make recommendations about the new command and control arrangements, the size of the command and its tasks, although not all were accepted in the SDR process.

'In World War Two, Korea, and elsewhere through to Bosnia today multi-Service co-operation did not just happen,' said AVM Niven at a ceremony in January 1999 to unveil the new command. 'We had to work on it. The JHC, however, will not undermine the single-Service ethos, each Service brings something to the new organisation.'

AVM Niven stressed that joint training would be a key factor in the success of the JHC. 'In the past the three Services have not trained together in an efficient way. You need close day-to-day integration. They are not my words, they are drawn from the joint vision.'

The new JHC provided a unified command structure for the integration of battlefield helicopters, air assault forces, and their related combat support and combat service support units. It drew together the operational units of the AAC, the Commando Helicopter Force of the Royal Navy's Fleet Air Arm and RAF Support Helicopters, previously assigned to its No. 2 Group. Senior JHC officers claimed the helicopter force in Bosnia in 1996 was 40 per cent bigger than it needed to be because of inter-Service roles and missions duplication.

The AAC brought the largest number of helicopters to the JHC, some 231 Gazelle AH.1s, Lynx AH.7s and Lynx AH.9s. Some eighty RAF Chinook HC.2s and Puma HC.1s were the initial RAF contribution, but Merlin HC.3s and Chinook HC.3s were to join when they entered service. The Royal Navy's Sea King HC.4s, Gazelle AH.1s and Lynx AH.7s were the Senior Service's contribution.

The day-to-day command of overseas-based units, such as the garrisons in the Falkland Islands, Northern Ireland, Cyprus, Brunei and the former Yugoslavia, was to be delegated to local headquarters.

Westland Puma HC.1 transport helicopters were a key capability for the new JHC until the arrival of the first Merlin. *(Tim Ripley)*

Support for Royal Marine amphibious forces was a core task of the new JHC. *(Tim Ripley)*

The JHC was also to look after logistic units, such as the Royal Electrical Mechanical Engineers (REME) and Royal Logistic Corps (RLC) elements, which provide maintenance and fuel supply support for AAC units; the RAF Tactical Support Wing, which provided refuelling and other in the field support; and the Joint Helicopter Support Unit (JHSU), which specialises in loading out-sized cargoes on support helicopters.

According to AVM Niven, a 'key part' of the JHC was 16 Air Assault Brigade, which was to be formed by merging the AAC helicopters of the old 24 Airmobile Brigade and the parachute-trained elements of 5 Airborne Brigade.

The JHC did not command the Royal Navy's anti-submarine and anti-surface and airborne early warning helicopters. RAF and Fleet Air Arm Search and Rescue (SAR) helicopters remained under current single Service command arrangements.

The JHC headquarters was to be manned by eighty military personnel, drawn from all three Services, and civil servants. These were being drawn together in early 1999 from the existing headquarters that commanded battlefield helicopters, Headquarters No. 1 Group RAF, Headquarters Flag Officer Naval Aviation (FONA), and the Army Aviation staff branch at HQ LAND. AVM Niven said that when the JHC stood up it would result in a 15 per cent saving in military manpower.

Aircrew selection, basic and type conversion of aircrew remained single Service responsibilities, but with the joint Defence Helicopter Flying School (DHFS) continuing to operate as before. The JHC worked closely with the Defence Helicopter Support Agency at Yeovilton, which then managed logistic support for all the Services' helicopters.

The main task of the JHC is to provide a range of helicopter forces to meet operational commitments. When an operation was to be launched, the JHC would delegate command of helicopter assets to field commanders. The JHC was be closely involved with the Permanent Joint Headquarters (PJHQ), at Northwood, on helicopter matters of contingency planning and crisis management.

Royal Navy Westland Sea King HC.4s of the Commando Helicopter Force were a major
element of the JHC. *(Tim Ripley)*

Refuelling and other helicopters logistic support elements of the RAF, Royal Logistic
Corps and Royal Marines are co-ordinated by the JHC. *(Tim Ripley)*

'In the past the Services created single Services solutions in the battlefield area – we
will create joint solutions, particularly in logistics,' said AVM Niven. 'In logistic support
the three Services created three solutions – we will have a single logistic chain to support
our operations.'

The JHC was to set performance standards, control training and oversee logistic
support. It was also to produce advice on personnel issues, doctrine, operational
requirements, operating and engineering regulations and working practice. AVM Niven,
however, stressed that the final say in personnel matters would remain under the control
of the individual Services.

AVM Niven was the first commander of the JHC but it was intended in the future that
the command would be open to officers from any of the three Services.

After the JHC was up and running, its impact was intended to stretch beyond the
scheduling of exercises and preparing forces for overseas deployments. AVM Niven
alluded to the JHC's impact on the doctrine and procurement process when he said it
'would have a major impact on the successor to the Lynx, Puma and Future Amphibious
Support Helicopter (FASH)'. It was the intention of the study team that the JHC would
become the focus for doctrine and procurement advice on battlefield helicopter issues. A
joint approach to helicopter doctrine was to be the start of this, harmonising for example
the Royal Navy and the RAF's view of the employment of support helicopters. The Royal
Navy and the AAC also had differing views on the use of armed and observation
helicopters. This was then expected to determine operational requirements that would
drive the shape and size of the replacement for the ageing Puma, Lynx and Sea King HC.4
fleets.

A major influence would also be the level of budgetary freedom given to the JHC, to influence debates over the through-life costs of any new helicopters and their logistic support. While the creation of the JHC went a long way to addressing the institutional disconnects that hampered British helicopter forces during the 1970s and 1980s, it did not entirely remove the conflicting inter-Service rivalries and financial pressures that remained in different forms.

For the British Army, the heart of the SDR was the requirement to sustain a single division-sized formation of 10,000 to 20,000 troops overseas for short term or surge major operations. The solution to this was a device known as the force readiness cycle, which was in effect a rotation process whereby each branch of the Armed Forces had to have forces trained and equipped for operational deployment overseas. This allocated time to train up to the required standard, time on alert or deployed overseas and was followed by a period of post-operational rest and re-organisation. In the later 1990s as Britain was sustaining large contingents of troops in the Balkans, priority was given to having the army divisions in Germany (1 UK Armoured Division) and the UK (3 UK Mechanised Division), each having three armoured or mechanised brigades so they could maintain a full rotation cycle, with both divisions having a brigade at high readiness at any one time.

The down-side for the air mobile and airborne forces was that this meant that either 5 Airborne or 24 Airmobile Brigades would have to be disbanded to allow a new mechanised brigade to be formed to make the force readiness cycle process work for the UK-based 3 (UK) Division, which up to then only had two mechanised brigades.

So as a result of the SDR, the army announced that 5 Brigade and 24 Brigade were to be combined into a single formation that would eventually contain some 8,000 troops. Under the SDR plans Colchester would be the home of the new Brigade, with the Parachute Regiment battalions that would form its core having to move to the Essex city from their traditional home in Aldershot to make room for the soon to be formed 12 Mechanised Brigade. The new Brigade headquarters was to be established in Colchester during the summer of 1999 and the bulk of its troops would follow over the subsequent year.

The move to Colchester would cause considerable angst in ranks of the Parachute Regiment because it was combined with the closure of its own recruit training depot at Browning Barracks in Aldershot. Potential paratroopers would now undergo their basic training at the Infantry Training Regiment at Catterick alongside recruits from line infantry regiments. Some in the Parachute Regiment considered this a dangerous watering down of their ability to select and train their own 'Airborne Soldiers'. However, the famous P Company course to qualify soldiers as fully fledged paratroopers remained undiluted and fully under the control of the Airborne Forces. The potential offered from joining the new air assault brigade was enough of a carrot to the leadership of the Parachute Regiment for them not to cause too much trouble over the changing of the basic training regime. The disbandment of one of the Parachute Regiment's two Territorial Army battalions was also a price the Regiment had to pay. Not all three Regular Parachute battalions would be available for duty with 16 Brigade at any one time because one battalion was always to be assigned to Northern Ireland duty.

The new 16 Air Assault Brigade was to combine the airborne role of the Parachute Regiment and deep strike capabilities of the attack helicopters. The new buzzword was air manoeuvre rather than air mobility, which covered the moving of troops by helicopter and

The anti-tank variant of the Lynx was scheduled to be replaced by the AH-64D Apache early in the 21st Century. *(Tim Ripley)*

fixed wing air transport, supported by attack helicopter strikes.

Lieutenant General Mike Jackson, who was then Colonel of the Parachute Regiment, described the new Brigade as the 'focus for those who go by air to battle'.

Air manoeuvre operations were thought of as a spectrum involving a mix of 16 Brigade's central components, AAC attack helicopters and air assault infantry of the Parachute Regiment. On the battlefield it was to conduct a number of distinct roles to move rapidly across impassable terrain or deep behind enemy lines. These included:

- Attack helicopter raids against high-value targets behind enemy lines. They were to be conducted in tandem with long-range artillery fire and fixed wing air support, principally against targets not able to be attacked by other means.

- Air assault, seen as an infantry-led operation, which was to be more ground- than air-focused. Whilst being infantry-led, they could rely on a combination of insertion means – parachute or helicopter – and forms of combat support including fixed wing, army aviation attack or artillery to achieve their aim. Aviation would support the air assault infantry, perhaps by escorting, clearing and then screening an objective for subsequent infantry action. The ultimate ambition was to deliver an air assault infantry battalion 150 kilometres behind enemy lines by helicopter or tactical air transport.

● Theatre entry where troops are delivered by tactical air transport if out of support helicopter range, with the aim of seizing an airhead or bridgehead for future use. It could be strategic or tactical and parachuting troops to seize strategic objectives was an option. As a rapidly deployable light formation, the Brigade would be utilised as an early or rapid effect force. This could be an independent action or as the lead element of a larger force. 16 Brigade was to be outside the force readiness cycle and held on alert to spearhead this type of mission.

These concepts of operation are also considered applicable to peacekeeping or guerrilla warfare scenarios where there are no fixed frontlines and the battlefield situation is very fluid.

Behind the scenes in the new JHC and within the services, a great deal of work was taking place to develop the tactics and procedures to mesh together all the new air manoeuvre capabilities into 16 Brigade. At the same time, a lot of effort was made to bring coherence to the various helicopter and other equipment procurement projects that could be of use to the new Brigade. This was happening at the time the UK procurement organisation was being overhauled as a result of SDR, with single Service requirements processes being merged into a single joint-Service Equipment Capability (EC) organisation. This brought army, navy and air force officers together into joint teams to work out the equipment requirements.

In the late 1990s several important equipment projects were under way, which were very specifically required by air manoeuvre forces and there were others that were closely related. Some, such as the Apache and Merlin helicopter purchases, were under contract and production was under way. Others were in development and had yet to be contracted.

US Army Apache operations in Bosnia were closely studied by the JHC for lessons on how to bring the attack helicopters into service. *(NATO/SFOR)*

The SDR process meant some of these projects were merged and new projects were launched. While the SDR appeared to offer the prospects of much new air manoeuvre equipment and capabilities, the defence procurement budget was severely stretched at the turn of the century. The Labour government's new Chancellor of the Exchequer (finance minister), Gordon Brown, imposed very strict cash controls on the Ministry of Defence. Projects to build new Astute nuclear attack submarines and Nimrod maritime patrol aircraft were running several hundreds of millions of pounds each over budget and Brown insisted that there would be no extra money to bail out the Ministry of Defence. The result was that existing procurement projects had to be stretched out over the coming decade and any new projects had to be launched by cutting spending on existing projects. This meant 16 Brigade's full air manoeuvre capability was to be achieved in a series of four main incremental steps, with the intention of them all being complete by a 2010/2012 timeframe.

The main big budget item for the air manoeuvre forces was the Apache attack helicopter, which was costing almost £2.9 billion. In the 1998–2002 period this was designated the British Army's priority procurement item to field the full force of three Apache regiments by 2003. Production was ramping up at Westland Helicopters' Yeovil site at the turn of the century. Some twenty-two Merlins were also due to delivered to the RAF between 2000 and 2002 under a contract worth nearly £800 million. In the longer term the RAF and Royal Navy hoped to replace their existing medium-lift helicopters with seventy new machines by the end of the decade under the Support Amphibious and Battlefield Rotorcraft (SABR) project. This brought together the RAF plans to replace its Pumas and the Royal Navy's replacement for its Sea Kings – dubbed the Future Amphibious Support Helicopter (FASH). These new helicopters would allow 16 Brigade and 3 Commando Brigade to operate simultaneously to their full potential. Some 124 Lynx and forty-five Gazelle helicopters were to be replaced under the £1 billion Battlefield Light Utility Helicopter (BLUH) project from February 2008. It was envisaged that more than 200 new helicopters were needed under these plans, which were expected to cost in excess of £5 billion over a ten-year period.

To support these efforts a series of enabling capabilities were needed. Large off-road Oshkosh fuel tankers were on order, as was a system of communications gateways to link the Apache fleet to the army's Bowman radio system. Funding was also not yet confirmed for more forward arming and refuelling points (FARPs). The availability of fuel at FARPs in forward zones of the battlefield was essential if the Apache force was to have sufficient time on station to find and destroy their assigned targets.

Combining the air mobile and airborne forces into 16 Brigade meant tactical and strategic air transport was now a key part of air manoeuvre. However, this aspect of air manoeuvre capability remained firmly under the control of the RAF's No. 2 Group. Half of the 1960s vintage Lockheed C-130K Hercules airlifters were in the process of being replaced by the newer C-130J variant. Problems getting the new variant certified or released by the air worthiness experts of the Defence Evaluation Research Agency (DERA) at Boscombe Down, meant the older C-130Ks would bear the brunt of the effort to support 16 Brigade until 2005. It had been hoped to replace the rest of the Hercules with the new European A400M but political wrangling delayed the contract signing until May 2001 and meant that it would not be ready until 2011/12 at the earliest.

The delays with the A400M did prompt the Ministry of Defence to move to lease four

Boeing C-17 Globemaster strategic airlifters from 2001. These aircraft arrived just in time for 16 Brigade's first operation.

It was envisaged that 16 Brigade would benefit from the British Army's ambitious plans to field a new generation of artillery and rocket systems. Dubbed Indirect Fire Precision Attack (IFPA), this was an integrated system of sensors and weapons that was intended to dramatically improve accuracy and firepower by a factor of ten, cut manpower requirements in half and simultaneously reduce logistic support to a tenth of the current level. This latter factor was particularly important for air manoeuvre forces because artillery ammunition is very heavy and bulky, taking up large amounts of space on transport aircraft or helicopters. Under the £1.2 billion IFPA project, it was envisaged that new lightweight 155-mm howitzers and Multiple Launch Rocket System (MLRS) wheeled launchers that could be carried in a C-130 or under a Chinook would be purchased for 16 Brigade and the Royal Marines. Precision-guided munitions would reduce the number of rounds required. The first elements were to enter service by 2008 to hit targets out to 70 kilometres and the full system would be in-service by 2015 to hit targets out to 150 kilometres. Targets for these weapons were to be located by a variant of the Swedish Ericsson Arthur lightweight fire-locating radar – dubbed the Mobile Artillery Monitoring Battlefield Radar (MAMBA) under IFPA. Enemy radio communications were to be monitored by new portable equipment to be purchased for the 16 Brigade's Light Electronic Warfare Team (LEWT).

The Watchkeeper tactical unmanned aerial vehicle (UAV) was to enter service in 2008 and the new joint RAF/Army Raytheon Sentinel R.1 Airborne Stand-off Radar (ASTOR) was to come on line in 2006. This latter system was similar to the US Air Force's Joint-STARS ground surveillance radar aircraft, which could monitor huge areas of terrain and pin-point moving targets in the way that Airborne Warning and Control System (AWACS) aircraft monitored aircraft movements.

This network of advanced intelligence, surveillance targeting and reconnaissance (ISTAR) systems was meant to give the commanders of 16 Brigade an unprecedented 'real-time' view of the battlefield. This would allow them to fine tune their manoeuvres, to keep away from enemy threats and to bring firepower to bear against key enemy positions, prior to assault by friendly ground units. For lightly equipped air manoeuvre forces, having a real-time view of the battlefield meant commanders could feel confident that they would not be surprised by superior enemy forces. For the British Airborne Forces, the experience of World War Two when paratroopers were trapped and all but destroyed at Arnhem in September 1944 by superior German armoured forces was an ever present worry.

The final element in the future equipment plans of 16 Brigade was the introduction of the Bowman digital radio communication system. This was aimed at providing the British Army with a battlefield internet-style communications system and replacing the 1960s vintage Clansman radios. These were very unreliable and liable to eavesdropping by the enemy. It was hoped that the Bowman would transform the British Army's radio communications and for the first time give junior commanders secure radios. With this standard of communications the viability of air manoeuvre operations deep behind enemy lines would be transformed. A key element of the full Bowman system was real-time location beacons embedded in each radio that would allow battalion and brigade headquarters to automatically track where their troops were on rapidly moving battlefields. This would dramatically increase the ability of 16 Brigade commanders to quickly bring long-range precision-guided weapons and air power to bear because they would know exactly where all their troops were, making so-called friendly fire a thing of the past.

By bringing a communications system on line that offered internet-style capabilities, the view of the battlefield available to 16 Brigade's commanders would be unprecedented. The intelligence feeds from the various ISTAR systems and the Longbow radar of the AAC's Apaches could be merged into a single real-time 'picture' of the battlefield. This offered the potential to dramatically speed up the pace of 16 Brigade's operations, giving it a battle-winning advantage over opponents.

The British Army's ambition to conduct air manoeuvre operations out to 150 kilometres behind enemy lines was based not just on the purchase of additional long-range heavy helicopters under the SABR project. The ability to project combat power was judged to be a combination of attack helicopters, transport helicopters, intelligence gathering, long-range precision fire support, communications, air transport and logistic support. Air manoeuvre capability was created by moulding together several key elements into a coherent whole. It would be many years until all these elements came on line to allow 16 Brigade to operate to its full potential.

The SDR process led to the UK at last developing a coherent concept for using the helicopter to achieve a decisive effect on the battlefield. The air manoeuvre concept was ambitious and offered British operational commanders a powerful battlefield tool. For the first time specific headquarters – the Joint Helicopter Command and 16 Air Assault Brigade – was given responsibility for delivering the most important elements of the British Armed Forces' air manoeuvre capability.

While this was a major advance it was not yet supported by any indication that the British Ministry of Defence had secured the funding to turn the air manoeuvre vision into reality. At the turn of the century, 16 Brigade was still short of vital helicopters, artillery, long-range rockets and communications systems and it looked like it would be well towards the end of the next decade before these shortages would be overcome.

CHAPTER 5

By Helicopter to Kosovo

Along the main road into Kosovo all eyes were skyward as the first wave of five Pumas and eight Chinooks passed low overhead. As dawn was breaking on 12 June, in the crowded tented camps just south of the border, thousands of Kosovar Albanian refugees stood and watched the British RAF helicopters fly northwards up the narrow Kacanik gorge, hoping their country would soon be liberated. On the road below, the tank crews of the British Army's 4 Armoured Brigade were poised to pour across the border once the paratroopers and Gurkhas crammed inside the helicopters could secure and clear the bridges and tunnels on the only main road into Kosovo. Television news crews aimed their cameras at the helicopters, beaming live pictures around the world to signal that Kosovo would soon be free.

Even before the ink was dry on Prime Minister Tony Blair's Strategic Defence Review (SDR) document that set in train the establishment of the Joint Helicopter Command and 16 Air Assault Brigade, events in the Balkans

RAF Boeing Chinook HC.2s landing in Kosovo's Kacanik gorge to pick up paratroopers of 5 Airborne Brigade. *(Kevin Kapon/KFOR pool/Tim Ripley)*

would lead to the British Army and RAF launching one of the most dramatic helicopter-borne operations to date in British military history.

The signing of the Dayton Peace Accords in December 1995 had brought an end to the Croatian and Bosnian wars, but the Serbian-ruled province remained restive. Its Albanian-majority population continued to demand independence from the Serbian-dominated Yugoslav government in Belgrade. For Yugoslav president and Serbian strong man Slobodan Milosevic, Kosovo was a prize that could not be given away easily. The province was the ancient home of Serbian nationalism and he had risen to power on the back of a wave of nationalistic rhetoric.

In March 1998, tensions boiled over and the Albanian guerrilla fighters of the Kosovo Liberation Army (KLA) began an insurgency aimed at expelling Serb troops from the province. Unsurprisingly, Milosevic unleashed his security forces, backed by Serb

Allowing Kosovar Albanian refugees to return to their homes was a central objective of the NATO campaign against Serbia. *(NATO/AFSOUTH)*

PONOSEVAC, SR
GEO COORD:422400N0201700E
DOI: 17 OCT 98

APPROX 45 PERCENT OF VILLAGE DESTROYED

Tunnels in the Kacanik gorge were mined for demolition by Serbian forces. *(Tim Ripley)*

paramilitaries, against the KLA. In true Balkan fashion, civilians bore the brunt of this conflict. Homes were torched and hundreds of thousands of Albanian civilians sought sanctuary in Kosovo's hills and forests.

US envoy Richard Holbrooke attempted to repeat his success at Dayton in a series of negotiations during the autumn of 1998. Under the threat of NATO air strikes, Milosevic agreed to a cease-fire to be monitored by international observers.

The deployment of the Organisation for Security and Co-operation in Europe (OSCE) monitors in Kosovo in October 1998 brought a temporary respite but fighting resumed with a vengeance in January 1999. The major western powers attempted to broker a negotiated solution at the Rambouillet peace talks. NATO offered to provide peacekeeping troops to enforce any settlement agreed at these talks. In February, it authorised the deployment of so-called enabling forces to neighbouring Macedonia, led by the headquarters of the Allied Command Europe (ACE) Rapid Reaction Corps or ARRC, under the command of Britain's Lieutenant General Michael Jackson. The G3 Air Operations branch of ARRC headquarters would soon be up and running in the 'Shoe Factory' complex on the outside of the Macedonian capital, Skopje. It would play a key role in future allied helicopter operations throughout the southern-Balkan theatre.

RAF Chinooks being prepared for operations at Petrovec airport in Macedonia. *(Tim Ripley)*

On 20 March, the Kosovo crisis went critical. The peace talks at Rambouillet had broken down and the OSCE monitors were ordered to withdraw to the relative safety of Macedonia. Within four days, NATO bombers and cruise missiles were in action against Serb targets. For almost the next two months, NATO troops in Macedonia and Albania were pre-occupied with responding to the expulsion of hundreds of thousands of Albanians from Kosovo by the Serbs.

Back in the UK, 5 Airborne Brigade, had been monitoring the escalating crisis. There was great uncertainty about what would happen. The OSCE monitors could have required rescuing or Serb forces could have attacked Macedonia, to head off NATO action. Once the NATO air strikes got under way, the Brigade's readiness was raised by the Ministry of Defence. As the full horror of Serb retaliation against the Albanian civilian population emerged in the days after the air campaign began, the British government looked desperately for options. There was talk of setting up 'safe havens' for refugees inside Kosovo, with NATO troops to protect them. The rapid landing of British and US paratroopers was proposed as one way to make this happen. British military planners explained to their political masters that the lightly armed paratroopers would soon find themselves being attacked by 50,000 heavily armed Yugoslav army troops and Serb paramilitaries. Casualties would be heavy and Kosovo's unique geography meant it would be very difficult for reinforcements to arrive. The province was bounded on its northern, western and southern borders by high mountain ranges, with only a handful of good roads

US Army AH-64A Apache attack helicopters flew from Albania to join 5 Airborne Brigade's insertion operation into Kosovo. *(US DoD)*

or railway lines. To the north of Kosovo was the Yugoslav republic of Montenegro so NATO forces could not pass through it. To the west was Albania. Although its government was supportive of NATO and the KLA, the road infrastructure was non-existent in the border region to support the presence of NATO forces. Only to the south in Macedonia were NATO forces present in strength. In March 1999, there were only some 8,000 NATO troops in Macedonia, who had fewer than thirty tanks, so they were unable to offer much support in a stand-up fight with the Yugoslav army, which had more than 300 tanks in Kosovo. Even if there had be more NATO troops in Macedonia, the only metal road into Kosovo ran up the narrow ten-kilometre long Kacanik gorge. British Army officers who carried out a detailed reconnaissance and terrain analysis of the gorge concluded that only a few dozen determined defenders could hold up thousands of attackers for months. The road ran across six bridges and through two tunnels that the Yugoslav army had prepared for demolition.

With no means of rapid reinforcement, any airborne operation would be a high-risk gamble that could have led to heavy military and civilian casualties. NATO's political leaders therefore decided to stake everything on a strategic bombing campaign. US President Bill Clinton publicly rejected the use of land forces. Although British Prime Minister Tony Blair toyed with the idea of mobilising a huge land army to invade Kosovo, the huge cost and risks of ground operation meant the British government in the end stuck with the air power option.

On 15 May, NATO's North Atlantic Council met in Brussels and authorised Kosovo Force (KFOR) to be expanded to 50,000 troops in anticipation of the Serbs agreeing to allow international peacekeeping troops into Kosovo. Within days a 'force generation conference' was held at the Supreme Headquarters Allied Powers Europe (SHAPE) and allied governments offered up a variety of forces, including the formation of a multi-

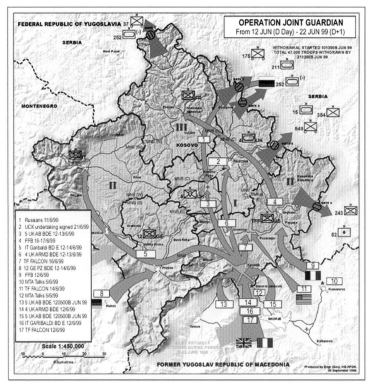

KFOR's move
into Kosovo
(KFOR/NATO)

national aviation task force made up of transport and liaison helicopters. Belgium, Canada, France, Germany, Italy, the UK and the US all promised to send extra helicopters for the peacekeeping force. General Jackson in Macedonia was to command the initial insertion operation and subsequent peacekeeping mission once the Serbs had pulled out. At this stage there was no indication of a Serb climb-down and the efforts to muster troops for KFOR seemed to have little urgency.

In the UK, 5 Airborne Brigade was alerted that it could be part of this expanded force, although there was not yet any firm idea what it would be actually called upon to do. The Brigade conducted a large training event, dubbed Exercise Corsican Lanyard, to practise co-operating with RAF helicopters and transport aircraft.

In the first week of June, much to everyone's surprise, the Serbs suddenly agreed to a joint Finnish–Russian peace plan to end the war. General Jackson entered into several days of intense negotiations to firm up the deal and on 10 June Operation Allied Force was called off. The race was now on to get the troops across the border

The ground component of the British invasion force was provided by 4 Armoured Brigade, which was already in Macedonia, and 5 Airborne Brigade. As well as being head of the ARRC, General Jackson was Colonel of the Parachute Regiment and he personally requested the services of 5 Airborne Brigade over its air mobile rival, 24 Brigade.

The airborne formation was allocated two battalion-sized battlegroups – the 1st Battalion, The Parachute Regiment (1 PARA), and the 1st Battalion, The Royal Gurkha Rifles (1 RGR) – for the Kosovo mission. They were ordered to Macedonia on 5 June after it became clear that the Russian and Finnish peace deal to allow Yugoslav forces to be replaced in Kosovo by NATO peacekeepers was going to bear fruit. RAF VC-10 aircraft flew the Brigade's personnel to Macedonia, while two giant Antonov An-124s were chartered to fly its vehicles to the operational theatre.

The Brigade was commanded by Brigadier Adrian Freer, a straight-talking paratrooper who was always known to call a spade, a spade. On more than one occasion he did not see 'eye to eye' with the British commander of KFOR, General Jackson, who was also a paratrooper. Known as 'mad Adrian' by some of his colleagues, Freer had a reputation for daring and not being afraid of action. He had several nicknames, including 'Angry of Aldershot'.

5 Airborne Brigade Order of Battle, June 1999

Headquarters 5 Airborne Brigade and Signals Squadron
Pathfinder Platoon
1st Battalion, The Parachute Regiment
1st Battalion, The Royal Gurkha Rifles
Tactical Headquarters, 7th Parachute Regiment, Royal Horse Artillery
G Battery, 7th Parachute Regiment, Royal Horse Artillery
Tactical Headquarters, 39 Engineer Regiment, Royal Engineers
9 Parachute Squadron, Royal Engineers
69 Squadron, Queen's Gurkha Engineers
613 and 614 Tactical Air Control Party
5 Airborne Brigade Logistic Battalion
23 Parachute Field Ambulance

Headquarters Support Helicopter Force

21 Signals Regiment, Royal Signals
27 Squadron, RAF, 8 x Chinook HC.2
33 Squadron, RAF, 6 x Puma HC.1
RAF Tactical Refuelling Wing

Headquarters KFOR

659 Squadron, AAC, 4 x Lynx AH.9

The Brigade's mission was vaguely envisaged as being to seize the bridges and tunnels in the Kacanik gorge to prevent Serb sabotage from hindering the movement of the main KFOR up the main road into Kosovo. At this stage General Jackson had yet to begin his marathon negotiating sessions with the Yugoslav army about the entry of KFOR into Kosovo. British officers serving in NATO's Shoe Factory headquarters describe this period as one of manic activity with new plans for the entry to Kosovo being written and ripped up on an almost hourly basis. Tension was rising as the negotiations with the Serbs dragged on but few NATO officers were getting much sleep. The permutations for the

Westland Lynx AH.9s of 659 Squadron AAC provided VIP transport for the Commander of KFOR, Lt Gen Michael Jackson. *(Tim Ripley)*

entry operation were immense and 5 Airborne Brigade had to plan a variety of scenarios, ranging from armed Yugoslav resistance to unopposed entry. Wild card action by KLA fighters or Serb paramilitaries could not be discounted. Helicopters were considered vital to allow 5 Brigade to seize the key points in the gorge before anyone could set off demolition charges. To help plan the operation, the RAF's Support Helicopter Force (SHF) headquarters was ordered to Macedonia to work with the KFOR.

The SHF headquarters, which was normally based at RAF Benson, in Oxfordshire, was tailor-made for this type of operation and brought together all the necessary support organisations to sustain helicopters in a tactical setting. These include the RAF's Tactical Supply Wing to refuel helicopters and vehicles; a mobile meteorological unit; Mobile Air Operations Teams (MOATs) to provide forward command and control at helicopter landing sites (HLS); the Joint Helicopter Support Unit to prepare under-slung loads,; the Aeromedical capability of the Tactical Medical Wing and the Mobile Catering Support Wing. Tactical communications were provided by the Army's 21 Signals Regiment. The SHF was led by Group Captain Al Campbell, who deployed from the home of the Chinook Force at RAF Odiham, where he was station commander. Wing Commander Wayne

The Russian occupation of Pristina airport was a major headache for NATO commanders. *(Tim Ripley)*

Gregory, the peacetime commander of the SHF headquarters, was designated chief of staff to the SHF Commander for NATO's Operation Joint Guardian, as the KFOR mission was code-named.

'Our mission was to provide effective air support to the Headquarters of KFOR, we were a KFOR asset,' recounted Gregory in June 1999. The SHF played a key role in the initial insertion of NATO troops into Kosovo and this operation was the biggest helicopter assault operation conducted by the British Armed Forces since Suez in 1956.

The outline concept was first for us to provide direct support to 4 Brigade but when we got here, right at the last minute we chopped to NATO command.

I arrive [in Macedonia] on 1 June with a reconnaissance and liaison team, along with logistic elements of the squadrons to make sure the package was correctly structured and basing sorted out. I went to briefings at Headquarters KFOR and Headquarters 4 Brigade. Eventually I had to completely revise these plans in order to guarantee initial operating capability to support ground operation. This was to provide a company sized lift of four Chinook and four Puma. Two Puma were already in theatre providing casevac (casualty evacuation) and medivac (medical evacuation) support to 4 Brigade. I then rang up RAF Strike Command in the UK and said this is what we needed, the order we need it in and we need it this weekend to make it happen. The stations then worked day and night to generate the aircraft and equipment. The aircraft self-deployed and got to Macedonia in time for the big event.

The 1st Battalion, The Parachute Regiment, reached Kosovo's capital Pristina on the second day of the insertion operation. *(Tim Ripley)*

A force package of eight Chinooks and four additional Pumas were flown out to Macedonia during the second week of June. There was a rest stop in Split, Croatia, to swap over Chinooks with the RAF Flight based there supporting NATO forces in Bosnia. No. 27 Squadron navigator, Flight Lieutenant Jeff Lindsay, recalls 'One Tuesday evening we got the call to go – 48 hours later we were in Split for an overnight stop.'

The SHF first set up its base at Prilep in southern Macedonia, as 5 Airborne Brigade arrived in the country ready to prepare for the insertion. Gregory recounted:

> I set up my initial Headquarters at Prilep. Our Advance Tactical Headquarters element located with 5 Brigade near [Macedonia's capital] Skopje. It then moved to the assembly area at Camp Piper, just to the north of Skopje and did detailed planning from there. We worked with 5 Brigade on Exercise Corsican Lanyard, in May, so we had a close working liaison with them and knew their procedures and people.

A leap-frogging of assets then occurred until Friday 11 June, when 5 Brigade and the SHF's helicopters were in Camp Piper ready to mount the operation. Fuel had been forward-based in bladders, MOAT teams were on hand to control the operation, the JHSU had more than 100 under-slung cargoes and groups, or chalks, of troops marshalled ready to board the helicopters, which were now based in what had previously just been a wheat field.

Squadron Leader Paul Bartlett, a forward planner with the SHF Tactical Headquarters, said the loading plan reflected 5 Brigade's tactical requirements – to secure the furthestmost part of the Kacanik defile, set up a reconnaissance screen, put in blocking and screening forces on flank, establish communications rebroadcast sites on the high ground and place explosive ordnance disposal teams at vulnerable points in the gorge to clear Serb mines and booby traps.

An important element of the British plan was escorting Apache attack helicopters of the US Army's 6th Squadron, 6th Cavalry Regiment (6-6 CAV). In early June, they were in neighbouring Albania attached to the controversial Task Force Hawk but the attack helicopter force was kept on the ground because of fears it would suffer heavy casualties and spark a land war with the Serbs. 'We had a campaign [plan] to roll back Serbs from the border to Pristina,' recalled Lieutenant Colonel George M Bilafer, commander of the 6-6 CAV. 'General Wesley Clark [NATO's Supreme Allied Commander] told us he was asking for us to go every day – we were stopped at a higher level.'

When the Yugoslav military authorities signed their agreement with NATO to pull their troops out of Kosovo, the race was on to muster powerful forces to move into the province to fill the security vacuum as Serb forces pulled out. The 6-6 CAV was mobilised to move into neighbouring Macedonia to join the KFOR. Within hours of receiving the order to move, a force of Apaches was flying towards to the existing US Army base at Petrovec airport, Camp Able Sentry, to the east of Skopje.

Bilafer recounted:

When the mission ended in Albania we deployed up here at short notice. Until we deployed [to Macedonia] we were task organised under the 12th Aviation Bde, then we formed Task Force 12 for this deployment on 10 June with twelve Apaches, eleven Sikorsky UH-60 Blackhawks and four Boeing CH-47D Chinooks. On 12 June we went into Kosovo with the UK 5 Airborne Brigade – Chinooks and Pumas of RAF Support Helicopter Force.

When we arrived here the task force operations officer went to Camp Piper for a face to face with the Brits who were planning the operation. We were ready to go the following morning. Our refuelling vehicles came by road but we brought enough spare parts and tools for 48–72 hours by Chinook and Blackhawk. Until the remainder of the task force's support vehicles crossed the treacherous mountain roads from Albania, the task force had to rely on a shuttle of helicopters to bring in its supplies.

As final preparations were being made for the insertion operation to secure the Kacanik defile, a high drama was unfolding on the diplomatic arena. Russian leaders were furious that they had not been allocated their own operational zone as part of the proposed NATO peacekeeping force. So to create 'facts on the ground', they secretly ordered 200 Russian paratroopers serving with the peacekeeping force in Bosnia to drive, via Belgrade, to seize Pristina airport to allow further reinforcements to arrive by air from Moscow. NATO Supreme Allied Commander Europe (SACEUR) General Clark was determined not to have their plans thwarted by Russian intervention, which might allow the Serbs to keep hold of part of Kosovo. General Jackson was not keen but allowed contingency planning to go ahead until he could persuade his political masters in London to get Clark to drop the idea, which he called 'barking', as in barking mad.

Western leaders, such as UK Foreign Secretary Robin Cook, were mobbed when they visited Pristina after the liberation. *(Tim Ripley)*

Brigadier Freer was ordered to prepare plans for a *coup de main* operation to seize the airport ahead of the Russians. At Camp Piper, the paratroopers, Gurkhas and SHF literally dropped what they were doing and prepared quick battle orders for the new operation. 'The helicopters were "burning and turning" when the stand-down order came through, fifteen minutes before H-Hour,' said one senior KFOR officer. Allied political leaders called off the operation with only minutes to spare when intelligence reports came in that 5,000 Russian paratroopers were in the air heading for Pristina. 'It was just like the scene from the movie *Ice Station Zebra*,' said one KFOR planner. 'Within minutes we could have been fighting the Russians – the prospect was too horrendous for anyone to contemplate and NATO "blinked".' With only fifteen minutes to go Clark cancelled the operation to allow the US President take the matter up with his Russian counterpart.

At Camp Piper, the British helicopter crews closed down their engines and the airborne brigade's soldiers returned to their improvised bivouacs. The plan to seize the Kacanik define was now back on. H-Hour was set for 0500 hrs on 12 June. 'We spent the Friday day sitting in field waiting for the operation to start,' said Bartlett. 'The aircraft were our home, we slept in them in sleeping bags.'

Lieutenant Colonel Paul Gibson, commanding officer of 1 PARA for the Kosovo and Sierra Leone operations. *(Tim Ripley)*

The first helicopter airborne was a Westland Lynx AH.9 of the Army Air Corps' 659 Squadron. Their four helicopter-strong detachment had been in Macedonia since February as a flying command post for General Jackson. This morning they took off at 4.30 am to carry Brigadier Freer so he could control the operation in the gorge.

British AAC and RAF officers assigned to NATO's G3 Air Operations Branch in the KFOR headquarters, then based in Skopje, Macedonia, created the insertion plan and controlled the overall air operation, making this the first time UK forces had control of attack helicopters during a 'real world' operation. As dawn broke on 12 June, the 6-6 CAV Apaches were airborne to escort the British Chinooks and Pumas, as they headed up the Kacanik gorge into Kosovo. Once across the border, they fanned out to protect the flanks of the British force as it headed deeper into Kosovo.

Bilafer recalled:

When we went in we did not know for sure if Serbs would resist, if everyone had been notified of the terms of the withdrawal. As far as we concerned it was combat. As we flew past the tanks and the anti-aircraft artillery it was very tense. We were fully armed and all switches were hot – if someone flinched or moved to operate a weapon system we would have taken them out. But they all had 'hands off' when we flew by. The Brits just kept leap-frogging their troops forward – they flew 100 sorties, just turning assets. Their objective was Pristina and they did a great job, it was real easy working with them. As we moved forward we saw the Serbs departing, we saw houses burning as they rolled out, and lots of convoys rolling out. At 05.00 am we could see into Pristina – there were no fires, by 10.00 am individual buildings were in flames,

A 1 PARA radio operator in Pristina. Parachute Regiment officers complained that their 1960s vintage Clansman radios were inferior to commercial mobile phones. *(Tim Ripley)*

then we saw a whole city block go up in flames. That was real tough for us.

Lindsay recalled:

When we knew we would go at dawn we had little sleep. We pitched up early in the morning. We had a briefing and were given our formation numbers and detailed loads. Five Pumas and two escorting US Army Boeing AH-64A Apache attack helicopters were first over the border. I was in the first Chinook of eight, which were next over the border. Before we crossed the border we could see thousands of people in the refugee camps and roads but when we flew across the border there was no one to be seen.

The define is almost ten kilometres long and the seizure intact of the main road through it was vital to General Jackson's tactical plan to push NATO peacekeeping troops rapidly into Kosovo. Although Serb military commanders had promised to allow NATO free access to the road, key bridges and tunnels had been rigged for demolition and no one was taking any chances on rogue Serb elements trying to sabotage the NATO advance. In the end, the Serbs offered no resistance.

Lindsay continued:

My drop was just south of Kacanik. We put 20 guys and a Land Rover with a trailer on a road. The gorge was so steep we had to land with the back wheels on the road. A few aircraft put the ramp to 90 degree so the guys could step off onto the road. The road was empty, we didn't see anyone for a long time. It took three and a half hours to put all 5 Brigade in. We shifted back and forth, we used the right side of the defile as the route in and the left hand side as the route out. Later in the day we saw the tanks move. It was what we train to do. To be at the centre of all the headlines that weekend was fabulous. It was exhilarating and exciting to be in the world's eye. All we saw as we crossed the border were satellite dishes [of TV news crews].

As the RAF Chinooks and Pumas dropped off paratroopers and Gurkhas along the gorge, the Lynx helicopters of 659 Squadron were shuttling back and forth, dropping off bomb disposal experts and Royal Engineers. 'We were lifting explosive ordnance disposal and engineers to do route clearance on the tunnels and bridges in the Kacanik [gorge],' said Major Richard Leaky, the squadron's officer commanding. 'Another aircraft was flying ahead [up] Route Hawk doing route clearance.'

With the gorge now clear and the route open for British armour to roll forward toward Pristina, the famous intervention of Russian paratroopers at the city's airport now complicated NATO's plans. 5 Airborne Pathfinder Platoon was at the front of the huge road convoy snaking through the Kacanik gorge and it was now ordered to race to the airport to find out what the Russians were doing. A small command team from 5 Brigade went forward to negotiate with Moscow's men. In the meantime, the remainder of 5 Brigade was held at Kacanik waiting on events, with SHF helicopters parked on the roads ready to lift troops forward.

Brigadier Freer had soon established good relations with the Russians and it seemed they would allow NATO troops access to the heavily damaged airport. 1 PARA was ordered to prepare to quickly fly forward to secure the airfield and soon paratroopers were boarding their helicopters parked on the road.

Then out of the blue General Jackson, on orders from Downing Street media 'spin-doctors' in London, arrived at the airport in his personal Westland Lynx AH.9 helicopter, of 659 Squadron, to hold a press conference. The Russian commander was furious at not being consulted and any idea of moving NATO troops into the airport was lost. 1 PARA was stood down again.

Major Leaky said:

In the afternoon two aircraft flew up to Pristina airfield with Gen Jackson for his press conference in the rain. I flew him. It was quite exciting because we were very uncertain of the role of the Russians. How would they respond? It was an uncertain atmosphere. I never felt under threat but there was direct menacing attitude [from the Russians]. The eyes of the world were on us.

The following day the SHF was in action again, lifting 1 PARA over the British tanks to the heart of Pristina ready to begin the liberation of the city from withdrawing Serb forces. The Battalion's commanding officer, Lieutenant Colonel Paul Gibson, led the operation with a small tactical headquarters and his C Company. By 3 pm the battalion was complete on the edge of the province's capital and after quick verbal orders, patrols of paratroopers began fanning out to occupy Pristina to a heroes' welcome from the city's remaining Albanian population.

The arrival of 1 PARA in Pristina is now the stuff of legends. Serb forces were in full retreat and the city's Albanian population emerged from hiding to greet their liberators. The scenes were reminiscent of the liberation of Paris after World War Two. Small groups of Serb paramilitaries were left behind and the paratroopers killed a handful in a number of incidents around the city, to cheering from crowds of watching Albanians.

The province was tense as hundreds of thousands of Albanian refugees returned from

Battlefield mobility was provided by 1 PARA's Pinzgauer light vehicles. *(Tim Ripley)*

exile. Ethnic murder was rife as old scores were settled with the Serb population that remained after the Yugoslav army pulled out of the province. 1 PARA was ordered to launch a series of patrols around the city to clamp down on revenge attacks. A key priority was to prevent the KLA from setting up a rival government to the international administration being set up by the UN so 1 PARA ordered all KLA fighters and other armed men to stay off the streets. In one famous incident a group of armed Albanians was parading around the city in a convoy of cars, firing their AK-47s in the air. They drove into a patrol from 1 PARA and two ended up dead.

The paratroopers took over a series of schools and other public buildings as patrol bases and set about dominating the city. They were soon given air support from 408 Squadron of the Canadian Armed Forces, with their eight Bell CH146 Griffon helicopters. Their commanding officer, Lieutenant Colonel Bruce McQuade, recalled:

> We did reconnaissance, surveillance, casevac, general utility tasks, moving commanders around. We flew 30 hours a day. A lot of our missions were flown under G2 (intelligence) direction – doing reconnaissance with the British Parachute Regiment. They taught us a lot of Northern Ireland tasks. Our crews learnt a lot. Some days the Paras put an officer in our aircraft, to act as an airborne command post to run their operations.

Gurkha troops secured Pristina airport while 1 PARA moved into the Kosovo capital. *(Tim Ripley)*

The helicopters of 408 Squadron featured prominently in a CNN news report from Pristina, when the global television network was filming a supposedly secret KLA training session. The event was interrupted by the arrival overhead of Griffons loaded with British paratroopers.

As 1 PARA grabbed the international limelight in Pristina – including hosting the visit of Prime Minister Tony Blair – the remainder of 5 Brigade, including the Royal Gurkha Rifles, was pre-occupied with securing the area around Pristina airport and the nearby town of Lipljan. This was traditional peacekeeping work, helping refugees return to their homes and preventing revenge attacks on small groups of Serbs by KLA fighters. The Gurkhas and the Pathfinders also had the additional task of setting up a security cordon around the Russian garrison at the airport to stop them being attacked by rogue KLA elements. The RAF SHF force pulled back to Petrovec airport to rest and reconfigure to support the main KFOR peacekeeping effort.

Gregory recounted:

Commander KFOR gave us priorities of operation and took us back under operational control after we chopped to 5 Brigade for the insertion operation. We were to support his air mobile reserve, which was a company of Gurkhas. We were on 30 minutes' notice to move them and a couple of times when things heated up we had the pilots in the cabs with rotors turning but things then calmed down. We sustained and supported 4 and 5 Brigades, so one of our six Pumas was on standby for casevac/medevac with 2 Armoured Field Ambulance to move its immediate response team. That helicopter was based in Pristina on a 24-hour basis. We also undertook theatre tasks as issued by Commander KFOR. We co-ordinated through G3 Air Branch at Headquarters KFOR in Pristina. All other helicopter assets worked for specific national contingents. We were the only helicopter assets Commander KFOR directly controlled.

The Chinooks flew daily shuttles up to the new KFOR headquarters outside Pristina and contingents of British troops operating around Pristina and northwards to the boundary with Serbia.

After good relations were at last established with the Russians, it was possible to relocate the SHF to a hardstanding area on the eastern side of Pristina airport to improve servicing and operating conditions. They were then joined by Belgian Agusta A109 liaison helicopters and a contingent of Russian Army Aviation Mil Mi-8 Hip transport and Mi-24 Hind attack helicopters.

By the end of August, the bulk of 5 Brigade and the SHF's helicopters were pulled back to the UK. The dramatic operation to seize the Kacanik gorge was an undoubted success and a dramatic opening gambit in NATO's move into Kosovo. The operation was mounted live on global twenty-four-hour rolling news channels and was evidence of NATO's military prowess, demonstrating to the Serbs and Albanians that the western alliance meant business. It set the conditions for the remainder of the KFOR operation and instilled respect for NATO among the local population. A lot was at stake and if the initial phase had faltered, the whole deal to force the Serbs to pull out of Kosovo could have unravelled.

Although it pre-dated the creation of 16 Air Assault Brigade, the Kacanik operation was a vivid demonstration of the potential of air manoeuvre. The air manoeuvre lobby in the British Armed Forces had a major feather in its cap. 5 Airborne Brigade's Kosovo deployment had been conducted without loss, except for two Gurkha engineers who were killed in an accident with unexploded ordnance on 21 June. Crucially, from the point of view of the Parachute Regiment, light role infantry units had successfully participated in a peacekeeping operation, which up to then had been almost the exclusive preserve of British Army armoured or mechanised infantry regiments. Light role infantry units, backed by helicopters, had proved they could cut it in complex operational environments. Perhaps more importantly, the air manoeuvre forces, particularly the Parachute Regiment, had caught the attention of senior government ministers and the media. Whenever there was a crisis in the next few years, the cry 'send for the Paras' would go up in the media and parts of Whitehall. The Airborne Forces had established their reputation as a 'can do organisation'. General Jackson would soon be appointed as Commander-in-Chief of Land Command, the army main frontline headquarters, and Lieutenant General John Reith, another senior Parachute Regiment officer, would be appointed Chief of Joint Operations at the Permanent Joint Headquarters. The newly formed 16 Brigade would have friends in high places.

RAF Chinooks operated a shuttle service to Pristina from Macedonia in the early days of the KFOR mission into Kosovo. *(Tim Ripley)*

CHAPTER 6

Sierra Leone, 2000

At 10 am on 5th May, the decision was made to send the Operational Reconnaissance and Liaison Team. We left at 6 pm and after a refuelling stop we arrived at Lungi airport in Freetown at 6 am the following day. Government forces were rapidly falling back on the capital. The rebels were a major threat. The UN troops were the last line of defence but were in near panic. There were violent demonstrations in the capital and everyone was afraid of a coup. Brigadier Richards tried to bring together all the government leaders. On 7th May, we asked the lead company of 1 PARA to deploy. By 15th May, the situation had changed dramatically.

Lt Col Neil Salisbury, Chief of Staff, UK Joint Force Headquarters

16 Air Assault Brigade was only nine months' old when it got the call to send troops into the heart of one of Africa's bloodiest civil wars. Few members of the Brigade had heard of Sierra Leone in May 2000, as reports began to circulate in the Ministry of Defence in London that the country's government was in danger of being toppled by a brutal rebel group known as the Revolutionary United Front (RUF).

Buoyed by the success of his 'ethical foreign policy' in the Kosovo crisis, Prime Minister Tony Blair was taking an increasing interest in the problems of Africa. The former British colony of Sierra Leone was seen by Blair and his then Foreign Secretary Robin Cook, as a failed state that needed to be rescued. For more than a decade, the West African country had been convulsed by civil war, as rebel groups vied for control of the lucrative diamond mines. The RUF had gained a notorious reputation for brutality and its trademark was the amputation of a prisoners' limbs by machete. For much of the 1990s, Sierra Leone had no viable government and its population had lived in fear as rival militia groups fought for control of the country and its mineral resources. While billions of dollars-worth of diamonds was illicitly exported from the country, the population's standard of living hovered near the bottom of most international league tables.

In 1995, the Sierra Leone government was so desperate it employed the services of the South African mercenary company Executive Outcomes and managed to drive the rebels back from the capital Freetown. The British private security company Sandline then provided more assistance with the tacit approval of the Foreign Office in London. Stalemate on the battlefield had allowed the UN to negotiate a cease-fire and begin the deployment of a peacekeeping force, dubbed UNAMSIL. British diplomats played an important role in setting up the UN-led peace process and London was watching its progress closely.

RAF Boeing Chinook HC.2s were the mainstay of the UK mission to Sierra Leone. *(Patrick Allan)*

During April 2000, the civil war re-ignited and more than 5,000 RUF fighters appeared to be advancing on the capital. Other rebel forces took hundreds of UN peacekeepers hostage and besieged the remainder in their bases. The whole country and the 11,000-strong UN force looked like being on the verge of collapse.

In London, the Blair government decided this was shaping up to be a test of British commitment to the people of Sierra Leone. The Permanent Joint Headquarters (PJHQ) at Northwood was ordered to dispatch part of its Joint Force Headquarters (JFHQ) to Freetown on 5 May to monitor events and prepare contingency plans for British intervention. An Operational Reconnaissance and Liaison Team (ORLT), led by PJHQ's Chief Joint Force Operations Brigadier David Richards, arrived the following day and more JFHQ personnel followed soon afterwards. The JFHQ is a small, highly mobile headquarters team that is held on two days' notice to fly anywhere in the world to co-ordinate UK intervention missions. It has enough communications equipment and

Sierra Leone (*CIA*)

The RAF Lockheed Martin C-130 Hercules force provided key tactical airlifts during the insertion phase of the operation. (*JFHQ Pool/Tim Ripley*)

supplies to run a brigade-sized operation for a couple of weeks before it has to be replaced by a better-equipped headquarters.

Richards led the British participation in the UN mission to East Timor late in 1999. He had a reputation for being very self-confident and relishing missions that apparently had little chance of success. The former Royal Artillery officer radiated optimism and was always cheerful, according to visitors to the British High Commission or embassy in Freetown during the UK intervention.

Over the weekend of 6 and 7 May, Richards sent a stream of reports to London that the rebels were within days of capturing the capital. Hundreds of UK passport holders were at risk, the government looked like it would fall and the UN troops were cowering in their bases.

Blair decided to act. PJHQ was ordered to dispatch an intervention force, initially to evacuate British passport holders, but the scope of the mission soon expanded to include supporting the Freetown government and the UN mission. Richards would command the operation from Freetown but PJHQ and Land Command turned to the newly formed 16 Brigade at Colchester to provide the initial land forces for the operation. The newly formed Joint Helicopter Command at Wilton would have to generate four Boeing Chinook HC.2 helicopters to provide the force with tactical mobility and RAF Strike Command's No. 2 Group was tasked to get the force to Sierra Leone. This was just the type of mission 16 Brigade was designed to conduct and it would soon be held up as a 'classic intervention'

Securing Lungi airport was the first object of the 1st Battalion, The Parachute Regiment.
(JFHQ Pool/Tim Ripley)

mission. The pace of the operation was such that 16 Brigade's headquarters would not get
the chance to deploy to the West African country but several of its major units were in the
thick of the action from the very start of the crisis until the autumn of 2000.

Richards' team hunkered down in the High Commission in Freetown using its satellite
communications equipment to bounce ideas back and forth to planners at Northwood
during the days running up to the launch of the intervention. The plan went through
numerous evolutions, as different force configurations, deployment schedules and tactical
plans were considered, thrown out, modified or adapted. Central to all the planning was
control of Lungi airport on a peninsula to the south of Freetown. With control of the
airport, UK and UN forces could sustain themselves, bring in reinforcements and conduct
evacuations of civilians. A second key requirement was securing a forward-operating base
in a friendly, neighbouring country from which to mount the force. On 6 May, Senegal
agreed to host the UK force and preparation ramped up considerably. Alan Jones, British
Ambassador in Freetown, and Richards then got what was left of the Sierra Leone
government to 'request' British military assistance.

Early on the morning of 5 May, the alert status of the 1st Battalion, the Parachute
Regiment (1 PARA), had been raised and its commanders warned that they could soon be
heading to Sierra Leone. It was then the UK Spearhead Lead Element, and was held at
seventy-two hours' notice to move, but the spearhead battalion was rarely mobilised for
real. Spearhead duty is usually characterised by a stream of false alarms and chaotic
preparations for operations that never happen. So not surprisingly, when news spread

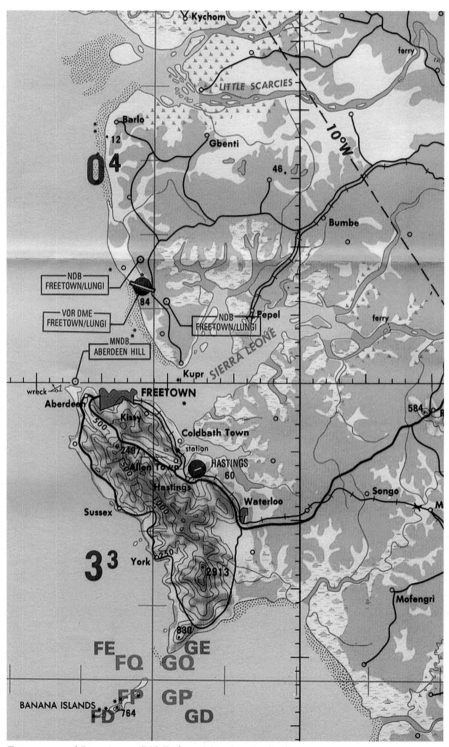

Freetown and Lungi area *(US Defense Mapping Agency)*

Brigadier David Richards masterminded the UK's intervention in Sierra Leone. *(NATO)*

around the battalion's Aldershot base after the Sierra Leone mission, morale rocketed. The Toms of 1 PARA began a period of frenetic activity to get themselves ready for action.

They moved to the UK's Operational Mounting Centre at South Cerney in Wiltshire on the evening of 6 May to prepare to be loaded on board RAF aircraft in a 'tactical configuration'. Lieutenant Colonel Paul Gibson was expecting his men to go straight into action as soon as they got off their aircraft in Freetown. On Sunday 7 May, Gibson and his battalion flew from RAF Brize Norton in Oxfordshire in RAF Lockheed TriStars to Dakar in Senegal.

One of 1 PARA's three rifle companies was on a training exercise in Jamaica as the crisis developed and could not get home in time, so 16 Brigade offered up a company of one of its air assault battalions, 1st Battalion, The Royal Irish Regiment, to replace it. The Royal Irish company got as far as Brize Norton before Gibson declined the offer of its services. This was to be a Parachute Regiment only operation. More than 200 troops of the 2nd Battalion, The Parachute Regiment, would be used to reinforce 1 PARA over the coming week.

No. 2 Group and JHC were also ramping up their preparations. Over the weekend of 6/7 May, eight RAF Hercules from 47 and 70 Squadrons took off from Lyneham bound for Dakar. Four Chinooks then left RAF Odiham early on 6 and 7 May to fly to the British forward base in Dakar, via Portugal, Gibraltar and the Canary Islands. After a brief

Lungi airport became the main base of 1 PARA and other British forces in Sierra Leone. *(Patrick Allan)*

refuelling stop, the helicopters were airborne for Freetown on 8 May to support the evacuation operation.

The first phase was the insertion into Freetown – in a classic Tactical Air Land Operation (TALO) – of C Company of 1 PARA during the evening of 7 May. Richards called them forward to Lungi airport when rumours spread of a *coup d'état* in Freetown. The single Hercules was packed with 102 fully armed paratroopers whose job was to seize the airport ahead of the main body. It took them two hours to fly to Freetown from Dakar and the arrival of the paratroopers caused much surprise among the hundred Nigerian UN personnel who were still nominally in control of the airport.

The following morning, Ambassador Jones formally requested the start of the evacuation operation. At 10.30 am, four Hercules carrying D Company of 1 PARA and Gibson's Tac HQ, as well as the heavily armed troops of 16 Brigade's Pathfinder Platoon, landed at Lungi. Just ahead of them was a pair of Chinooks flown by 7 Squadron pilots. At the High Commission in Freetown, Richards and his team were getting ready to begin evacuating up to a thousand UK passport holders and other foreign nationals from the city.

With the arrival of the Chinooks, at 7 pm Gibson started to fly his troops from the airport peninsula to reinforce the High Commission in Freetown and begin the evacuation from a UN-run assembly area. The 75-mile road into the city went through what was thought to be rebel-held territory so the Chinooks were vital to the success of this phase of the operation. The evacuees were picked up by Chinook and then shuttled to Lungi airport, from where they were transferred to Hercules and flown to Dakar. This phase of the operation received much publicity at the time and the Blair government publicly declared this was the only mission of UK forces in Sierra Leone. Blair's spin doctor, Alistair Campbell, was reportedly worried about how the wider intervention mission would be reported by the media so he ordered the focus to be on the rescue mission.

As the evacuation was under way, Gibson's troops were pushing in-land from Lungi airport to set up a screen of blocking positions around the capital. They were not ordered to attack the rebels, just to hold their ground and return fire if attacked. There were little more than 500 paratroopers on the ground at this time but as they moved forward through the suburbs of Freetown, the effect on the population was electric. People came out to cheer. The presence of hundreds of heavily armed British troops rallied the morale of the government and its rag-tag army. Richards told them the British were not going to leave them in the lurch. The scope of the operation now began to expand and Blair in London decided that the British troops would stay to prop up the Freetown government and help the UN.

Lungi airport was not bustling with British activity. Some twenty-one Hercules flights over two days brought in 1 PARA and its vehicles, as well as evacuating British passport holders. It had taken 1 PARA sixty-four hours from getting its first call on 5 May to having its first troops on the ground in Freetown. The paratroopers were amazed at the speed of things, which had been organised mainly through a series of telephone calls and quick verbal orders. Some veteran paratroopers were even heard praising the speed at which the RAF had managed to get its aircraft and helicopters to Freetown. They were a tough audience to please.

Two giant Antonov An-124 airlifters were chartered from the Ukraine to fly from Brize Norton to Dakar with more of 1 PARA's vehicles on 8 May. Back in the UK, PJHQ and 16 Brigade were preparing a second wave of reinforcements. A medical detachment of the Brigade soon followed 1 PARA. A battery of 105-mm Light Guns from 7 Parachute Regiment Royal Horse Artillery was sent to South Cerney and a Scimitar squadron of the Household Cavalry Regiment was ordered to prepare to deploy. The RAF had no heavy-lift aircraft to carry the armoured vehicles and artillery ammunition to Africa so the Americans were asked to help. They could not provide any aircraft in time but PJHQ decided not to press the issue because a Royal Navy carrier group, centred on HMS *Illustrious* and a Marines amphibious task group, based around the amphibious assault ship HMS *Ocean* with 42 Commando Royal Marines' were only a few days' sailing away from West Africa.

In the outskirts of Freetown, the rebel fighters of the RUF had not yet picked up fully on the fact that the British were now committed to defend the city. B Company of 1 PARA set up three blocking positions to the east of the airport and the Pathfinders moved past them to set up an early-warning post at Lungi Loi. When a group of RUF fighters approached the Pathfinder position during the night, they were engaged. The small group of British troops fired some 1,800 rounds. The rebels, many appearing to be high on drugs, could not return accurate fire and soon fled. The following morning, when the

At the end of May Royal Marine Commandos relieved 1 PARA. *(Patrick Allan)*

Pathfinders cleared the enemy positions, they found four dead rebels. Many more were believed to have been killed.

The impact on the rebels of this setback was profound. Their morale collapsed, just as the spirits of the government forces were raised by the arrival of the British forces. RUF troops were now in headlong retreat from the capital, with government troops in hot pursuit.

British forces continued their build-up at Lungi airport and continued to sustain a high profile around the capital to maintain civilian morale. Conditions were primitive and 1 PARA found Sierra Leone's equatorial climate more of a challenge than the RUF. The sudden nature of the battalion's deployment meant that it had not been able to secure enough of the right sort of anti-malaria tablets for its troops. Some twenty paratroopers and RAF pilots contracted the tropical disease.

By the end of the month, the Royal Marines had arrived off the coast and the hand-over with 1 PARA took place on 28 May. The RAF then flew the battalion back to the UK via Dakar. The operation was hailed as a great success. For no loss of UK life, 1 PARA had successfully stabilised a dangerous situation and contributed to the rout of the rebels.

Britain's involvement in Sierre Leone was only just beginning. The RAF Chinook detachment remained and the British government decided to deploy a strong training team to build up the Sierra Leone army.

On 10 July, the RAF Chinooks took part in a daring mission to lift Indian Special Forces to relieve an Indian UN garrison, which had been under siege for several weeks in the interior of Sierra Leone

The 1st Battalion, The Royal Irish Regiment, got its chance to deploy to Sierra Leone in the summer of 2000. It was tasked with establishing three company-sized groups of soldiers to act as training teams to the Sierra Leone army. The 'training teams' would be very different from other such missions in that they would be deployed as formed units that would be able to fight their way out of trouble in a crisis. Trouble soon found the Royal Irish.

By August, the RUF had evaporated after its apparent non-stop stream of set-backs but the interior of the country was still dominated by heavily armed militia groups of very shifting loyalty. One such group was known as the West Side Boys (WSBs), which had supported the government during the fighting with the RUF earlier in the year. The Royal Irish mounted regular vehicle patrols around Freetown to gather intelligence and try to establish some sort of contact with these militia groups.

On one such mission, an eleven-strong patrol was surrounded and captured by the WSBs. The soldiers were held hostage in a jungle camp, while the WSB leadership tried to negotiate with the British government. As these talks were going on, the British were preparing a rescue plan. A large contingent of Special Forces was moved in conditions of great secrecy to Freetown and was reinforced by A Company of 1 PARA. When the negotiations collapsed, the Special Forces were ordered to attack in order to rescue the hostages early on the morning of 10 September 2000.

The SAS and SBS rescue force was landed by Chinook and Lynx AH.7 on top of the village, while the paratroopers were landed at a nearby village to block any WSB escape routes. As soon as the first helicopters landed, a fierce firefight broke out. The hostages were soon freed but one SAS man was killed. Outside the main village, A Company were soon trading fire with rebels and the company commander and platoon commander were injured after British 81-mm mortar rounds detonated prematurely after hitting the jungle canopy.

One of the Chinook pilots afterwards told *RAF News*:

The fundamental key to the success of the operation was that the two-pronged assaults on the north and south camps had to be simultaneous. The Chinook was literally crammed full of paratroopers, all apparently totally focused on what they had to do, despite being in the unenviable position of having no control over their destiny while on board the aircraft. Approaching the target, we could see the enemy tracer being fired towards the aircraft. Fortunately, the Army Lynx did a superb job of suppressing the enemy positions, although seeing tracer passing above us did make us contemplate exactly what we were letting ourselves in for. The landing site turned out to be a waist-high swamp. Therefore after we lifted, we returned fire onto the enemy positions with the M-134 mini-gun, which firing at 4,000 rounds a minute, had a devastating effcct.

The SAS neutralised all resistance in the village and the paratroopers helped clean up the objectives after the operation. The now-liberated British vehicles were under-slung under Chinooks to be returned to their rightful owners.

Although Britain's intervention in Sierra Leone did not directly involve the Brigade headquarters of 16 Air Assault Brigade, many of its major units were involved. The operation was a classic example of the type of rapid intervention mission that 16 Brigade, and other elements of the Joint Rapid Reaction Force, was formed to undertake. The combination of lightly equipped paratroopers, helicopters and air transport worked well, but some in the Armed Forces worried that British forces did not really face a first-class opponent in Sierra Leone. Many British soldiers were worried that they still lacked many items of battle-winning equipment that would make the difference against more determined and better-armed opponents.

CHAPTER 7

Exercise Eagle's Strike, 2000

West Freugh airfield in southern Scotland had been under covert observation for several days by patrols from 16 Air Assault Brigade's Pathfinder Platoon. Over the next few days, they called in four RAF British Aerospace Harrier GR7 strike aircraft to bomb enemy positions around the key airbase. With the enemy's main air defence systems out of action and his supplies dwindling, it was now time for the 4 Regiment Army Air Corps' Aviation Battlegroup to go into action.

Their job was to neutralise the remaining enemy ground defences, to allow airborne troops to seize the airbase for peacekeeping operations to be mounted in the region. Using the woods and rolling hills around the airbase for cover, four Westland Gazelle AH.1 scout helicopters and four Westland Lynx AH.7 armed anti-tank helicopters quickly attacked targets that had been pinpointed by 16 Brigade's electronic warfare assets. Soon, volleys of TOW missiles were in the air, aimed at enemy armoured vehicles and troop positions. Three RAF Boeing Chinook HC.2 support helicopters used this covering fire to approach the edge of the airbase to drop off a company of US Army airborne troops from the 101st Airborne Division to secure a parachute drop zone. The commander of the Aviation Battlegroup reported the airbase to be now clear of the enemy and the arrival of the main force could proceed, protected by his screen of helicopters.

Circling out to the east, a pair of Westland Lynx AH.9 helicopters, carrying Brigadier Peter Wall and his key command staff, were monitoring the progress of the operation. It was now time to decide whether or not to commit the main assault force of the 2nd Battalion, The Parachute Regiment (2 PARA). Some 100 miles to the south, fourteen Lockheed Martin C-130 Hercules were in-bound carrying paratroopers and pallets of combat stores. After reports from the troops on the ground that the wind speed was beyond safety limits, the Brigadier ordered a tactical air landing operation (TALO). The rapid change of plan was relayed via a RAF Boeing E-3D Sentry AWACS to all the key players in the operation. Minutes later, a stream of eight RAF and USAF Hercules was rolling along West Freugh's runway, before halting to disgorge hundreds of heavily armed British and German paratroopers. Exercise Eagle's Strike was under way.

Less than a year after its formation in September 1999, the British Army's only air manoeuvre formation was put through its paces in its largest field training exercise or FTX. Every effort was put into generating aircraft, helicopters, fast jets, troops and command and control equipment to allow the Brigade staff to train to conduct complex air manoeuvre operations. This was a fraught time for the Brigade and it was far from easy to get all the resources it needed. Large British forces were still policing the Balkans and only a few months earlier British troops had intervened in Sierra Leone. Airlift aircraft and helicopters were in short supply but getting 16 Brigade up and running was a high

The flightline at West Freugh as vehicles, cargo and personnel are unloaded from an RAF Hercules. *(Tim Ripley)*

priority, so the Americans were even asked to loan some Hercules for the exercise.

Leading the Brigade in its first major FTX was its first commander, Brigadier Peter Wall, who was an airborne combat engineer or sapper, who had served in 5 Airborne Brigade's 9 Squadron Royal Engineers. A physically large man, who had a larger than life persona, Wall was not known for taking no for an answer. He was known for his ability to bulldoze aside military and civilian bureaucracy to get things done. Although he would not lead his Brigade into action, his time in command was seen by the army hierarchy as a major success because he got 16 Brigade up and running. Given the potential obstacles in terms of equipment shortages, diversion of personnel to support operations and sheer bureaucratic inertia in the Ministry of Defence civilian organisation, many observers considered it a miracle that Exercise Eagle's Strike and other 16 Brigade training events even took place in 2000.

Wall was soon on the fast track to promotion. In the 2003 invasion of Iraq, he played a key roll masterminding the British operation as chief of staff of National Component Headquarters based in the Gulf state of Qatar, before taking over command of 1 (UK) Armoured Division during the first months of the occupation of southern Iraq. He then moved to be chief of staff of the Permanent Joint Headquarters at Northwood outside

Brigadier Peter Wall,
Commander 16 Air Assault
Brigade, at West Freugh airfield
during Exercise Eagle's Strike
2000. *(Tim Ripley)*

London, where he was in day-to-day control of UK military operations in Iraq and Afghanistan. By 2007, he was a Lieutenant General and assistant chief of the defence staff, based in the Ministry of Defence in London. Wall has been described as 'one of Britain's best wartime generals' by a senior member of the Parachute Regiment. Wall had a reputation for displaying a clear understanding of the requirements of twenty-first century warfare, particularly using the media to project psychological warfare messages. He blazed a trail in 16 Brigade for ambitious senior officers, who soon recognised that a tour in Colchester was guaranteed to be eventful and a good place to get you recognised for future promotion.

During Exercise Eagle's Strike, Wall held a media briefing and unveiled much of the British Army's thinking about how its new brigade would operate.

We now have no boundaries between the old 5 Airborne Brigade's capabilities, which we have taken on, and what 24 Airmobile Brigade did. The [Army] aviation capabilities is where all the changes are taking place, more so after the Westland WAH-64 Apache arrives. The Strategic Defence Review brought the capabilities of the two brigades together to allow us to think more broadly. Both capabilities are mutually supportive. This is a happy conjunction of a number of initiatives, which live off one another, and we are pulling them together as a one star, brigade-sized joint force.

The onus [is] very much on early entry, moving quickly with light agile forces.

[Army] aviation is weaved-in in a larger scale, to give a lot more combat potential and flexibility in the way we deploy [Army] aviation and infantry. 5 Brigade, for example, never thought to perform TALO with an Aviation screen. We are working hard to give our [Army] aviation elements the 'logistic legs' comparable to the range of a C-130. [The] Apache will not have such a problem.

The exercise scenario saw the Brigade deploying from its bases in East Anglia on an imaginary peacekeeping mission to help a friendly nation threatened by a hostile neighbour. An integral part of the exercise was the move to the exercise area that was choreographed to represent deploying the Brigade in a realistic way.

Exercise Eagle's Strike Air Assets

Fixed Wing

8 Squadron, RAF	1 x Boeing E-3D Sentry AWACS
13 Squadron, RAF	2 x Panavia Tornado GR4A
Joint Force Harrier, RAF	4 x Harrier GR7
47/70 Squadrons, RAF	11 x Lockheed Hercules C1P/C3
37th Airlift Squadron USAFE	3 x Lockheed C-130E Hercules

Helicopters

18 Squadron, RAF	5 x Boeing Chinook HC.2
33 Squadron, RAF	1 x Westland Puma HC.1
654 Squadron, 4 Regt AAC	4 x Westland Lynx AH.7
	4 x Westland Gazelle AH.1
659 Squadron, 4 Regt AAC	5 x Westland Lynx AH.9

RAF Wing Commander Gavin Davey, then Air Staff Officer of 16 Brigade, commented:

Air operations began two days before the air assault with low level tactical reconnaissance by two Tornado GR4A of 13 Squadron flying from RAF Marham, using infra-red line scan. The tactical reconnaissance imagery was exploited by the Brigade at its Operational Mounting Base at South Cerney, near Cirencester in Wiltshire. It was down-linked by secure internet data link from the Reconnaissance Interpretation Centre at RAF Marham to 16 Brigade's headquarters. This contributed to the joint intelligence, surveillance, target and reconnaissance (ISTAR) picture to allow the tactical air-landing commander to plan his operation.

The operation started with simulated deep interdiction to gain and maintain air superiority, suppression of enemy air defence and then close air support attacked targets in depth. We had first established a forward operating base at Carlisle airport, on the England–Scotland border. When it was complete we got on the ground quickly to establish a forward Brigade headquarters and airhead in order to subsequently project power forward. The Brigade main headquarters spent four days

RAF Boeing E-3D Sentry AWACS aircraft acted as a key communications node during Exercise Eagle's Strike 2000. *(Tim Ripley)*

in a holding location at South Cerney planning the operation. They then projected the Pathfinders forward by C-130 using high altitude-low opening (HALO) parachuting techniques and covert night operations by helicopters. They had eyes on the objective from the high ground above the target. Meanwhile the RAF and AAC had set up a forward arming and refuelling point (FARP) within striking range of West Freugh, to support the helicopter operations in the battle area. The operation was what we call a composite air operation or COMAO.

A week of predominately ground operations followed in the Galloway Forest region, involving helicopter movement of troops and company-sized parachute drops mounted from West Freugh. The DERA-owned airfield was transformed into a forward operating base for both C-130s and helicopters, with RAF tactical air traffic control personnel from the RAF Tactical Communications Wing at RAF Brize Norton running the tower. The Brigade then reversed the operation for its move back to East Anglia, with a series of leap-frogging FARPs being set up to support the Aviation Battlegroup and RAF SHF. This phase was controlled by the NATO Combined Air Operations Centre (CAOC) at RAF High Wycombe, with a variety of fixed wing aircraft in support, including Dutch F-16s.

'Eagle's Strike is not comparable with an airborne exercise,' said Davey. 'This is air manoeuvre – it is more integrated, more effects-based, more joined up and it has more scope.'

USAF Lockheed C-130E Hercules aircraft augmented the RAF airlift force for Exercise Eagle's Strike 2000. *(Tim Ripley)*

A major element of the exercise was practising new and innovative command and control procedures to integrate the fixed wing, helicopter and ground elements into what Brigadier Wall called 'three dimensional warfare'.

Airspace control was at the centre of these efforts, with procedures being practised for the dynamic handover of control of blocks of airspace as the operation to seize West Freugh developed. The commanding officer of 4 Regiment controlled the airspace over south-west Scotland for the first phase of the operation, directing interdiction air strikes. A high density control zone was then established around West Freugh for the AAC helicopters, with other aircraft having to get specific permission from 4 Regiment before entering it. Artillery fire into or through the zone also had to be cleared with 4 Regiment. Once the ground force was established at West Freugh, airspace control passed to the commanding officer of 2 PARA.

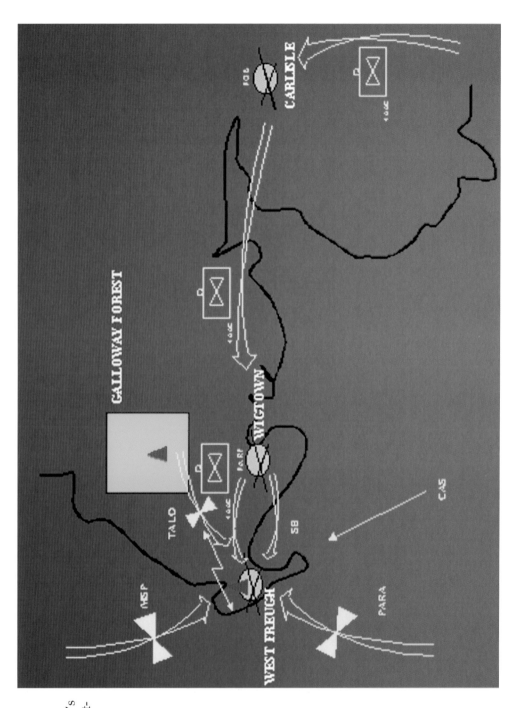

Exercise Eagle's
Strike 2000 out-
line concept
(Tim Ripley)

Exercise Eagle's Strike – The Battle

Scenario: A friendly nation represented by south-west Scotland has been blighted by civil war. British and allied forces are ordered to deploy on a peace-enforcing mission, moving by air to seize the designated main operating base at West Freugh airfield.

Phase 1 – Preparation of Battlefield

- 16 Brigade concentrates at South Cerney.

- Hercules aircraft drop reconnaissance patrols from 16 Brigade's Pathfinder platoon by HALO (high altitude, low opening) parachutes to observe West Freugh.

- Tornado GR1s conduct reconnaissance missions of West Freugh, results electronically transmitted to 16 Brigade's headquarters.

- Harrier aircraft strike targets located around West Freugh.

- RAF Support Helicopter Force and 4 Regiment Army Air Corps establish forward operating base at Carlisle airport.

Phase 2 – Insertion

- Under control of airborne command element in E-3D AWACS, air manoeuvre operation mounted to seize West Freugh.

- RAF Support Helicopter Force and 4 Regiment Army Air Corps set up Forward Arming and Refuelling Point (FARP) at Wigton to allow 4 Regiment's Aviation Battlegroup to dominate West Freugh area, neutralising enemy air and ground defences.

- 3 x Chinooks land Company of US 101st Airborne Division to secure outer perimeter.

- 2 x 47 Squadron Hercules make tactical air landing to seize runway and land tactical air control party.

- 6 x 70 Squadron Hercules parachute drop heavy combat stores.

- 3 x 70 Squadron Hercules and 3 x 37th Airlift Squadron C-130E make rapid air landing to deliver main body of 2nd Battalion, The Parachute Regiment (2 PARA), to West Freugh.

Phase 3 – Ground Operations

- RAF Support Helicopter Force and 4 Regiment Army Air Corps move 2 PARA into Galloway forest to hunt down enemy forces.

- West Freugh turned into Aerial Port of Disembarkation (APOD) for 16 Brigade, with helicopter and fixed wing movements controlled by RAF Tactical Air Traffic Team.

- RAF and USAFE Hercules launch company-sized parachute drops from West Freugh.

Phase 4

- After successful completion of ground operations, the Brigade re-deploys to Wattisham in Suffolk using air transport and leap-frogging series of FARPs.

- Fixed wing aircraft, including Dutch Lockheed Martin F-16, support air move co-ordinated by NATO Combined Air Operations Centre (CAOC) at RAF High Wycombe.

An airborne control element (ACE) flying on board the AWACS was employed for the first time to tie together all the component parts of 16 Brigade during the seizure of West Freugh airbase.

Brigadier Wall said that 'the AWACS was pivotal in drawing together such a complex plan – I was given tactical control of air assets for the first time. In the past this was not the case.'

Davey said the ACE concept was being developed in conjunction with the RAF's Air Warfare Centre at RAF Cranwell. He said:

…the ACE consisted of a RAF wing commander who was team leader, there was an Army Air Corps Major (from 4 Regiment AAC) and a brigade liaison officer. Brigadier Wall was airborne throughout the operation in a Westland Lynx AH.9,

Westland Lynx AH.9 utility helicopters were used as airborne command posts by Brigadier Wall and other senior commanders. *(Tim Ripley)*

RAF Chinook helicopters were key players in Exercise Eagle's Strike 2000 moving troops around the exercise area. *(Tim Ripley)*

along with myself, the commanding officer of 7 Royal Horse Artillery or 'CO Guns', the Brigade Plans Officer and the commander of the SHF.

It was an aspiration of the Brigade to have a data link in its headquarters to allow the recognised air picture (RAP) to be downloaded from the AWACS to give the Brigade commander the option of commanding his force from a ground location rather than having to be airborne. A dedicated command post helicopter was also being considered, with an extensive communications suite. A helicopter of EH101 Merlin or Chinook class is considered ideal for this mission because of the need to carry large command staffs and communications equipment.

AAC helicopter crews were particularly impressed at the way the AWACS significantly transformed the distances they were able to operate over. 'It relayed all our communications,' said one Lynx pilot. 'Previously comms had been a major weakness during this type of operation.'

Davey said:

The development work for the exercise was done with the RAF during NITEX in March 2000, which was a 1 PARA exercise that saw them assault RAF Kinloss in north-east Scotland. The planning mechanism was modified from that. We are pioneering new battlespace management procedures, 'CO Guns' and my team have been doing most of the work on them.

US Airborne troops of the 101st Air Assault Division board RAF Chinooks during Exercise Eagle's Strike 2000. *(Tim Ripley)*

Brigadier Wall said an 'increasing number of agencies were coming to the [air manoeuvre] party', including the AWACS community and electronic warfare. He continued:

> The evolving capability is very encouraging. A big thrust is the development of tactical doctrine and procedures. There is increasing integration with RAF Support Helicopter Force (SHF) and the tactical deployment capability of the Hercules fleet. The general thrust is joint awareness, in the Joint Rapid Reaction Force (JRRF) context. The fact that SHF and 16 Brigade are in the new Joint Helicopter Command (JHC) helps enormously.
>
> We are taking a joint approach to tactical communications, for combined RAF–Army operations. We also have a joint logistic theme for [Army] aviation and also for engineering support. In our exercise in Canada this autumn we will seek to have a mixed task force of Army and RAF helicopters, with joint fuel supplies and mixed technicians.
>
> US involvement in Eagle's Strike was very helpful. We had a US infantry company from the 101st Airborne Division and C-130s from Ramstein. We are trying to forge closer links with the 101st. In the past all 5 Brigades liaison officers were posted to the 82nd Airborne Division.
>
> There is a shading of 5 Brigade skills into 24 Brigade skills, into a new cocoon,

The command group of the 2nd Battalion, The Parachute Regiment, establish themselves at West Freugh after the Tactical Air Landing Operation (TALO) phase of Exercise Eagle's Strike 2000. *(Tim Ripley)*

a new package. This has been spurred on by the recent validation of light forces in Kosovo and Sierra Leone. 1 PARA's deployment to Africa was a model of the sort of approach to readiness we are trying to emulate. This was matched by the SHF's achievement of a thirty-hour self-deployment to Freetown. Readiness is an attitude of mind. Sierra Leone proved it in spades. There is an aspiration to work with the Royal Navy's amphibious readiness group. We are developing concepts to operate alongside our Commando cousins. Our capabilities are complementary, particularly in the littoral, such as taking down airfields. There are wider JRRF aspirations to make this happen. Opportunities might take place next year.

Over the four to ten year period we are expecting [a] new combat net radio, which will answer a lot of our communications problems, especially in the ground-to-air role. We are also looking at new light artillery, either 155 mm or rockets, new electronic warfare assets and embellishments to our infantry's firepower. Every time you evolve new ideas, you identify new equipment aspirations to glue the thing together. If we are allocated the Boeing C-17 Globemaster, it will transform our ability to take our heavy elements (artillery and helicopters) to within C-130 range of an area of interest. The potential is to use them as strategic airlift, not to operate in a tactical way.

We are evolving. There are three signposts on the route to our full operational capability. First will be the drawing together of the best capability up to brigade level

RAF Boeing Chinook HC.2s move vehicles away from West Freugh as 16 Brigade troops begin offensive operations from the airfield. *(Tim Ripley)*

The 2nd Battalion, The Parachute Regiment, secures West Freugh during the Tactical Air Landing Operation (TALO) phase of Exercise Eagle's Strike 2000. *(Tim Ripley)*

with the in-service equipment we have at the moment. Then when the first operational Apache squadrons arrive in the Brigade from 2002 onwards we will start training with them as part of their evolutionary programme. In one year's time [we] hope to see small deployable packages training with us. Finally, when all Apache are in the Brigade, we want to explore the utility of their huge potential. This will be in four to five years' time. There will then be sufficient numbers to use them en masse and to look at war fighting operations, deep raids, as well as UK participation in multi-national operations.

Brigadier Wall was pleased with the progress demonstrated on Eagle's Strike. 'We are off to a good start – all we need now is an operation,' he concluded, impatiently.

CHAPTER 8

Operation Essential Harvest

As the giant US Army Chinook helicopter approached the small field next to a makeshift rebel assault course, local ethnic Albanian villagers, rebel fighters and British paratroopers tried to ignore the dust cloud. Minutes later the helicopter was airborne, leaving a party of Macedonian members of parliament and journalists on the ground. They had come to see the rebel fighters of the National Liberation Army (NLA) hand over their arms to the paratroopers and looked very nervous being so far behind enemy lines. The flight up to the weapon collection site had taken them over bombed out villages from the eight-month long war but the arrival of NATO troops had at last calmed the situation. NATO helicopters were now flying freely over the frontlines, where only a few weeks before rebel and government forces had been confronting each other in the last Balkan ethnic war.

A US Army Boeing CH-47D Chinook delivers British paratroopers to the Brodec weapon collection point in Macedonia. (*Tim Ripley*)

British troops of NATO's Task Force Harvest count weapons handed in by NLA rebels.
(Tim Ripley)

Compared with the Balkan conflicts of the 1990s, the brief war in Macedonia in the summer of 2001 was a small-scale affair. Fewer than 100 people were killed and its impact was restricted to a relatively small area of the country. Eventually, international peacekeeping efforts resolved the conflict before it could spark widespread bloodshed. NATO military intervention was spear-headed by 16 Air Assault Brigade, in its first operational deployment. The operation proved a major success, with 16 Brigade deploying rapidly by air to the Balkans, then leap-frogging around the Macedonian countryside by helicopter to oversee the collections of weapons from rebel fighters. The political impact of the operation was significant, allowing a precarious peace accord between the rebels and the Macedonian government to take hold. NATO officially launched the operation on 22 August 2001, opening the way for more than 4,500 NATO troops from thirteen allied countries to move into Macedonia to establish weapons collection points to allow rebels to voluntarily handover their arms.

Brigadier Peter Wall did not get his wish to lead 16 Brigade on operations, before he was promoted to Major General and appointed as Chief of Joint Force Operations at the Permanent Joint Headquarters at Northwood. His successor, Brigadier Barney White-Spunner could not have been a more different character. He is the only 16 Brigade commander to date who has not had a Special Forces or Airborne Forces background. As a former commanding officer of the Household Cavalry Regiment, White-Spunner was initially treated with some caution by the Parachute Regiment veterans in 16 Brigade. His laid back 'Cavalry' style of command took some time to get used to but his willingness to protect his staff and soldiers from interference from remote headquarters back in the UK soon won him many friends within the Brigade. White-Spunner had gained a lot of experience of NATO peacekeeping operations during his time in staff jobs in the Ministry

Villages around Tetovo were heavily damaged in fighting between Albanian rebels of the NLA and Macedonian government forces.(*Tim Ripley*)

of Defence so was well versed in the intricacies of this new Balkan mission.

The first major operational item in the new Brigade Commander's in-tray was the brewing conflict in the former Yugoslav republic of Macedonia. Ethnic tension in the country had been smouldering since the 1999 Kosovo conflict. This had pitted predominantly Serb government forces against Albanian rebel fighters of the Kosovo Liberation Army (KLA) and eventually resulted in hundreds of thousands of Albanian refugees fleeing to safety in Macedonia. The subsequent NATO intervention and establishment of an international protectorate had been very unpopular in Macedonia, where its majority Slav population feared their own Albanian minority might try to break away to join their ethnic cousins in Kosovo and Albania, to form a so-called 'greater Albania'. The Albanians in Macedonia in turn complained that they were denied education rights, were economically disadvantaged and not treated as full 'Macedonian' citizens.

In the spring of 2001, former KLA fighters rebranded themselves as the NLA and launched an insurgency against the Macedonian government. They demanded equal rights for Albanians. This in turn prompted a surge in popularity for hard-line Slav nationalist parties and the appointment of Ljubco Georgievski as Macedonian Prime Minister, as well as putting another fierce nationalist, Ljube Boskovski, in charge of Interior Ministry and its paramilitary police forces. This polarisation of Macedonian politics and society continued during the late spring as rebel forces staged a series of provocative attacks close to the capital Skopje. Western governments were desperate to prevent this conflict spilling over and destabilising the southern Balkan region but the Macedonian government would not countenance any negotiations with the Albanians, who it termed 'terrorists'. NATO dispatched a negotiating team to the region, which opened discrete negotiations with the

Rebel fighters of the NLA occupied large areas of Macedonia by August 2001. *(Tim Ripley)*

NLA and Albanian politicians associated with it. The Macedonian President Boris Trajkovski was a moderate who quietly encouraged the NATO mediation effort and acted as a counterbalance to his hard-line Prime Minister. This confused political situation meant it was difficult to get the Macedonians to agree to anything. As one exasperated NATO diplomat commented, on leaving yet another meeting with Skopje government ministers, 'this is a ten-year-old country, with ten-year-old politicians'.

British Prime Minister Tony Blair was keen for NATO to pre-empt any outbreak of full-scale civil war and the fall of the Macedonian government. He wanted British forces to lead any peacekeeping mission and 16 Brigade was offered to NATO as a so-called 'framework headquarters' to lead the proposed multinational intervention force.

Task Force Harvest Troop Strength

Poland	10
France	539
Greece	413
UK	1,706
Italy	762
Turkey	141
Czech Rep	120
Netherlands	250
Spain	91
Norway	12
Canada	110
Belgium	66
Germany	480
Total	**4,700**

Contingency planning for the operation began in earnest in late June, when 16 Brigade was nominated as the tactical headquarters by NATO. Its commander, Brigadier White-Spunner, and his planning staff conducted four reconnaissance missions to Macedonia during July to get the lie of the land and work out how they would conduct their mission. Unfortunately, the UK armed forces were scheduled to start a major training exercise in the Middle East in the autumn and 16 Brigade had had to transfer equipment to other units to allow them to participate in this event. The bulk of the RAF's Chinook helicopter force, particularly scarce refuelling tankers and vital packs of spare parts, was already committed to the exercise and most of the aircraft were already *en route* to the Middle East by ship. Other nations would be asked to fill these capability gaps.

NATO peace negotiators were hard at work during July and into August trying to bring the two sides together as the war seemed to be escalating out of control. Heavy fighting was taking place in Macedonia's second city, Tetovo, and the rebels planted mines that killed several government troops near the capital, which prompted retaliation by paramilitary forces loyal to the Interior Minister. He was subsequently prosecuted by the Hague war crimes tribunal for this incident. Time was rapidly running out. US and European Union negotiators were able to drag the parties to sign the so-called Ohrid Framework Agreement for Peace on 13 August. To capitalise on the momentum of the peace deal, Britain pushed NATO into agreeing to deploy 16 Brigade headquarters ahead of a durable cease-fire being in place, which had previously been a NATO condition for launching Operation Essential Harvest.

The operation was designed as a confidence-building measure to try to persuade the Macedonian Slav population that the NLA could be trusted to keep to the cease-fire, ahead of peace negotiations. It was also intended that NATO forces would not get bogged down manning 'separation lines' between the two sides that might be used to mark ethnic boundaries. Rather than set up bases in tense frontline areas, it was decided that the collection sites would be temporary in nature. This reduced the time they were exposed to hostile fire and ensured NATO troops would not have to build fixed positions in sensitive frontline areas. For these reasons, 16 Brigade was to leapfrog troops out to weapon collection points by helicopter or vehicle before pulling

The Commander of 16 Air Assault Brigade, Brigadier Barney White-Spunner. *(Tim Ripley)*

A US Army 101st Air Assault Division door gunner on a Chinook bound for a weapon collection site. *(Tim Ripley)*

them back to bases around Skopje and Petrovec airport. For the NATO soldiers participating in Operation Essential Harvest, the experience was unlike any other previous Balkan mission. In Bosnia and Kosovo, NATO's mandate and legal powers were enshrined in internationally agreed treaties; whereas in Macedonia the Skopje government remained the sovereign authority and alliance troops were only present in the country to carry out a limited mission, as agreed between the signatories of the Ohrid agreement. Task Force Harvest (TFH), as the new NATO force was dubbed, was a political tool. It was designed to facilitate the handing-in of rebel arms, which would trigger responses from the Macedonian government and parliament. Its command structure was configured for this role, with the one-star headquarters of the UK's 16 Air Assault Brigade providing tactical command of the allied troop contingents assigned to the task force's Multi-National Brigade, and the two-star task force headquarters acting as the military-diplomatic interface. The main Task Force Harvest headquarters was co-located within the existing NATO Kosovo Force (KFOR) Rear Headquarters building at the Shoe Factory on the outskirts of Skopje.

On 16 August a small element of 16 Brigade's command team flew to Naples to confer with NATO's southern regional commander, US Navy Admiral James Ellis, before flying into Skopje's Petrovec airport the following day in a blaze of publicity. Handling the arrival of the aircraft carrying 16 Brigade's equipment, vehicles and personnel, was a small French Air Force team that ran NATO's Airport of Disembarkation (APOD) at

Task Force Harvest's Brigade headquarters at the Free Trade Zone near Petrovec airport. *(Tim Ripley)*

Petrovec, Macedonia's principal civil and military airport.

The newly arrived headquarters team moved to set up its command post in the deserted 'Chinese' Free Trade Zone at Bunardzik a few kilometres north of Petrovec airport, which had been built several years before with funding from the Taiwanese government in a failed bid to win the Skopje government's support for its UN membership. The empty building was soon packed with tents containing planning cells and operations rooms. Its drainage system could not cope with the hundreds of soldiers now in residence and Royal Engineers had to be called in to put in new water supplies.

The first task of Brigadier White-Spunner and his troops was to set up a system of liaison between the rebel and government forces to cement the tenuous cease-fire. On 18 August, in the first operational sortie by the new Boeing C-17A Globemaster II of the RAF's 99 Squadron, three AAC Westland Lynx AH.7s, of 657 Squadron, were delivered to Petrovec. They were needed to carry British Special Forces teams deep into rebel territory to establish contact with the commanders of the NLA. They were soon joined by two 654 Squadron AAC Gazelles and two RAF Westland Puma HC.1s of 33 Squadron, detached from the main British NATO force at Pristina in Kosovo to help 16 Brigade.

Hard-line Macedonian nationalists were far from happy with the arrival of NATO troops in their country and they set about making life as difficult as possible for Task Force Harvest. A group of protestors blocked the main road from Kosovo into Macedonia, preventing NATO KFOR troops in the UN-administered Yugoslav province from providing logistic support for the new task force or receiving supplies from the huge NATO logistic base at Petrovec. Allied troop contingents now began to set up a fixed wing and helicopter airlift to overfly the protestors. Central to this effort were the four Boeing CH-47D Chinooks of the US Army's 101st Airborne Division based at Camp Bondsteel

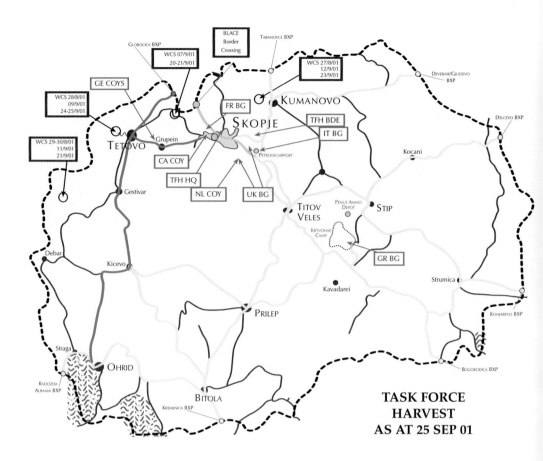

Weapon collection operations by Task Force Harvest *(TFH/NATO)*

in southern Kosovo. Bravo Company of the 101st Division's 7th Battalion was soon flying an hourly shuttle with under-slung loads back and forth between Camp Able Sentry at Petrovec to Bondsteel and other locations in Kosovo.

The first four days of the operation saw just over two dozen sorties by RAF Lockheed Hercules C.1Ks of the Lynham Transport Wing and six C-17A sorties. With the help of Brize Norton-based Vickers VC-10s, the Hercules and C-17 force moved almost 400 British personnel to Macedonia to allow 16 Brigade's commander to get his headquarters fully operational. Dozens of allied aircraft were also soon heading for Petrovec. First to arrive were two Czech Antonov An-26s carrying a company of paratroopers to guard the TFH brigade headquarters. A French Air Force CASA CN235 followed soon after with a small group of staff officers heading for 16 Brigade's headquarters.

On 20 August NATO's Supreme Allied Commander Europe, USAF General Joe Ralston, made a brief visit to Skopje to meet allied commanders and diplomats to assess if conditions were right to give the go ahead to formally launch Operation Essential Harvest. Despite almost nightly breaches of the cease-fire and political in-fighting within

Task Force Harvest's Brigade headquarters. *(Tim Ripley)*

the ranks of the Macedonian government, the North Atlantic Council, NATO's supreme political authority, accepted General Ralston's recommendation to begin the operation. A formal activation order was issued and the first troop contingents began moving late on 22 August.

First to arrive was a contingent of French Foreign Legion infantrymen. They were flown to Petrovec on French Air Force Douglas DC-8s and C.160 Transalls. A RAF VC-10K of 101 Squadron brought the first elements of the British Army's 2nd Battalion, the Parachute Regiment (2 PARA), into Macedonia in the early hours of the following day. More British troops followed during the day on eight flights as Lockheed TriStars of 216 Squadron joined the airlift. Dutch Fokker 60s and McDonnell Douglas KDC-10s, German C.160s, as well as Canadian and Spanish Hercules, were much in evidence moving their contingents. Canada hired giant Antonov An-124 airlifters to help move the Light Armoured Vehicles (LAV) of its contingent from Bosnia to Petrovec.

Task Force Harvest Order of Battle, September 2001

Task Force Harvest Headquarters
Gazella Metall Factory, Skopje
Commander Major General Gunnar Lange (Danish Army)

Task Force Harvest Multi-National Brigade
Headquarters 16 Air Assault Brigade
Commander Brigadier Barney White-Spunner

British Contribution

216 Signal Squadron, Royal Signals
RHQ 7th Parachute Regiment Royal Horse Artillery (7 Para RHA) Aldershot
Elements 30 & 14 Signals Regiments
Pathfinder Platoon
G Squadron, 22 Special Air Service Regiment
654 Squadron Army Air Corps, 2 x Gazelle AH.1
33 Squadron RAF, 2 x Puma
657 Squadron Army Air Corps, 3 x Lynx AH.7
Squadron, Scots Dragoon Guards
9 Parachute Squadron and 65 Field Support Squadron, Royal Engineers
Elements 13 Air Assault Support Regiment, Royal Logistic Corps
Elements 16 Close Support Medical Regiment and 5 Medical Regiment
Elements 7 Battalion and 8 Close Support Company, Royal Electrical & Mechanical Engineers
156 Provost Company, RMP
RAF Mobile Air Operations Team
47 Air Despatch Squadron, Royal Logistic Corps
29 Regiment, Royal Logistic Corps (airport unloading)
2nd Battalion, The Parachute Regiment (UK) (680 men), including
1 x Dutch Company, from 11th Battalion of Airmobile Battalion (250 men and SISU APC)

Multi-national Contributions

US

F Company, 159th Aviation Battalion, 4 x CH-47D Chinook
Bravo Company, 7th Battalion, 101st Airborne Division, 4 x CH-47D
2 x UH-60 Blackhawk (medevac)
Task Force Hunter, 6 x Hunter unmanned aerial vehicle (UAV)

OTHERS

Canada Force Reconnaissance Squadron (200 men)
Czech Republic Airborne Company (140 men)
2nd Foreign Legion Infantry Regiment (2 REI) (France) (500 French and
   120 vehicles), including 1 x Spanish Legion 'Austria' Company (120
   men and 20 APC)
2 x German Mechanised Companies (each 150 men), 150 armoured
   vehicles. Plus 200 strong support element
Greek 525th Mechanised Battalion (410 men)
Italian 'Sassari' Mechanised Regiment (450 operational + 250 support,
   including 1 x Turkish Company (150 men))

The existing NATO base at Petrovec could not cope with the new arrivals and the first TFH troops were moved into a series of improvised bases in disused industrial sites or farm complexes around the Skopje area. 2 PARA were sent to a former peanut factory, which they dubbed Camp Arnhem. The facilities were primitive and the British Army was found to be sorely lacking in portable showers, washing and cooking facilities. The poor quality of the British Army's expeditionary infrastructure equipment was brought to the fore. The paratroopers mucked in and made the best of their lot. Up the road the French Foreign Legion were living in relative luxury thanks to their pre-packed containers of tents, showers, camp beds and other kit they had ready for such missions.

RAF Hercules were sent to Pristina on 26 August to pick up the Scimitar armoured reconnaissance vehicles of the Scots Dragoon Guards, which had been stopped from joining 16 Brigade because of the border blockade. They were then flown southwards to Petrovec.

An aviation element of the Task Force Harvest Multi-National Brigade grew as the NATO mission gathered pace. The US Army offered to make Bravo Company's Chinooks available for troop and cargo movement tasks. A further four other Chinooks were deployed to Camp Able Sentry from Germany to take over the border re-supply tasks, freeing Bravo Company to fully support Task Force Harvest. Two UH-60s were also placed on alert at Camp Able Sentry, to fly casualty evacuation missions for the new NATO force. Surveillance support for Task Force Harvest was provided by six IAI/TRW BQM-155A Hunter unmanned aerial vehicles (UAVs) of Alpha Company, 15th Military Intelligence Battalion (Aerial Exploitation), already based at Petrovec airport.

With cease-fire violations threatening to unravel the peace deal, the commander of Task Force Harvest, Danish Major General Gunnar Lange, and Brigadier White-Spunner, were keen to get the thirty-day weapon collection operation under way as fast as possible. Three phases of weapon collection were planned to coincide with votes in the Macedonian parliament to ratify elements of the peace plan or changes to the constitution, so each phase was conducted under conditions of considerable political pressure and tension.

Reconnaissance and planning went into high gear on 25 and 26 August to prepare for the first weapon collection operation. Hunter UAVs were sent to scour around the target areas in the village of Otlija, north-east of Skopje. At the same time 657 Squadron was moving British Army liaison teams from 7th Parachute Regiment Royal Horse Artillery

16 Brigade's Pathfinder Platoon provided a key element of the Harvest Liaison Teams working with rebel and government forces. *(Tim Ripley)*

(7 RHA) and the Special Forces to meet rebel and government military commanders to ensure they were ready for what was about to happen.

At the heart of Task Force Harvest's efforts to ensure the weapons-collection phases went smoothly were its liaison efforts to establish contacts, at all levels of command, with all the military, police and rebel elements in Macedonia. Under the command of Lieutenant Colonel Duncan Francis, commanding officer of 7 RHA, within hours of 16 Brigade arriving in Macedonia on 17 August, what became known as the Harvest Liaison Teams (HLT) were spreading out to set up contacts on both sides of the frontline.

Lieutenant Colonel Francis said:

> Our mission was to ensure there was an open ground picture for both sides. So nothing was hidden, there were no surprises. That's when you get incidents. We had teams with both sides at all levels, from guys in the trenches to Ministry of Defence and Interior Ministry. We started off doing initial recces, established likely key points of contact at highest levels, and then worked down in the NLA and Macedonia Army. We had liaison officers with the OSCE, international organisations and non-governmental organisations, to try to draw them into the picture. What drives such missions is identifying key people on either side.

The 200-strong HLT operated as a distinct element of 16 Brigade, with 7 PARA RHA providing the command element with many of its forward-observation personnel re-roled as self-contained liaison teams. Three Lynx AH.7 helicopters of 657 Squadron supplied the airlift element of the HLT and 16 Brigade's Pathfinder Platoon provided a mobile element of the HLT in frontline areas. British and Norwegian special forces troops also participated in the HLT, as did other allied personnel.

NLA rebels hand in their weapons to Task Force Harvest. *(Tim Ripley)*

On 26 August, the first elements of the Foreign Legion and 2 PARA were flown in by US Army Chinook to secure the first collection site. The operation proper got under way the following morning when the bulk of the force was delivered by Chinook to establish a wide perimeter to allow the rebels to hand over their arms unmolested. An RAF Mobile Air Operations Team (MAOT) team was on hand to control the helicopters as they flew in and out of landing zones near the collection site.

As this operation was getting under way, a British soldier was fatally injured by a mob of Macedonian nationalist youths who dropped a slab of concrete on his Land Rover from a bridge over the main road into Skopje. His colleagues flagged down a US Army convoy and the wounded soldier was taken to the US Army medical centre at Camp Able Sentry. He was then flown by a US Army Blackhawk to the US medical facility at Bondsteel but they could not treat him, so he was then flown back to Skopje's main civilian hospital for neuro-surgery. He died nine hours later. The incident cast a shadow over the day's events and proved a source of continuing tension, as British commanders suspected that the Macedonian police, under orders from the Interior Minister, were not investigating the case with much vigour.

With only lightly equipped infantry units from Britain and France in Macedonia at this stage in the operation, to set up the first collection sites, Bravo Company's Chinooks were essential. They moved the troops into position, removed containers of collected weapons and recovered the forces after their mission. The first collection site was opened north of Skopje on the morning of 27 August by the French Foreign Legion and 2 PARA. As it was only ten kilometres north of the main NATO bases at Petrovec airport, it was supported by a number of allied armoured vehicles. When the column of vehicles approached the site, Macedonian troops started firing on NLA positions in an attempt to get the collection effort halted. British SAS troops and Foreign Legionnaires moved into fire positions and the Macedonians backed off and caused no more trouble.

By early afternoon the weapon collection activity was well under way. American Chinooks, British Gazelles and Pumas and French Army Aviation Eurocopter Super Pumas flew in a VIP and media party to view the proceedings.

British paratroopers lived in very basic conditions in a former factory during the Macedonian mission. *(Tim Ripley)*

Even as that operation was continuing, a far more ambitious mission was under way to set up a collection point in the village of Brodec, high in the mountains of western Macedonia. Unlike the Otlija operation, where vehicle-borne troops were also involved, the operation set for 28 August would be undertaken completely by helicopter. As before, Hunter UAVs were sent to scout of the lie of the land for 2 PARA and on 27 August an advance guard of British paratroopers and Dutch air mobile troops were inserted by two Chinooks. In the early hours of 29 August, eight Chinooks delivered the main body of 2 PARA to establish the collection site. Night vision goggles were used to ensure the helicopters delivered their cargo under the cover of darkness. Later in the morning the Chinooks then delivered ISO containers for the rebel weapons to be loaded into.

16 Brigade's support helicopter liaison officer, RAF Flight Lieutenant Al Richie, recalled:

The collection points out in western Macedonia were very inaccessible by road so we were not able to get in vehicles. We inserted advance elements of our battlegroup on two Chinooks loaded with troops the day before the collection began. They were the enabling force for the operation.

The following morning we inserted eight Chinook loads of troops, then the security party, specialist engineers to collect weapons, ISO containers to carry out weapons, as well as the media and VIPs. We ran the operation to a timetable. Each air operation was a concentrated package – not so much an air assault, more a logistic move in nature, getting enablers in place.

US Army Chinook instructor pilot, warrant officer CW3 Matthew Carmichael, recalled, 'I flew the night vision goggle portion of the mission. We took off at 5.30 am lifting troops and containers for weapons.' Chinooks were on task for the remainder of the day moving senior commanders, VIPs and media parties into the site to view the proceedings, before finally extracting the force back to base.

Carmichael said Bravo Company's aircraft flew sixty hours' flight time during the first three-day phase of the operation, lifting French Foreign Legionnaires, British paratroopers and Dutch air mobile troops. Carmichael said:

> The British and Dutch have Chinooks and knew our aircraft, while the French had [been] used to Boeing CH-46 Sea Knight[s] but the Czech paratrooper quick reaction force needed to have static land training before we could work with them. The British Army loading crews were good – they were real quick at slinging loads.

The commanding officer of 2 PARA, Lieutenant Colonel 'Chip' Chapman, said co-operation with the US Army helicopters was 'excellent' and 'flawless'. He attributed this to the excellent interpersonal relationship formed by the long-established practice of posting exchange officers between the 101st Division and the British Parachute Regiment. Chapman said the mountainous and wooded terrain restricted the availability of helicopter landing sites, so his troops had to be channelled through a handful of them.

> An advance party would be dropped off ahead of the main body to establish links to NLA. Then we would surge in as short as possible time, then the boys would bomb-burst from the landing site to their objectives. Then we would drive in the road party overland to establish the weapon collection site. I could not land observation parties on the hills above the site, there was nowhere to land.

Phase one of the weapon collection mission was completed the following morning when a company-sized group of 2 PARA was airlifted to south-western Macedonia at Tamuse. These three operations netted more than 1,200 weapons and set the stage for NATO's diplomats to apply pressure on the Macedonian parliament to begin implementing the constitutional changes as required under the peace plan. This took longer than expected and it was not until 6 September that the parliament passed the vital vote.

16 Brigade's limited command and

Lieutenant Colonel 'Chip' Chapman, commanding officer of the 2nd Battalion, The Parachute Regiment. *(Tim Ripley)*

control assets were stretched thin during the operation, with the small air cell in the headquarters not only being responsible for air mobility operations, but also establishing a liaison regime with the Macedonian military and civil aviation authorities. This monitored compliance with cease-fire restrictions on where Macedonian aircraft could fly. An RAF MAOT deployed with the ground units to act as the air cell's eyes on ground, co-ordinating helicopter movements near collection sites and carrying reconnaissance of the ground for helicopter landings zones.

Two US officers were assigned to the Brigade air cell to receive tasking requests from the British. They in turn passed them to a special headquarters set up in Camp Able Sentry to co-ordinate all US support for Task Force Harvest.

Richie said:

We have been very busy. We had to set up how to run airspace. We are a small unit running a compact operation as [an] air cell, we were almost operating as a one or two star level headquarters, a Air Operations Control Centre (AOCC) or a Combined Air Operations Centre (CAOC).

Task Force Hunter

Operation Essential Harvest was the first time 16 Brigade was able to use unmanned aerial vehicles in a realistic setting and they proved an important element in the success of the mission.

Major Dennis Griffin, the commander of Task Force Hunter, commented:

We had a training day with British G2 cell before Brigade began operations. The Joint Broadcast System sends our imagery to the TFH HQ. They could turn on a TV and watch 'Hunter TV'. The British used us more in an Intel role than US, where the pressure is to use us by G3 operators. The Brits are always using us to look ahead at operations one or two days' ahead. We were not relaying imagery live from first weapon collection operation. [A US commander would have used us to watch the operation.] The Brits say we are mission critical, more in G2 channel, their collection cycle.

An IAI/TRW RQ-5 Hunter unmanned aerial vehicle at Petrovec airport. *(Tim Ripley)*

A major communication challenge for 2 PARA was how to get a satellite television into the Peanut Factory to allow them to watch the World Cup qualifying match between England and Germany on 1 September. England won 5 to 1, producing a major boost in morale among the Toms of 2 PARA.

In the run up to the key parliamentary vote on 6 September, Macedonian hard-liners continued to stage incidents in the flash point town of Tetovo to destabilise the peace plan. 657 Squadron was much in evidence flying surveillance missions over Tetovo in its Lynx to support the 16 Brigade Pathfinder Platoon patrols monitoring the cease-fire line. US Army Blackhawks also ferried NATO negotiators to the main rebel base at Sipkovica high above Tetovo to ensure continued rebel compliance.

Within hours of the parliamentary vote on 6 September, 2 PARA began its operation to set up a collection point at Radusa, north-west of Skopje, inserting reconnaissance teams during the evening. The main helicopter-borne operation went smoothly with some 150 weapons handed in by the NLA's 115th Brigade on 7 September. It was the turn of the French to run the next collection site between 8 and 10 September at Brodec in Operation Tapanar. US Chinooks again played a key role flying the main body of the force into location.

During the morning of 11 September NATO staff officers and soldiers were in the process of preparing for the next day's operations when television screens in their headquarters started to show the live coverage of the Al Qaeda attacks on New York and Washington DC. In the main 16 Brigade headquarters there was a stunned silent as personnel stood around watching the television coverage of the events in the USA. 'Everything we were doing here seemed insignificant compared to what was happening in America,' commented one British soldier present.

The events in the USA also had a distinct effect on the Albanians and Macedonians. Television news crews started leaving to head for Afghanistan. International diplomats suddenly found their political masters had more important things to do than listen to the whinging of politicians in Skopje. The Albanians and Macedonians realised quickly that the US and NATO had lost patience with them and they could no longer procrastinate. The world had changed and the Balkans were no longer at the centre of global events.

Even so, Operation Essential Harvert had to continue. The Italian and Turkish battlegroups opened their collection site at Otlija on 12 September, moving mainly by vehicle from their bases at nearby Petrovec airport. Gurkha paratroopers attached to 2 PARA got the opportunity to open the final collection site of the second phase of Operation Essential Harvest when they flew to open a site at Tamuse in western Macedonia on 12 September. This phase of the operation netted more than 1,000 weapons.

The final round of weapons collection began on 20 September with French troops moving by road to Radusa. The Gurkhas were airlifted high into the mountains at Tamuse in Bravo Company's Chinook and Italian 412s the following day in the 'snap' operation. A day later, the Italian battlegroup opened the Otlija collection site in a ground operation. It was down to 2 PARA to conduct the final collection operation at Brodec, after moving by road to a forward staging area to reduce the flying time to the objective and time between lifts. 2 PARA remained on the ground for over twenty-four hours and pulled back to base during the afternoon of 25 September.

On 25 September NATO Secretary General George Robertson was flown by Chinook to the large German base at Erebino for a ceremony to mark the end of Operation

Essential Harvest. As he was announcing that NATO had received 3,875 weapons compared with the projected 3,300 weapons, a constant stream of Chinooks could be heard flying overhead, ferrying 2 PARA back from Brodec to Petrovec airport.

In a concentrated thirty-day period, Bravo Company's Chinooks flew some 204 hours in 182 sorties, carrying 3,988 passengers, twenty-six containers of weapons and twenty-nine vehicles. The Hunter UAVs flew twenty-six missions, totalling 196.2 hours, in support of Task Force Harvest, before it began re-deploying back to its home base in early October.

For 16 Air Assault Brigade, the operation was a major success. It had pulled off a complex mission that had the potential to go seriously wrong, without firing a shot in anger. Macedonia's politicians were now talking about their country's future. Within months the hard-line nationalists on the Slav side were gone from government and the former guerrilla leaders of the disbanded NLA were soon wearing suits to signify their transformation into political leaders.

Although some of the doctrine purists in 16 Brigade insisted the use of helicopters during Operation Essential Harvest did not qualify as true air manoeuvre, undoubtedly strategic airlift and battlefield helicopter transport were instrumental to NATO's success. The Brigade had deployed all its personnel and the bulk of its vehicles by air at very short notice, making use of the RAF's new C-17s for the first time in a real operation. Some vehicles had gone by ship but this did not delay the start of the operation. The lack of life-support equipment for British troops was identified as a major shortcoming. Fortunately, NATO already had a large logistic footprint in Macedonia, supporting the NATO-led Kosovo Force (KFOR), so 16 Brigade and many of the troop contingents were able to benefit greatly from the massive base-infrastructure around Petrovec airport, east of Skopje – enabling Task Force Harvest and 16 Brigade to hit the ground running. In less benign environments, the shortage of mobile showers, laundry units, camp beds, washing bowls and chemical toilets would have been more of a problem.

By the end of September, NATO had activated Task Force Amber Fox in Macedonia with the task of providing protection for unarmed civilian monitors who were to patrol the country's still tense ethnic conflict zones. Until it was fully up and running in mid-October, Lieutenant Colonel Francis, the Pathfinder and the HLT headquarters remained in Macedonia. The rest of TFH was already heading home and 2 PARA was back in Colchester by 11 October.

There was a mood of frustration among 16 Brigade personnel that they were still in Macedonia, while a new war was about to start in Afghanistan. Lieutenant Colonel 'Chip' Chapman of 2 PARA summed up this mood during the final weapon collection mission to Brodec, when he was heard declaring that 'hunting down Osama bin Laden in the caves of Afghanistan would be the pinnacle of his military career'. Unfortunately, he was not to get his wish, although the Colonel would soon be in Afghanistan.

CHAPTER 9

Afghanistan, 2002

Kabul in January 2002 was a hot bed of intrigue. Politicians, warlords, foreign diplomats, bounty hunters, secret agents and special forces operatives were all manoeuvring for influence and information in the power vacuum caused by the sudden collapse of the Taliban regime a few weeks before. The US and its allies were backing newly installed Afghan President Hamid Karzai. Keeping him in power would depend on the arrival of a strong force of western troops.

Waiting around for delayed aircraft and shivering in freezing cold tents is how most 16 Air Assault Brigade's soldiers recall their three month-long mission to Afghanistan in the first months of 2002.

Operation Fingal opened the way for the international peacekeeping troops to arrive *en masse* in the Afghan capital, Kabul, but it was more of a test of 16 Brigade's logistic and survival skills, than its combat power.

In the aftermath of the Al Qaeda attacks on New York and Washington DC on 11 September 2001, the UK offered the US military help to hunt down and destroy Osama bin Laden's forces in Afghanistan. By early October 2007 US troops, assisted by British aircraft, Tomahawks fired from nuclear attack submarines and special forces on the ground, had penetrated Afghanistan. Barely six weeks later, the Islamic fundamentalist Taliban regime, which had been harbouring the Al Qaeda chief and his associates, had been toppled.

US troops and allies from local militia allies had swept into Kabul and then moved south and east to mop up the final pockets of Taliban and Al Qaeda resistance. The then US Defence Secretary Donald Rumsfeld was keen to keep the number of American troops in Afghanistan to a minimum and had little interest in them doing anything but hunting down Osama bin Laden.

A sentry from the 2nd Battalion, The Parachute Regiment, on guard in Kabul.
(Private Collection)

The Al Qaeda attacks on New York and Washington DC in September 2001 led to US-led intervention in Afghanistan. *(US DoD)*

A strong contingent of British Special Forces, assisted by units of Royal Marine Commandos, had fought alongside the Americans during the brief campaign against the Taliban and Al Qaeda. A small UK base had been established at Bagram airbase to the north-east of Kabul to support Special Forces operations. Planners at the UK's Permanent Joint Headquarters (PJHQ) at Northwood, outside London, had developed a number of contingency plans to move large combat forces to join the battle in Afghanistan. Most were out of date before the ink was dry on them. These plans all centred on either 3 Commando Brigade or 16 Air Assault Brigade. As 16 Brigade was still recovering its troops and equipment from Macedonia during October 2001, the Royal Marines got the first bite at supporting the Special Forces in October. During early November, 16 Brigade had its readiness state raised in preparation for a possible Afghan deployment to relieve the Royal Marines, although at this stage the type of operation it would undertake was very unclear. There was a spate of media reports speculating that the Parachute Regiment would soon join the hunt for bin Laden in the caves of the Tora Bora mountain range.

Amid the chaos of the collapse of the Taliban regime a power vacuum was developing in Kabul, so international leaders wanted to set up a process to form a new broadly based Afghan government. This would bring together the predominately Tajik warlords of the local militia allies with Pushtun tribal leaders from the south and east. The Americans and British were keen to install a pro-western Pushtan guerrilla leader, Hamid Karzai, as the new Afghan president. A conference was called in the German city of Bonn on 6 December to hammer out a deal to line up international support behind Karzai's new interim administration. It was then intended to hold an Afghan tribal grand assembly or Loya Jirga to formalise a new constitution and open the way for national elections. A key element of the so-called 'Bonn Process' was the setting up of an International Security

RAF Boeing C-17A Globemaster aircraft could only land at US-run airfields in
Afghanistan at night to avoid enemy missile threats. *(US DoD)*

Assistance Force (ISAF) in Kabul to oversee this political process and protect the new
Afghan government.

British Prime Minister Tony Blair saw an opportunity to influence events in
Afghanistan and he quickly offered British troops to lead ISAF. Within days, Major
General John McColl, commander of 3 (UK) Division, was on his way to Kabul with a
300-strong team of staff officers and communications personnel to set up his headquarters
to run the still to be formed ISAF. The British government then offered 1,500 troops to
serve in the 6,000-strong ISAF for an initial three-month period, although at this stage
there was little idea what these troops would do.

McColl arrived in Kabul in the middle of December to find the city in turmoil. Rival
militia groups were occupying key points around the city, government buildings were
deserted and public utilities were functioning erratically. Out in the countryside, US troops
were still finding and fighting by-passed groups of Taliban and Al Qaeda fighters. The newly
installed President Karzai controlled little more than his palace. McColl quickly 'borrowed'
some Royal Marines from the Special Forces at Bagram to guard Karzai's inauguration on 22
December and then to mount joint patrols with newly recruited Afghan police.

RAF Lockheed Martin C-130 Hercules aircraft were able to operate from Kabul International Airport after British engineers cleared war debris in late January 2002. *(KMNB Pool/Tim Ripley)*

Back in Colchester, Brigadier Barney White-Spunner and his command team were trying to work out what they would do in Afghanistan. Beyond being allocated the 2nd Battalion, The Parachute Regiment (2 PARA), there was little guidance from the Ministry of Defence or PJHQ on the role or composition of ISAF. It was intended that 16 Brigade would form the core of what was dubbed ISAF's Kabul Multi-National Brigade (KMNB). The force would have two battlegroups or battalions, plus a variety of support elements, drawn from fourteen troop-contributing nations. The whole force would have to deploy and be sustained by air because of the lack of local infrastructure in Afghanistan. Initially, the force would be inserted into Bagram airbase until Kabul International Airport was cleared of war damage and reopened.

Afghan President Hamid Karzai relied on US and NATO troops to secure his regime in the early days of 2002. *(US DoD)*

FRONT

Hunting down Al Qaeda chief Osama bin Laden remained the main priority of US troops in Afghanistan in early 2002. *(NATO)*

BACK

PUSHTO		DARI
UP TO A $25,000,000 REWARD FOR INFORMATION LEADING TO THE WHEREABOUTS OR CAPTURE OF THESE TWO MEN.		UP TO A $25,000,000 REWARD FOR INFORMATION LEADING TO THE WHEREABOUTS OR CAPTURE OF THESE TWO MEN.

A brief reconnaissance mission to Kabul in the middle of December did little to help clarify the situation because events on the ground were moving too fast.

16 Brigade's troops had Christmas at home but within days the Brigade headquarters staff were on their way to the UK's Forward Mounting Base (FMB) at Thumrait in Oman. The desert airbase had been turned into the UK's main air transport hub for the Afghan mission and all the troops heading for Operation Fingal would pass through it. On arrival at Thumrait, it became clear to White-Spunner and his team that actually getting to Afghanistan was easier said than done. The US Air Force controlled Afghan airspace and Bagram airbase. They were strictly rationing landing slots at Bagram because of the lack of parking space and fuel at the base. At this stage of the campaign, the Americans were also not allowing aircraft to land at Bagram during daylight because of the threat of Al Qaeda surface-to-air missile attacks.

The final shape and size of the British contribution to Operation Fingal was not even confirmed when the 16 Brigade command team got to Thumrait. Several frustrating and confusing days therefore followed as planners tried to firm things up and then persuade the Americans to make the required landing slots available.

Back in Britain, a KMNB force planning seminar was held in South Cerney in

Afghanistan *(CIA)*

Gloucestershire on 27 December to hammer out the details of international participation in ISAF. Canada, Denmark, France, Germany, Greece, Italy, Jordan, New Zealand, the Netherlands, Spain and Turkey all sent delegates to the meeting.

On the same day, White-Spunner and his small command team were airborne from Thumrait to Bagram. They found the Afghan capital gripped by freezing winter weather and locked in political intrigue as the members of the interim government jockeyed for position.

Over the next two weeks, the remainder of the Brigade routed via Thumrait to Afghanistan. The pressure to get troops on the ground in Kabul to shore up Karzai's government was immense. This was often at the expense of logistic supplies, vehicles and other items considered non-essential. The British Army's stocks of mobile showers, washing bowls, toilets, heated tents and camp beds, or expeditionary infra-structure equipment as the essential kit was dubbed, proved to be minimal. Hardly any of this sort of material could be bought locally in war ravaged Afghanistan so the resultant living conditions for the British troops in Kabul were primitive. Royal Engineers building camps for 16 Brigade had to scavenge for wood and other materials from bomb-damaged buildings because it had low priority on the air transport plan. It was a similar situation with food and water, so for most of their time in Kabul, 16 Brigade ate army ration packs

Freezing winter weather made life miserable for British troops in Kabul during January and February 2002. *(Private Collection)*

rather than fresh food. Giant Antonov An-124 airlifters were chartered to lift 16 Brigade's vehicles but only a few flights a week were possible until the RAF and Royal Engineers opened Kabul airport later in January. The convoluted air transport chain plagued the deployment and bureaucratic problems meant the first wave of 2 PARA arrived in Afghanistan without live ammunition.

In spite of the logistic problems, the first paratroopers patrol took place in Kabul on 11 January. This coincided with an agreement with several warlords to move their troops out of the capital and the storage of their heavy weapons. Senior ISAF officers and international diplomats brokered this deal and then had to maintain a constant round of meetings to keep the leaders of the new Afghanistan on side.

For the ordinary soldiers of 16 Brigade, the experience of living in Kabul was sobering, even for veterans of Balkan war zones. Large parts of the city had been devastated from more than two decades of war. The population lived in abject poverty and the breakdown of utilities after the fall of the Taliban added to their privations. British troops became involved in several charity projects, including setting up ambulance services and children's hospitals.

In the middle of February, the Brigade helped organise a football match between the ISAF and an Afghan team. The UK Football Association, led by the Executive Director David Davies and Lawrie McMenemy, the former Northern Ireland coach who once served in the British Army as a Coldstream Guardsman, and Gary Mabbutt, the former England and Tottenham Hotspurs player, flew to Kabul to help coach the two teams. The match was played on 15 February, before a massive crowd in the stadium, estimated to number at least 30,000. There was also some disturbance outside the stadium as huge numbers of enthusiastic Afghan football fans tried to get into the stadium.

Two days later, an observation post of 2 PARA came under fire by unidentified assailants. A paratrooper returned fire, unfortunately killing a pregnant women passing by in a taxi. There were similar incidents on 20 and 27 February but they were attributed by British intelligence to criminal gangs rather than Al Qaeda or the Taliban. These were the only 'contacts' by the paratroopers during their tour in Kabul. Five German and Danish soldiers were killed by an unexploded bomb on 6 March. These were the only fatal casualties suffered by the KMNB.

By the middle of March, 16 Brigade had begun to hand over command of the KMNB to the German army. At the same time, the 1st Battalion, The Royal Anglian Regiment, was arriving to relieve 2 PARA. As this was happening, US troops were locked in heavy combat in eastern Afghanistan with hardcore Al Qaeda fighters. US commanders asked 7th Parachute Regiment Royal Horse Artillery if they could deploy their 105-mm Light Guns to support the battle against Al Qaeda, but they had been left back in the UK. Understandably, morale in 2 PARA slumped when it became clear they would not be able to join the battle. Securing Kabul was still considered a high priority by the British government.

As the troops of 16 Brigade started to pack up and begin to move home, news emerged in London that the Ministry of Defence was to send 3 Commando Brigade out to Bagram to help US forces hunt down Al Qaeda fighters in eastern Afghanistan. This was a further blow to the morale of 2 PARA, to see their rivals in the Royal Marines selected for what appeared to be another high-profile combat mission.

Operation Fingal proved a major test of the ability of 16 Brigade to operate at the far end of a very convoluted supply chain, in extreme weather conditions and a very confused political-security situation. These lessons would be very useful when it was next called into action. The Brigade held the ring in Kabul during a tense period in Afghanistan's history but its fighting capabilities had hardly been tested.

CHAPTER 10

Invading Iraq, 2003

Iraqi artillery and tank shells were exploding amid the Scimitar armoured vehicles of the Household Cavalry Regiment (HCR). A flight of Lynx and Gazelle helicopters led by Captain Richard Cathill arrived overhead to give fire support. With visibility obscured by sand thrown up by the Iraqi fire, Cathill manoeuvred his Lynx to behind the Scimitars so he could line up his helicopters to fire along the path of 30-mm tracer rounds fired by the HCR vehicles. He spotted the muzzle flash of an Iraqi self-propelled artillery piece and guided a TOW missile onto its targets. This required him to fly his helicopter straight and level as shells exploded around it. This bravery won Cathill the Distinguished Flying Cross.

On another part of the Iraqi battlefield, the gunners of the 7th Parachute Regiment Royal Horse Artillery were fighting an artillery duel with Iraqi batteries. I Battery moved forward to engage the Iraqis when they came under fire. To cover their withdrawal, F Battery moved up to engage the Iraqis. It too came under fire from the enemy. As the gunners dived for cover, the battery commander, Captain Grant Ingleton, realised his men's best defence was to keep firing to neutralise the incoming fire. He defiantly took

Westland Lynx AH.7s armed with TOW missiles were used by 16 Air Assault Brigade to hunt down Iraqi tanks and artillery during the brief combat phase of Operation Telic. (*AgustaWestland*)

Iraq *(CIA)*

his helmet off and replaced it with his maroon beret and walked around the gun position to encourage his men back to their weapons. The citation for his Military Cross, said Ingleton's 'infectious sense of humour and selfless leadership drew the men back to their guns, where they maintained their rate of fire and allowed the other battery to withdraw safely without casualties'.

Further north, a patrol of 16 Air Assault Brigade's Pathfinder Platoon had passed through American lines *en route* to Qalat Sikar airfield. This was to be the target of a major air assault operation by the Brigade and the Pathfinders were to help secure it. As they drove through the night, Iraqi Fedayeen fighters in pick-up trucks opened fire on the British Land Rovers. Then they tried to block their escape route. Sergeant Nathan Bell led his patrol off into the desert to escape the attention of the fanatical Iraqi militiamen. Manning the General Purpose Machine Gun in the front of his vehicle, Bell shot up several Iraqi positions as they headed south towards friendly forces. For his bravery that night Bell was awarded the Military Cross.

Although 16 Air Assault Brigade had deployed on operations to Macedonia in 2001 and to Afghanistan a few months later, these were peacekeeping or peace support missions that did not test its war-fighting capabilities. In December 2002 the Brigade was alerted that it could soon be heading to the Middle East to fight in the coming war against Iraq.

RAF Boeing Chinook HC.2 heavy-lift helicopters were never allocated in large numbers to support 16 Brigade. *(Private Collection)*

This would be a severe test of 16 Brigade and see it eventually used in a way that had not been originally envisaged by its commanders and senior officers. A dramatic air manoeuvre operation to seize an airfield nearly 200 kilometres inside Iraq was cancelled at the last minute, leaving the Brigade to secure oil infrastructure, while the bulk of the British forces besieged Basra. The Brigade's three infantry battalions ended up conducting only one large-scale combat operation – 3rd Battalion, The Parachute Regiment's (3 PARA) assault on Basra city centre – under the command of 7 Armoured Brigade. Yet it destroyed more than eighty-six enemy tanks and successfully dispersed a whole Iraqi armoured division. The aggressive use of artillery fire and strikes, under the control of only a couple of dozen highly specialised teams of observers, was responsible for this success.

Ali Al Salem airbase in Kuwait was the centre of the build-up of British Army and US Marine Corps helicopters in the run up to the war. *(Tim Ripley)*

AAC technicians reload a TOW missile on a Lynx AH.7. *(AgustaWestland)*

The outcome of the brief war that led to the fall of Iraqi President Saddam Hussein's regime was not as neat and tidy as some of the conflict's originators in the Bush administration in Washington DC had expected. This resulted in 16 Brigade's troops finding themselves in a difficult and chaotic situation in southern Iraq.

Britain's role in planning the invasion of Iraq stretched back to the visit of Prime Minister Tony Blair to US President George Bush's ranch in Crawford, Texas, in April 2002. The US President told Blair of his intention to deal with Iraq and sought British support. Blair agreed to join with this endeavour but stressed the need for a last diplomatic effort at the UN to isolate the Iraqi regime and build international support. Saddam Hussein's alleged efforts to acquire weapons of mass destruction were to be at the heart of Blair's policy because he needed to deflect criticism at home of his war strategy.

For British officers involved in the war-planning with the Americans, this political manoeuvring by the Blair government had a feeling of make believe, with their US counterparts never giving any hint that the final conclusion of their efforts would be anything but a US-led invasion to depose Saddam Hussein. When Bush announced the deployment of more than 100,000 US troops to the Middle East in December 2002, war seemed only a matter of weeks away, even though Blair continued to insist that the UK was not committed to any form of military action. In public, the British Prime Minister continued to talk up his belief in getting UN approval for military action but at the same time was promising the US President that come what may, the UK would be with the Americans when they started the war.

The US war-planning was led by General Tommy Franks, head of Central Command, which controlled all US operations in the Middle East. The Texan General was crafting an aggressive plan to bring down the Iraqi regime in a matter of weeks. He wanted to race three strike forces to Baghdad, from Turkey in the north, Jordan in the west and Kuwait from the south, to depose the Iraqi President in the hope that his regime would come crashing down once its leader had been overthrown or fled. Britain sent a liaison team to Franks' headquarters in Tampa in Florida in May 2002 and soon afterwards a small secretive team at the UK's Permanent Joint Headquarters at Northwood outside London started to work out options for British involvement. The political sensitivity of this work meant it was defined as 'close hold' and few of the commanders or units being considered for participation were given any hint that they could soon be going to war. At the same time the Blair government was engaged in a bitter industrial dispute with the Fire Brigade's union, which soon led to some 19,000 UK military personnel being deployed on fire-fighting duties between October 2002 and March 2003.

In the last three months of 2002, war-planning gained intensity as the US moved to deploy its combat forces around Iraq. The UK's initial commitment was to provide an amphibious brigade, of some 3,000 to 5,000 troops backed by a naval task group, to help the US Marines secure Iraq's oil infrastructure on the Al Faw peninsula. This then grew to offering a division of troops to help a US offensive from Turkey into northern Iraq. At this point, 16 Brigade began to become actively involved in the war-planning when one of its

3 Regiment AAC moved into a desert assembly area in the run up to the invasion of Iraq. (*AgustaWestland*)

Scimitar CVR(T)s of the Household Cavalry Regiment formed the first 16 Brigade unit to link up with the US Marines to take over responsibility for the security of the Rumaylah oil field. *(US Marine Corps)*

army aviation units, 3 Regiment AAC, was warned that it could be sent to join the British division deploying to Turkey. The paranoid security clamp down ordered to prevent leaks to the media about British war-planning meant that only a few senior officers in the regiment were told about their potential involvement. The 16 Brigade staff had no idea that one of their major units had been assigned a war role. Some of the Brigade's specialist communications equipment was also transferred to the Special Forces who were at the heart of British war-planning at this stage. Four of 16 Brigade's major units were also committed to Operation Fresco, as the fire-fighting mission was called, and a large number of its vehicles had been left behind in Afghanistan in the spring and had not been replaced. All this combined to leave 16 Brigade in a difficult position when the order to deploy to the Middle East was given. Vital operational training and the requesting of specialist equipment had to be done in a matter of days.

In the middle of December 2002, the war-planning grew in scope and the new commander of 16 Brigade, Brigadier Jonathan or 'Jacko' Page, and his senior officers were let in on the secret. Brigadier Page had commanded a platoon of 2 PARA during the 1982 Falklands war and then a tank squadron in the 1991 Iraq war. He was considered the most innovative tactician ever to have commanded 16 Brigade, as well as having a reputation for being hyperactive and being able to survive on only three hours' sleep a day for weeks at a time. Not surprisingly, considering his background he had little time for staff processes and military bureaucracy. He was subsequently promoted to Major General and commanded NATO forces in southern Afghanistan at the height of fighting against the Taliban in 2007. Page was without doubt the most media-shy of 16 Brigade's commanders.

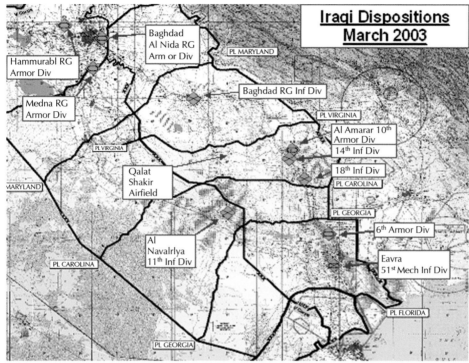

US and Coalition forces surge into Iraq, March 2003. *(USDoD)*

The 16 Brigade staff were tasked to co-ordinate with their counterparts in the US 82nd Airborne Division, who were planning a series of dramatic operations to seize Baghdad and other cities in Iraq in the event of what was termed 'regime collapse' before the war started. These were classic air manoeuvre operations involving parachute drops and air-landing assaults from C-130s to capture Baghdad airport ahead of rapid moves to take control of key government buildings, oil fields and, most importantly, alleged weapons of mass destruction sites. Not surprisingly, senior Parachute Regiment officers were enthusiastic about being at the centre of offensive operations against Iraq.

Although the Brigade was told of its possible involvement just before Christmas 2002, the Turkey option was not yet confirmed because the Ankara government had decided to let its parliament vote on its participation in the coming war with Iraq. During this time, 16 Brigade ramped up its planning and training but without a firm indication of its exact role in the war plan, its troops could not make detailed preparations.

A month passed until the British government decided that the Turkey option was a no go. The UK would now deploy an armoured division of 28,000 troops to Kuwait to support the southern axis of the advance into Iraq. The Chief of Joint Operations, Lieutenant General John Reith, promised his American counterparts that the British division would be ready for action in the Middle East by 24 February.

What the British force would do once it got to Kuwait was still a matter of great debate. Throughout January, Brigadier Page and his staff held planning conferences with the commander of the British land force, Major General Robin Brims, to try to convince him

Oil field flares lit up the sky as 16 Brigade moved into the Rumaylah oil field. *(US Marine Corps)*

to use 16 Brigade in a number of air manoeuvre operations. Even though the General was a former commander of 24 Airmobile Brigade and understood air manoeuvre capabilities, his staff had little exposure to what 16 Brigade could do. They were pre-occupied with planning armoured operations and 16 Brigade staff officers complained that they had explain everything to them in very basic terms.

British war-planning was now constrained by strategic guidance from the British government, which limited 1 (UK) Armoured Division to operating within the so-called 'Al Nasariyah-Basra Box', which covered most of south-east Iraq. The Americans were convinced that the Iraqi military would have little stomach for a fight and would 'fold' or collapse as soon as US troops rolled into Baghdad. There was little consideration of the guerrilla or insurgent threat at this stage. British planners, particularly at Northwood and within the Ministry of Defence in London, were more cautious and did not share the confidence of their American counterparts that the Iraqi army would be quickly defeated. Government ministers were worried about heavy casualties if the British got involved in the Battle for Baghdad. Britain had long connections with Basra and it was thought that this would help in the post-war period. While perhaps most importantly, British Army chiefs were concerned that they could not set up enough supply lines to sustain an operation deep inside Iraq. Containing Basra seemed do-able and low-risk, so British forces were to be confined to 'the box' unless in exceptional circumstances.

The capture of the oil infrastructure on the Al Faw peninsula by 3 Commando Brigade was to be the UK's main effort and this operation was to begin at the start of the US-led assault on Iraq. The I Marine Expeditionary Force (I MEF) would then storm across the border from Kuwait to capture the Rumaylah oil field complex and then turn east to screen Basra, to allow the US Army's V Corps to start its drive on Baghdad. In the wake of I MEF,

Staff officers working inside the 16 Brigade headquarters. In the background is the blue forces tracking (BFT) display that showed the location of all coalition land forces in Iraq. *(Private Collection)*

7 Armoured Brigade, known as the Desert Rats, was then to take over the job of screening Basra and prepare to take on the Iraqi 6th Armoured Division, which was based to the north-west of the city up the Euphrates valley. 16 Brigade was tasked with taking over security of the Rumaylah oil field, which contained most of Iraq's oil reserves, from the US Marines. This area was criss-crossed with oil pipelines that could not be crossed by the heavy armoured vehicles of the 7th Brigade without causing huge damage to the oil pipelines. At the same time, 16 Brigade was to hold its airborne task force, based on 1 PARA, in reserve as the British armoured division's 'contingency force' to respond to unexpected events, such as a sudden collapse of the Iraqi regime, which might trigger a move out of 'the box' towards Baghdad. This force was also told to be ready to mount a helicopter-borne assault of Qalat Sikar airfield, which was located to the north of 'the box', to help protect the flank of I MEF's columns as they headed for Baghdad from counter-attacks by an Iraqi armoured division based at Al Amara, to the east of the airfield. Once the airfield was secured, a forward arming and refuelling point (FARP) was to be set up to enable the attack helicopters, C-130 Hercules and Harrier jump jets of the 3rd Marine Air Wing (MAW) to support the drive on Baghdad. The Qalat Sikar operation was by no means a certainty. It depended on the success of 7 Brigade around Basra and how the Iraqis reacted. The sensitivity of moving out of the 'the box' to take Qalat Sikar was such that it would have to be approved by the Prime Minister in London.

In the run up to the war, the Commandos and the Desert Rats were allocated all the RAF's eleven Chinoook heavy lift and seven Puma transport helicopters of the Joint Helicopter Force (JHF) to support their initial operations around Al Faw and Basra. The JHF was designed as a 'division asset' and so its helicopters were not placed under the control of 16 Brigade. This was almost all the Chinooks the RAF could muster and it showed dramatically the shortfalls in British helicopter strength. Only the Lynx and Gazelle helicopters of 3 Regiment AAC were permanently assigned to 16 Brigade.

US Marine Corps troops exchange fire with insurgents near the southern Iraqi city of Al Nasariyah. *(US Marine Corps)*

This cautious employment of the British division meant its main task during the war would be to guard the American lines of communication from Kuwait. It would not play any part in the capture and occupation of Baghdad, which set the scene for events that led to the start of insurgency that wrought havoc with British and American efforts to rebuild Iraq and led to the country being convulsed by years of violence.

Once 16 Brigade got the word to deploy on 20 January 2003, pandemonium ensued at its bases in Colchester, Wattisham and Canterbury. Quartermasters began to request huge quantities of desert uniforms and boots, body armour, extra vehicles, specialist communication equipment and nuclear, biological and chemical (NBC) protective suits. 3 Regiment's helicopters had to be modified with sand filters to allow them to fly in desert conditions and have defensive systems fitted to defeat shoulder-launched surface-to-air missiles. All this equipment was in very short supply and not all of it was ready by the time the Brigade moved into the desert at the start of the war in March.

The delays in authorising the Brigade's deployment and the short time frame before deployment meant all this preparatory activity had to be done in a few days to allow the 1,800 vehicles, cargo containers and twenty-two helicopters to be loaded onto cargo ships for the three-week voyage to Kuwait. All 16 Brigade's heavy equipment had to be moved by ship because there was no spare air transport capacity.

When the ships carrying the Brigade's equipment arrived in Kuwait the docks were full with US and British ships unloading cargo. It took weeks to sort out whose containers belonged to whom and this process was not complete by the time the war started on 19

A US Marine Corps CH-46E Sea Knight helicopter overflies Al Nasariyah during the height of the fighting against Saddam Fedayeen fighters in March 2003. *(US Marine Corps)*

March. Equipment shortages meant that when the war started some 20 per cent of the Brigade's soldiers did not have body armour, nearly half did not have desert boots, anti-malaria tablets quickly ran out and, most worrying, its chemical weapon detection equipment only had enough spare filters to last two weeks' of continuous operations in a contaminated environment. This left many members of the Brigade wondering if the British government was really serious about going to war.

As all this was going, on a small team of staff officers flew out to Kuwait to take over six tented camps that contractors were building in the north of the country for 16 Brigade. The Kuwaiti desert was being transformed into a huge encampment to hold more than 28,000 British and 200,000 American troops massing for the invasion. In early February the bulk of the Brigade started to fly out to Kuwait International Airport on commercial airliners and they were then bussed to their desert camps. This led some Parachute Regiment officers to complain that the troops were not being toughened up enough to live in the desert and fight a war. This attitude received a sharp jolt when the first of several dust storms engulfed the British camps in the Kuwait desert in the run up to the war. The dust from these storms penetrated inside armoured vehicles, and tents collapsed under the weight of sand deposited on them.

The Brigade staff and main battalion command groups spent most of February taking part in a series of planning exercises or rock drills with the I MEF and 3rd MAW staffs to work out their role in the invasion. Close co-operation was established with the 5th Marine Regiment who would initially capture the Rumaylah oil field before handing it over to 16 Brigade. Once the Brigade's vehicles started arriving, two field exercises were held to test driving and navigating long distances in the desert.

Bell AH.1W Cobra gunships flew many attack missions in support of 16 Brigade. *(US Marine Corps)*

16 Brigade deployed to Kuwait with two Parachute Regiment battalions, 1 and 3 PARA, the 1st Battalion, The Royal Irish Regiment, in the air assault role and 3 Regiment AAC, which was designated an aviation battlegroup. The PARA and the Royal Irish battalions each mustered around 700 soldiers, equipped as light-role infantry. They each had four infantry companies with around 120 soldiers. The three battalions all brought a couple of dozen DAF four-ton trucks with them to Kuwait and these proved the main means of moving their infantry companies around the desert, leading to the paratroopers jokingly nicknaming them 'Deliverers of Airborne Forces' or DAFs.

In addition to their infantry, the three battalions boasted support companies, containing 81-mm mortar, general purpose machine-guns, Milan anti-tank guided missile, sniper, reconnaissance and assault pioneer platoons. These platoons were all mounted in Land Rover or Pinzgauer 4 x 4 vehicles and provided their battalions with hard-hitting mobile strike forces, dubbed Mobile Support Groups (MSGs) that spearheaded the invasion of Iraq. These drew their inspiration from World War Two long-range desert group patrols that packed heavy firepower with high-speed desert mobility.

1 PARA was designated an airborne task force (ABTF) and it took all its parachutes and drop equipment to Kuwait. A detachment of four RAF Hercules transport aircraft deployed to a US Marine Corps airstrip in the Kuwaiti desert to be ready to launch the ABTF.

The aviation battlegroup contained a mix of Lynx AH.7 helicopters armed with TOW wire-guided missiles, a Lynx AH.9 liaison helicopter, which was used as a airborne command post, and Gazelle AH.1 scout helicopters. It was usual to have a company of paratroopers or Royal Irish infantry attached to 3 Regiment to provide protection for FARPs or to hold ground.

A gunner of the 7th
Parachute Regiment
Royal Horse Artillery
in action during
fighting around the
Rumaylah oil field.
(BAE Systems)

The Brigade's Offensive Support Group contained the bulk of its long-range firepower, including four batteries of 105-mm Light Guns of 7th Parachute Regiment Royal Horse Artillery (7 RHA), augmented later in the Iraqi campaign by two batt-eries of AS-90 155-mm self-propelled howitzers. Crucially, the OSG also contain-ed all the Brigade's surveillance systems to find targets and groups of artillery and forward air controllers (FACs) who were qualified and equipped to call in artillery fire and close air support. All these teams were connected to the central firepower control centre within 16 Brigade's headquarters so artillery and air support could be rapidly massed against targets. Three new Swedish-made MAMBA mortar and artillery locating radars from 5 Regiment Royal Artillery were attached to 16 Brigade for the Iraq mission. Electronic eavesdropping teams and Phoenix unmanned aerial vehicles were also assigned to the OSG so 16 Brigade could look for targets dozens of miles behind Iraqi lines.

The Forward Observer Officers and Tactical Air Control Parties who went looking for targets in heavily armed Land Rovers, were also supported by two specialist units of the Brigade. The Pathfinder Platoon was a forty-strong group of reconnaissance specialists

16 Air Assault Brigade Operations - March-April 2003

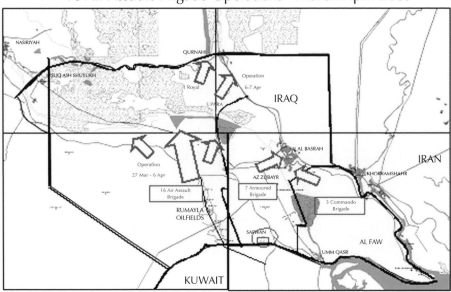

16 Air Assault Brigade operations in Southern Iraq, March to April 2003 *(Tim Ripley)*

mounted in heavily armed Land Rovers. D Squadron, The Household Cavalry (HCR), was the only armoured unit assigned to 16 Brigade. It had twenty Scimitar Combat Vehicle Reconnaissance (CVR(T)) lightly armoured scout vehicles, which had specialist night vision equipment fitted to help their crews find targets at night. Both the Pathfinders and HCR were lavishly equipped with communications equipment and contained a large number of personnel trained as FOOs and FACs to call down artillery fire and air strikes.

The final element of the OSG was the assignment of a US Marine Corps ANGLICO (Air Naval Gunfire Liaison Company) unit, which provided the vital link to 3rd MAW's air power. ANGLICO teams worked in 16 Brigade headquarters and other teams were assigned to each of its four main battlegroups and the OSG. They had highly secure satellite radio links to 3rd MAW's headquarters and US Marine Corps aircraft on patrol above the UK sector, to allow strike aircraft and helicopter gunships to be directed to emerging targets in a matter of minutes.

Comic moments were rare, as the build-up to war seemed unstoppable. A visit to the Brigade by the Leader of the Conservative Party, Iain Duncan-Smith, provided a rare chance to see one of the government's spin doctors humiliated. The government was paranoid about negative publicity concerning troops not having enough equipment in the run-up to the war and was trying to limit media contact with the troops. Duncan-Smith had supposedly agreed not to hold any 'political events' during his visit and Alistair Campbell classified this as including press conferences. When the Conservative leader started holding a press conference at one of 16 Brigade's camps, Simon Wren, the spin doctor, phoned his boss Alistair Campbell in Downing Street for instructions and was told in no uncertain terms to stop the event happening. Wren turned to a group of paratroopers

Many Lynx missions were flown at night to hunt down tanks and artillery batteries of the Iraqi 6th Armoured Division. *(AgustaWestland)*

and ordered them to stop the press conference, to which the giggling soldiers replied, 'what do you want us to do mate, shoot them?'

By mid March, the Brigade had all its major units and most of its equipment in place as the countdown to war speeded up. The commander of I MEF, Lieutenant General James Conway, held a morale-boosting parade in a desert camp under arches made from artillery gun barrels. In an exercise in psychological warfare 1 PARA held a parachute drop – while wearing full NBC protective clothing – to deceive the Iraqis into thinking thousands of British paratroopers would soon be descending onto strategic locations.

Confidence was high that the Iraqi resistance would collapse as soon as the first US and British troops crossed the border. Preparations were accelerated for the Qalat Sikar air manoeuvre and air drop operation by 1 PARA. Eight RAF Chinooks were allocated for the mission once they had completed landing the Royal Marines on the Al Faw. US Marine AH.1W Cobra helicopter gunships were to fly close escort for the RAF helicopters to neutralise any threats to the mission and the 3rd MAW had promised lavish fixed-wing air support from F/A-18 Hornet bombers and AV-8B Harrier jump jets. RAF and US C-130 Hercules were ordered to standby to fly Tactical Air Land Operations (TALO) support for the mission after the helicopter-borne troops had secured the Iraqi airfield. Brigadier Page decided he would fly in behind the assault helicopters to set up his tactical headquarters to direct the battle against the Iraqi armoured division based in Al Amara.

16 Air Assault Brigade, Order of Battle, March–April 2003

Brigade Headquarters
216 Squadron Royal Signals

Major Combat Units

1st Battalion, Royal Irish Regiment
1st Battalion, The Parachute Regiment
3rd Battalion, The Parachute Regiment
3 Regiment Army Air Corps (662, 663 Squadrons), 12 x Lynx AH.7/9
   and 10 x Gazelle AH.1

Operational Support Group

D Squadron, Household Cavalry Regiment,
7th Parachute Regiment Royal Horse Artillery (RHA) (18 x 105-mm
   Light Guns, attached 2 x batteries AS-90 (D Bty, 3 RHA and 17/16
   Bty, 26 Regiment RA))
21 Battery, Royal Artillery (HVM)
Pathfinder Platoon
613, 615, 616 Tactical Air Control Party (TACP)
3rd ANGLICO Brigade Team (USMC)
Light Electronic Warfare Team (LEWT), 14 Regiment Royal Signals
MAMBA (Arthur) Weapon Locating Radar Troop, K Battery, 5
   Regiment Royal Artillery

Combat Support

23 Engineer Regiment (Air Assault), Royal Engineers (9 and 51
   Squadrons)
13 Air Assault Regiment, Royal Logistic Corps
7 Air Assault Battalion, the Royal Mechanical and Electrical Engineers
16 Close Support Medical Regiment
Element 47 Air Despatch Squadron, RLC
156 Company, Royal Military Police

After President Bush declared on 18 March that the Iraqis had not met his demands to disarm, all coalition forces in Kuwait were placed on a heightened alert. US commanders expected to launch their offensive by Friday 21 March but events in Baghdad conspired to force this to be brought forward by two days.

The Americans brought forward the start of war when they received intelligence that Saddam Hussein was to visit a farm complex to the south of the Iraqi capital on the evening of 19 March. President Bush authorised an air strike by F-117 stealth fighters on

Dozens of USAF A-10A Warthogs flew from Ahmed Al Jaber airbase in Kuwait in support of 16 Brigade. *(Tim Ripley)*

the farm but it later emerged that the intelligence was faulty and the Iraqi leader was nowhere near the location. The air strike meant the Iraqis could start retaliating against targets in Kuwait at any time so General Franks decided to move his land assault forward to the morning of 20 March. At 3 am, US Army and Marine Corps columns started bulldozing lanes through the sand ramp or berm along the Iraq–Kuwait border to open routes northwards. By dawn thousands of US armoured vehicles were heading towards Basra and Baghdad. Simultaneously with the land assault, 3 Commando Brigade had landed on the Al Faw to capture Iraq's oil installations. Guns of 7 RHA fired in support of their US Marine counterparts as they blasted Iraqi border defence posts.

In the Kuwaiti desert, 16 Brigade had moved out of its tented camps during the night of 19/20 March to a number of tactical assembly areas to reduce their vulnerability to Iraqi ballistic missile and rocket attacks. The Iraqis fired a number of ballistic missiles at the Kuwait desert, prompting coalition troops to don their full chemical warfare protective equipment on several occasions. For a day, the British Army waited in their assembly areas for the Americans to secure their objectives in southern Iraq. During the evening orders were issued for 16 Brigade to move forward and Royal Engineers of 51 Field Squadron began bulldozing a breach in the Iraqi berm in the early hours of 21 March. Scimitars of the Household Cavalry crossed into Iraq during the evening of 21 March to link up with the 5th Marine Regiment, which had secured the Rumaylah oil field complex. Iraqi resistance had been swiftly overwhelmed by the US Marines and they had captured the oil field before the elements loyal to Saddam Hussein had time to conduct any sabotage.

The Royal Irish under the command of the famous Lieutenant Colonel Tim Collins

More than eighty-six Iraqi tanks were destroyed by 16 Brigade. *(Tim Ripley)*

were the first to conduct a relief in place or RIP with the Americans and soon afterwards 3 PARA moved through the breach to take over security of the northern part of the oil field complex. As this was happening, 3 Regiment began to dispatch aviation reconnaissance patrols (ARPs) northwards to the Rumaylah bridge over the al-Hammar canal to try to give warning of a counter-attack by the Iraqi 6th Armoured Division, which was based to north of the canal. At first there was little sign of enemy activity.

Although the oil field infrastructure was secured intact, the whole of the 16 Brigade area was littered with the remnants of an Iraqi mechanised brigade that had been rolled over by the US Marines. Paratroopers and Royal Irish patrols fanned out to round up the prisoners, make contact with the local population and set up a security perimeter to stop any Iraqi counter-attacks. The size of the security zone was so big that helicopter patrols by 3 Regiment were the only way to monitor it all and give any kind of early warning of any Iraqi forces massing nearby.

As this clear-up and security operation got under way, the Brigade got its first taste of occupation duties. Power and water supplies in Rumaylah town needed to get back into operation and rumours began circulating that under-cover insurgent groups were still at large. Iraqi Ba'ath party loyalists, dubbed Fedayeen, were the core of these groups and they were said to be preparing an arms cache, ready to launch guerrilla-style attacks on British and American troops.

Scores of Iraqi
artillery pieces
were found
abandoned in
southern Iraq by
16 Brigade.
(Private Collection)

While 16 Brigade was mopping up in the Rumaylah oil fields, 7 Armoured Brigade
was moving north towards the outskirts of Basra and the US Marines were approaching
Nasiriyah. Iraqi forces in both of these cities were now starting to put up serious
resistance. By the evening on 23 March, senior British and American commanders were
beginning to realise that the Iraqi collapse was not going to happen in the next couple of
days and more resources were needed to deal with Basra and Nasiriyah.

For 16 Brigade, this meant that its air manoeuvre operation to Qalat Sikar was put on
hold to allow the British division to concentrate on reducing resistance in Basra. General
Brims was not yet ready to assault the city but he wanted to stage a series of operations
to specifically target centres of resistance. He did not want to fight a prolonged street
battle with the Iraqis that could cause heavy civilian casualties. 3 Regiment was ordered
to dispatch several of its Gazelle and Lynx helicopters to help 7 Armoured Brigade. They
staged a number of airborne raids, targeting Iraqi strong points in the city with TOW
missiles.

For five days, 1 PARA sat in its assembly area waiting to receive the order to launch
the Qalat Sikar strike before the operation was cancelled by the government in London.
Two British soldiers had been dragged from a Land Rover outside Basra and killed by
Ba'athist militia and US Marines were bogged down in series of bloody skirmishes
throughout Nasiriyah. The time was not seen as ripe by the government to surge British
troops deeper into Iraqi territory.

Senior British commanders in Iraq were keen to try to help their American allies and
lobbied hard to get the Qalat Sikar operation reinstated. On the morning of 26 March, it
was back on. Preparations were accelerated, air support organised and the RAF Chinooks
of 18 Squadron were issued with orders for the mission, which was to be launched during
the night of 27 March. US Marine Corps Hornets carried out reconnaissance flights over
the airfield and reported the presence of Iraqi anti-aircraft missile batteries. At the Joint
Helicopter Force (JHF) base in Kuwait the reports caused great unease among the RAF
Chinook and US Marine Cobra pilots. They estimated at least one Chinook would be shot

RAF Puma helicopters flew casualty evacuation missions in support of 16 Brigade.
(*Private Collection*)

down, with the loss of dozens of paratroopers. Protests were made to the 16 Brigade and 1 (UK) Division headquarters. The operation was placed on temporary hold as senior commanders debated what to do. By the late afternoon, General Brims gave the go-ahead and the operation was scheduled for that evening. In its assembly area, 1 PARA began final preparations and the Chinooks, with their escorting Cobras, were winding up to fly forward from Ali Al Salem airbase in Kuwait to pick them up. Just as darkness was falling, news came in that the US Marine Corps FARP outside Nasiriyah, where the helicopter force needed to refuel, was under sustained Iraqi artillery and mortar fire. The troops and helicopter crews were stood down. A few hours later, US Marine Corps troops heading for Baghdad approached the Qalat Sikar from the south and found it undefended. 16 Brigade's Qalat Sikar mission was cancelled and would never be resurrected.

One unforeseen side effect of the Qalat Sikar operation was that the G (Mercer's Troop) Battery of 7 RHA had been moving by road via Nasiriyah to support the assault on the airfield when it got caught up in the heavy street fighting in the city between US Marines and fanatical Fedayeen fighters loyal to the Baghdad regime. The Iraqi guerrillas had set up positions dominating two key bridges over the Euphrates River and were raking US convoys that were crossing them with rocket-propelled grenades and machine-gun fire. The British gunners set up their 105-mm Light Guns 1,500 metres from the bridges and as the US convoys raced over the bridges, they laid down a barrage of fire on the insurgent position. The 105-mm guns could switch fire in under two minutes, compared with the eight minutes it took the US Marines' 155-mm howitzers to engage new targets, so the American commanders attributed their British allies with saving scores of their troops' lives. After a day in action in the middle of Nasiriyah, the British divisional command to the east was increasingly worried about the battery suffering casualties and ordered them to pull back to Rumaylah.

The Pathfinders had also been ordered to move by road, via Nasiriyah, but they got through the town before the Iraqis started to put up major resistance to the US Marines. They started to drive north towards Qalat Sikar when they ran into a group of Fedayeen fighters and killed around fifty of them before extracting themselves to safety.

With its air manoeuvre operation cancelled, 16 Brigade was now ordered to focus on containing the Iraqi 6th Armoured Division north of the al-Hammer canal. The HCR, Pathfinders, MSG of 3 PARA and ARPs of 3 Regiment were ordered to probe along the canal to find the centre of Iraqi resistance and called down artillery fire and air strikes. Other OSG operatives huddled over television screens in the Brigade headquarters to look at live video feeds from Royal Artillery Phoenix UAVs to try to find targets. Other intelligence analysts used eavesdropping equipment to monitor Iraqi radio communications to try to find more targets.

For over a week, this battle grew in intensity as 16 Brigade pushed its reconnaissance forces further north from the al-Hammer canal towards the Euphrates River and the main defensive positions of the Iraqi division. The terrain between the al-Hammer canal and the Euphrates River alternated between palm groves and marshy ground, so there was plenty of opportunity for the Iraqis to hide their positions. Around the clock, the reconnaissance teams were calling down artillery fire from the OSG against Iraqi bunkers and tanks. 3 Regiment's Lynx joined the battle, engaging targets with TOW missiles or calling in artillery fire. US Air Force A-10A Warthogs and US Marine Corps' Harriers made daily

Thousands of Iraqi civilians came out to cheer 16 Brigade's troops as they surged forward into Maysan province in April 2003. *(Private Collection)*

Maysan province contained the famous marshes that were drained by Saddam Hussein in his attempt to crush rebellious tribesman. *(Tim Ripley)*

forays over the battlefield, striking at targets identified by 16 Brigade troops. They were also looking for Iraqi ballistic missile batteries that were still firing at Kuwait from palm groves along the Euphrates.

This was by no means a one-sided battle, with the Iraqis making extensive use of their own target location systems to control their return artillery fire. British Lynx pilots on an hourly basis had to dodge Iraqi tank and artillery fire that was aimed at their helicopters and if they got too close to Iraqi infantry, volleys of rocket-propelled grenades could be expected. Iraqi artillery spotters tried to infiltrate 16 Brigade positions on several occasions, including trying to surrender to troops of HCR before opening fire. For 16 Brigade's artillery fire spotters and forward air controllers, the attention of Iraqi artillery was very unwelcome and the best defence was a rapid withdrawal out of range in their vehicles, before they would re-group and try to find another way to approach their targets. The British reconnaissance teams often dismounted to move forward to occupy covert observation posts to watch their Iraqi opponents for days on end, relying on secrecy for protection. Occasionally, if targets presented themselves, Milan-guided missile firing posts were brought forward under cover to launch surprise attacks on the Iraqi positions. In a major success the Brigade identified the 6th Division's headquarters in Ad Dayr and directed a US Marine Corps jet to drop a satellite-guided Joint Direct Attack Munition (JDAM) on the site.

In effect, a few hundred members of 16 Brigade were playing a deadly game of cat and mouse with several thousand Iraqi defenders, who had by no means given up the fight. The 6th Division conducted a professional defensive operation and gave as good as it got on many occasions. Fortunately, US air power meant the Iraqis were pinned into their defensive positions and could not risk their tanks breaking cover. At the same time, the 16 Brigade reconnaissance teams had freedom of movement to pull back to safety and re-group. The Pathfinders used this confused situation to slip through Iraqi lines to monitor the movement of Iraqi reinforcement into Basra from Baghdad, down the Al Amara road.

The Iraqis were firing back with their South African-made G5 155-mm howitzers, which out-ranged 7 RHA's 105-mm guns, so 16 Brigade's OSG staged a series of artillery raids. The regiment's 105-mm batteries were raced forward to firing points close to the al-Hammer canal to engage the Iraqis, before they rapidly withdrew when it was feared the Iraqis had identified their positions and were directing artillery fire against them. Heavy self-propelled AS-90 155-mm guns were then called forward to counter the big Iraqi guns. Officers of 7 RHA attributed its success in its battle with the longer-range Iraqi artillery to the new MAMBA radars, which allowed it to rapidly pinpoint enemy batteries and bring down effective counter-battery. The MAMBAs were responsible for over 40 per cent

RAF Chinooks flew re-supply fights from Basra to Al Amara during 16 Brigade's brief occupation of Maysan province. *(Private Collection)*

of the fire missions fired by 7 RHA.

During this period, the bulk of 16 Brigade's infantry battalions was not engaged *en masse* and stood guard on the oil complex. A couple of small-scale attacks were mounted by 3 PARA to mop up resistance around the Rumaylah bridge but the bulk of the action was controlled by the OSG. In the course of this battle, 16 Brigade claimed the destruction of eighty-six Iraqi tanks and scores of enemy artillery pieces.

All through this battle 16 Brigade was very lucky and its reconnaissance teams managed to avoid suffering any casualties, but on 28 March an HCR patrol came under attack from USAF A-10As. The patrol was strafed twice by the American pilots, leaving one HCR soldier dead and four wounded before they were called off. The friendly fire incident eventually led to an inquest in Britain that blamed American pilots for unlawfully killing the HCR soldier.

The Brigade also continued to support the US Marines during this period and the Pathfinder Platoon was also inserted deep behind Iraqi lines by RAF Chinooks to watch routes towards Baghdad that the commander of I MEF was considering using. The teams were successfully extracted and were debriefed by senior US Marine Corps officers before the big US attack on Baghdad.

In the first week of April, American troops were closing in on Baghdad and General Brims was getting ready to make his assault on Basra. He ordered 16 Brigade to release 3 PARA to join this operation and it moved eastwards to be ready to help in what could be a huge street battle. Simultaneously, 16 Brigade was ordered to make preparations to assault the 6th Division's positions at Ad Dayr and Al Qurnah to seize key bridges over the Euphrates. Reconnaissance teams had closed up to these positions and were engaged in skirmishing with well camouflaged, apparently determined, Iraqi troops.

On 6 April, as US troops entered Baghdad, the leader of Iraqi resistance in Basra, Ali Hassan al-Majid (the infamous Chemical Ali), reportedly fled north from the city with several of his key lieutenants. This was the moment General Brims had been waiting for and he ordered 7 Brigade to sweep into the city. The old kasbah district of the city was 3 PARA's objective and the paratroopers moved forward expecting to meet heavy resistance. The advance proved an anti-climax, with cheering crowds of locals filling the streets to welcome the British troops. The Fedayeen were long gone.

Further north, 16 Brigade was scheduled to launch its strike the following day to neutralise the 6th Division and launch a drive towards Al Amara. During the night, as regime loyalists fled past them heading towards Baghdad, the morale of the 6th Division began to waver. At this point, Colonel Collins sent friendly tribal leaders across the lines in an attempt to persuade the Iraqi defenders around Al Qurnah to flee. Outside Ad Dayr, Brigadier Page and some of his staff made contact with local leaders to try to broker another peaceful withdrawal. Both attempts worked and by the following morning, 16 Brigade found its enemies had fled.

Thus began 16 Brigade's drive northwards. Convoys of Parachute Regiment and Royal Irish vehicles raced forward to capture intact the bridges over the Euphrates. Huge crowds of civilians lined the roads as the British troops surged forward into Maysan province. The Iraqi army had now collapsed.

British troops were assigned responsibility for securing the south-east of Iraq and they were ordered to move quickly to establish control of all major towns in the region. Brigadier Page was given the job of securing Maysan province, which has a population of over a million people. It included the famous marshes that Saddam Hussein had drained to try to flush out tribesmen staging a revolt against his regime.

US Marines had occupied the capital of Maysan, Al Amara, in the days after the fall of Baghdad but the Americans were keen to hand over to the British to allow them to concentrate on securing the Iraqi capital. Pathfinder Platoon patrols drove up to the city to establish liaison with the US Marines and a team of Central Intelligence Agency operatives who were trying to bring order amid a major outbreak of looting. On 12 April, the Royal Irish moved into Al Amara and 16 Brigade's headquarters followed a few days later. 3 PARA moved up from Basra to take over securing the southern part of Maysan, while 1 PARA remained in the Rumaylah oil fields. The Brigade headquarters was controlling operations across 17,000 square kilometres of southern Iraq.

This was a very chaotic situation. With rival militia and insurgent groups all vying for power in the province, looting was rampant and no police were to be seen. British soldiers took on trying to get public utilities working, clamping down on lawlessness and trying to tidy up the detritus of war. A company of 1 PARA also drove to Baghdad to secure and re-open the British embassy. The Iraqi capital was being convulsed by looting and sabotage of key infrastructure, leading to power and water supplies failing in most of the city. US troops were overwhelmed and they had few experienced infantry to enable them to put enough soldiers on street corners to take the place of the city's non-existent police force. British commanders in Iraq were worried that the impact of this chaos was threatening to undermine the whole project to rebuild the country. It was proposed to send the remainder of 16 Brigade's headquarters and 1 PARA to Baghdad to begin rebuilding the city's police force to fill the security vacuum.

At this point, just as 16 Brigade was getting into its stride in Maysan and plans were firming up to send 1 PARA to Baghdad, the British government ordered the British Army to start drawing down its forces in Iraq to around a third of the 28,000 strong force that had led the invasion in March. The move to Baghdad was cancelled only twenty-four hours from when the first troops were due to begin deploying from Al Amara. In the last week of April, the Royal Irish were ordered back to Kuwait and were soon on their way home. The bulk of the Brigade was on its way back to the UK by the end of May, except for 1 PARA, which was to remain controlling all of Maysan until mid July. It was then to hand over to the follow-on troops from 19 Mechanised Brigade, which arrived with only 9,000 troops.

Amid the euphoria of the fall of Baghdad, it seemed to the British and American governments as if the war was over. The problems with looting and infrastructure failures were viewed as minor difficulties. As US Secretary of Defense, Donald Rumsfeld, commented, 'stuff happens'. There was little appreciation of the scale of reconstruction needed and the importance of filling the security vacuum in the vital months after the fall of the old regime. For the British government the chance to stage photo-opportunities of victorious troops returning home to their families was too good to miss so 3 Commando and 16 Brigades were pulled home in May, leaving 7 Brigade to hold the ring until 19 Brigade arrived in Iraq in July. The new Brigade only had four lightly equipped infantry battalions to secure the area, which had been controlled by the three brigades of 1 (UK) Division. Although the Americans have taken a lot of criticism for losing control of the situation in Baghdad, at least unlike the British, they did not actually cut the number of their troops in Iraq.

The precarious situation in southern Iraq was amply demonstrated on 24 June when troops of the 1 PARA battlegroup came under attack in Majar-al-Kabir, to the south of Al Amara. A patrol of paratroopers came under attack on the outskirts of the town, while inside the town's police station six Royal Military Policemen were killed by a mob of tribesmen. Communications problems and limited intelligence-gathering capabilities because of the troop draw-down in Maysan province were all identified as contributing to this tragedy by a subsequent army board of inquiry.

The troops of 16 Air Assault Brigade returned home victorious but also slightly disappointed. They had not been able to put their air manoeuvre capabilities to the test after the Qalat Sikar mission was cancelled. Although many members of the Brigade had seen intense fighting, its three main infantry battlegroups had not been able to fight a full-scale stand-up battle with the Iraqis.

The Brigade had ended up securing the Rumaylah oil complex, fighting a holding battle against the Iraqi 6th Division and conducting peacekeeping operations in an area stretching from the Kuwaiti border to Al Amara. The battle against the Iraqi 6th Division was a very innovative battle that was fought without the Brigade's infantry battalions actually being engaged, relying instead on artillery and predominately US airpower. For the British Army this was a revolutionary form of warfare and the skills honed in this battle would be put to great use three years later in Afghanistan. 16 Brigade's 300-kilometre advance to Al Amara had been conducted largely by vehicle. Although this advance could be viewed as a classic *blitzkrieg* drive that had scattered the enemy through psychological warfare and speed of movement, it was not really an air manoeuvre operation. The shortage of helicopter lifts in the UK Armed Forces meant resources had to be prioritised and 16 Brigade was not considered the main effort by 1 (UK) Division. Also, the lack of long-range surveillance and artillery capabilities meant that when the Brigade was given the chance to mount an air manoeuvre operation against Qalat Sikar airfield, it had to be cancelled because threats could not be confirmed with any certainty or fire brought to bear against them. The guns of 7 RHA had insufficient range to hit the suspected enemy air defence site blocking access to the airfield.

The precipitate withdrawal from Maysan province added to the feeling that the Brigade had not really cut its teeth in Iraq and left plenty of unfinished business. The Brigade played a heavy price for its operations. It lost eleven dead during the battle for Iraq. One soldier died in the friendly fire incident, two were lost in road accidents, one to an unexploded bomb, one to a suspected negligent discharge and six RMPs in the Majar-al-Kabir incident.

CHAPTER 11

The Queen's Apaches

On 1 September 2003, the first frontline British Army pilots began conversion training to fly the AgustaWestland Apache AH.1 at the School of Army Aviation at Middle Wallop. This marked a major milestone in the history of the AAC and was also a major milestone in the effort to provide the British Army with an attack helicopter capability.

The olive green Apaches were soon to become a familiar sight in the skies around Middle Wallop in Hampshire and by the middle of 2004, they were flying regularly from the first frontline British attack helicopter base at Dishforth in North Yorkshire.

Britain's Apaches are unique and feature a large element of 'UK-specific' technology, which makes them very different from the Boeing AH-64D Apache Longbows currently in service with the US Army and a number of other air arms. In several respects, the British Apaches are more capable than their American counterparts. Westland Helicopters (now AgustaWestland) who assembled the helicopters at their Yeovil plant initially, dubbed them Westland Attack Helicopter (WAH-64) Apache Longbows and the British Army subsequently designated them Apache AH.1s. To the McDonnell Douglas (later Boeing) technicians who worked on the helicopters at the Mesa plant in Arizona, they were known as 'the Queen's Apaches'.

9 Regiment AAC ramped up training to convert to the AgustaWestland Apache AH.1 attack helicopters during the last months of 2003. *(AgustaWestland)*

For the British Army, the Apache programme represented its biggest, most expensive and most technologically challenging procurement effort in modern times. Never before had the British Army attempted to field such a complex and expensive piece of military hardware. Prior to the Apache, the AAC annually absorbed 7 per cent of the British Army's equipment budget. But in the late 1990s, at the height of the attack helicopter programme, it ran to 32 per cent of the equipment budget. The importance of the Apache can be gauged by the fact that in 2003, the AAC only accounted for 3 per cent of the British Army's personnel. For a variety of reasons, the programme slipped and the Apache's entry into frontline service was delayed by more than two years and it took a lot longer than expected to train up the required personnel to man the AAC's Apache regiments.

If the AH-64D was seen as the 'Rolls-Royce' solution to the AAC's requirements, it came at a price that the UK's Treasury (finance ministry) found difficult to swallow. The need to save money on the programme led to several attempts to cut corners that came back to haunt Ministry of Defence procurement managers later on in the programme. Crucially, hard-earned lessons about assigning a single prime contractor, with overall programme management powers, were ignored. The supply of the Apache munitions was hived off to Hunting (later InSys) to save just £30 million on a project worth billions of pounds. The Treasury considered Westland's bid to provide air and ground crew training far too expensive and negotiations dragged on for two years after the main airframe contract was signed in April 1996, in another bid to save a few dozen million pounds. When the training contract was signed in July 1998 the 'New' Labour Party had returned to power and it used Apache training as a vehicle for one of its experimental private

Apache attack helicopters being prepared for a training mission. *(AgustaWestland)*

finance initiative (PFI) strategies. This involved a 50:50 joint venture between Boeing and GKN-Westland being responsible for purchasing and building all the training devices and facilities, in return for a thirty-year contract to provide all training services for new aircrew and ground personnel.

A whole raft of 'UK-specific' items were included in the Ministry of Defence's shopping list for its attack helicopter programme, which made it a complex effort involving several different companies under a variety of complex contractual arrangements.

Westland was at the centre of the programme as prime contractor and co-ordinating design authority for the aircraft. It was responsible for the final assembly of fifty-nine of the aircraft at Yeovil, as well as the certification of the munitions, manufacture of transmissions, delivery of some training and support elements. The Yeovil company was also a 50 per cent stakeholder in the Aviation Training International Limited (ATIL) PFI company that was responsible for the provision of training services to the Apache programme. ATIL had to 'train the trainers' before the first AAC 'conversion to type' training courses could be run and it was then to take on continuation training of all aircrew, ground crew and maintenance staff.

McDonnell Douglas was designated as design authority for the air vehicle. It undertook initial assembly of the first eight aircraft and then shipped parts to Yeovil for assembly. The integration of the Rolls-Royce Turbomecca RTM-322 engines took place at McDonnell Douglas' Mesa plant in Arizona. This proved to be more of a challenge than imagined and it delayed the delivery of the first nine helicopters to the Ministry of

Extensive live-firing training was an important element of the conversion of 9 Regiment AAC to the Apache. *(AgustaWestland)*

The UK Apache has a unique defensive system dubbed HIDAS. *(BAE Systems)*

Defence by a year beyond the date announced at the procurement launch in 1995. The new engines are more powerful than the General Electric T700-GE-701 turbo-shafts used in the US Army's AH-64D, which is a bonus considering the extra weight carried by the British helicopters.

Martin Marietta (later Lockheed Martin) was responsible for supplying the Longbow radar and Target Acquisition and Designation Sight/Pilot and Night Vision Sensor (TADS-PNVS). These items were essentially the same as those fitted to US Army AH-64Ds. They are the key elements of the Apache weapon system and allow it to employ radio frequency (RF) or laser versions of the Raytheon AGM-114 Hellfire missile. The Longbow radar uses millimetre wave technology that can detect large metal objects, such as tanks and vehicles, in bad weather or at night. It then automatically downloads the target data into the RF AGM-114L Hellfires and guides them to their targets. Up to 100 targets can be tracked at one time and all sixteen Hellfires can be fired in a 'ripple' salvo. The UK purchased sixty-eight radars to allow one to be installed on every UK Apache, along with 204 missile launchers and 980 AGM-114Ls, which were to be built by Shorts (now Thales) in Belfast.

The British, however, opted for a home-grown solution to protect their Apaches from surface-to-air missile threats and selected GEC-Marconi (now BAE Systems Avionics) to supply the Helicopter Integrated Defensive Aids Suite (HIDAS). This features warning sensors to detect missile launches and automatic systems to employ countermeasures and decoys. HIDAS includes a Lockheed Martin (formerly Sanders) ultraviolet-infrared AN/AAR-57 Common Missile Warning System (CMWS), a Lockheed Martin AN/APR-48 radar frequency interferometer for emitter targeting, a BAE Systems Sky Guardian 2000 Radar Warning Receiver and Type 1223 laser-warning system, linked for automatic control to W Vinten Vicon 78 Series 455 chaff-flare dispensers. Provision has been made for the eventual fitting of an infrared jammer system, such as the standard Lockheed Martin ALQ-144 or the new Northrop AN/AAQ-24 Nemesis Directed Infrared Countermeasures (DIRCM) system. Greece and Kuwait later bought HIDAS to equip their AH-64D fleets.

HIDAS was the first third-generation defensive aids suite in the world and the AAC considered it to be far more advanced than the US counterpart. BAE Systems is pitching it for installation on Apaches operated by several non-US operators.

While the AAC's Apaches use standard RF and laser-guided Hellfire missions, as well as standard 30-mm cannon ammunition, the UK decided to adopt the CRV7 unguided rockets, made by the Canadian company Bristol Aerospace, as its area effects munition. It is also fitted to carry the Shorts (now Thales) Starstreak air-to-air missile but the actual weapons have not been purchased because of a lack of funding.

Smith Industries was contracted in April 2000 to provide a Health and Usage Monitoring system. Later that year, a £64 million contract was placed with Cubic and Inter-Coastal Electronics (ICE) to provide laser engagement training equipment to allow

The School of Army Aviation at Middle Wallop is where AAC pilots get their first taste of flying the Apache. *(Tim Ripley)*

Would-be Apache pilots make extensive use of simulators to train to fly the attack helicopter. *(ATIL)*

the Apache to participate in collective training exercises with ground troops. This includes laser detectors positioned around the helicopters to determine if the Apache has been hit by enemy fire and weapon effect simulators to all ground targets to be 'attacked'.

A UK-specific communications suite was also purchased based on Thompson (now Thales) SATURN AM/FM Have Quick II secure air-to-air radios, contracted in November 1999. Ground-to-air radios proved to be more of a problem because the Apache was ordered before the British Army had selected its long-delayed Bowman digital 'battlefield internet' capable radio system. As a stopgap, the UK Apaches were delivered with US Army standard ITT Industries Single-Channel Ground and Airborne Radio Systems (SINCGARS) VHF/HF air-to-ground radios. However, they were later found to be incompatible with Bowman when it was ordered from General Dynamics UK in 2000. The ability to download in real-time radar imagery from Longbow radar in ground force headquarters was considered vital by the British Army. In early 2003, they contracted General Dynamics and Aerosystems International (AeI) to provide a series of 'gateways' to allow digital data, including 'snapshots' of the radar 'target sweeps', to be downloaded by Improved Data Modem (IDM) Version 3.02 modems, which are carried as standard on Apaches, into the Bowman systems. Known as the Apache Bowman Connectivity (ABC) proposal, the IDM-based solution was to be on line by 2005 but it was seen only as a stopgap until full Bowman capability is introduced after 2012 at the earliest.

The first eight UK-standard Apaches were assembled and flown at Mesa under the supervision of McDonnell Douglas designers and engineers. Then a process to transfer assembly to Yeovil got underway. The first nine Yeovil-built Apaches were handed over to the Ministry of Defence in January 2001, only two weeks later than stipulated in the contract.

Production then ramped up with another six aircraft being delivered in May 2000 and by August 2002, some twenty-five Apaches had been handed over by Yeovil. The final aircraft had originally been due for delivery by December 2003 but this slipped by four months.

Problems getting the simulators to work properly delayed the introduction of the Apache into service. *(ATIL)*

The first eighteen aircraft were delivered in the so-called 'baseline configuration' without the full HIDAS, Health and Usage Monitoring System and communications suite. Aircraft Number 19 onwards had the full capability fitted as standard and the first eighteen Apaches were retrofitted with the full equipment by mid-2005.

In tandem with the delivery of aircraft to the Ministry of Defence, a process of trials was begun by the Defence Research and Evaluation Agency or DERA (now Qinetiq) at Boscombe Down to certify Military Aircraft Release (MAR) and clear the Apache for safe operations. The MAR process in effect certified that an aircraft performs to requirements stated in the contract.

Because of the large UK-specific nature of the British Apache, this proved far more drawn out than was originally envisaged in the 1998 Apache fielding plan. It took seven months longer than planned for Boscombe Down to clear the Apache for flying. Budget restrictions on funding for the MAR process also forced it to be spread over several years. The long drawn out trials process was not helped by the start of the privatisation of DERA from 2001, which led the US military to temporarily delay the handing over of performance data. A government-to-government memorandum had to be signed to overcome this problem.

By December 2001, the MAR process was re-evaluated and a new plan issued for the staged release of the operational and weapons systems aspects of the aircraft. By late 2002, MAR 3 and 4 were achieved, allowing limited weapon employment for training purposes. By the summer of 2003, MAR 5 allowed the use of the full communications system and collective training equipment. This was a key milestone because it opened the way for the first conversion-to-type training to begin.

By late 2004, MAR 6, full clearance of aircraft and its weapon system, was achieved. Early in 2004, clearance trials on ships were complete, although ice trials were only concluded in December 2006.

In an era of huge defence procurement delays and cost overruns, the building of the UK's Apache aircraft went largely to cost and schedule. The main aircraft contract was only £71 million over its £2.9 billion budget and the last aircraft were delivered within a few months of the target.

Training the personnel to fly and operate the helicopter has proved more challenging and has resulted in the British Army having to reschedule its programme to introduce the Apache on several occasions. It had originally been envisaged that all of its three attack helicopter (AH) regiments would be fully trained by the end of 2003 to coincide with the aircraft delivery schedule.

Selecting Pilots for Apache AH.1 Training

The initial training for all pilots who are selected for the AAC is the same, irrespective of the helicopter that pilots will ultimately go on to fly and command. This phase begins with an initial aptitude test carried out at RAF Cranwell in Lincolnshire. Here the candidates are required to complete a series of computer-based tests to evaluate their suitability and aptitude for flying. At RAF Cranwell, the candidates will undergo an initial medical to establish if they are fit to fly helicopters.

On successful completion of both the aptitude test and medical, candidates will arrive at Middle Wallop to carry out what is termed Flying Grading. This is conducted over a period of three to four weeks. If the candidates pass Flying Grading, they are then in a position to start the Army Pilots Course (APC).

The Army Pilots Course is approximately eighteen months long and consists of several different phases. The initial phase is conducted in conjunction with both candidates from the Royal Navy and the RAF and includes instruction on elementary flying training on light aircraft. Successful students will then move from RAF Cranwell down to RAF Shawbury to begin rotary aircraft training.

This begins with a period of ground school to bring the students up to speed on the aircraft upon which they will be training. Successful completion of this phase will see the students move through to the School of Army Aviation at Middle Wallop for the final phase, which teaches the students how to operate their aircraft in a military environment.

Having completed all the phases, the students will be presented with their 'Wings' and the pilots are then required to undergo the Conversion to Type Courses for the Gazelle, Lynx or Apache AH.1.

Candidates for Apache AH.1 training must satisfy additional selection criteria. These criteria consider rank, experience, the arm or service within the armed forces and further medical requirements.

The conversion course for the Apache AH.1 consists of two main phases: namely the Conversion To Type (CTT) and the Conversion To Role (CTR). The CTT focuses on individual training and is six months' long. This phase of the training is conducted under the auspices of the Army Training Agency (ATRA). The CTR focuses on the collective training and is also six months' long and is carried out under auspices of AH regiments and experts from the British Army's Air Manoeuvre Advisory Group.

AAC pilots begin their helicopter training at the Defence Helicopter Flying School at RAF Shawbury. *(FBS)*

Introducing such a complex helicopter into service as the Apache has obviously resulted in the British Army placing a very high priority on ensuring the AAC and the Royal Electrical Mechanical Engineers (REME) have enough trained personnel to utilise the full potential of the weapon system.

Aircrew conversion-to-type training, as well as ground crew and maintenance personnel training, was the responsibility of the ATIL PFI company, under a £1.05 billion contract. It soon had a large presence at the School of Army Aviation at Middle Wallop where the main conversion-to-type training for aircrew took place. Many of its 110 personnel had service backgrounds to give the training a 'military feel' and senior AAC staff work side by side with ATIL staff. Twelve Apaches were initially based at Middle

Training facilities for the Apache are run by the private company ATIL. *(ATIL)*

Wallop for use by the AAC AH Fielding unit, 651 Squadron, for operational evaluation and training. But in the long term it is expected that only nine aircraft will remain at the School of Army Aviation.

ATIL was also made responsible for providing full mission simulator services at the two main frontline Apache bases, Dishforth in Yorkshire and Wattisham in Suffolk, for continuation training of squadron air crew. ATIL was also to provide mobile deployable simulators that can be moved to exercise areas in the UK or on operations overseas for use as mission rehearsal tools. Some 550 AAC personnel were expected to pass through ATIL facilities each year at the peak of the training effort.

AAC ground crew began training at Middle Wallop on how to operate and service Apaches in purpose-built class room facilities fitted with advanced inter-active training aids. REME maintenance personnel are trained on comparable facilities at the Arborfield.

Delays in the delivery of full-mission simulators being built for ATIL by Boeing played havoc with the original Apache fielding plan and led to a two-year delay in the first conversion-to-type course for squadron aircrew starting. This resulted in aircraft deliveries getting way ahead of the training stream and the Ministry of Defence had to store dozens of Apaches at RAF Shawbury in Shropshire until crews were available to operate them from 2004 onwards. The AAC now had to totally recast the Apache fielding plan.

Under the second version of the fielding plan, 9 Regiment AAC's 656 Squadron was the first to go through the twenty-six-week conversion-to-type training. It was then followed by another of the regiment's sub-units, 664 Squadron. The fielding plan then called for 3 Regiment from RAF Wattishm to send its sub-units, 653 and 662 Squadrons, to Middle Wallop. Finally 4 Regiment's 654 and 669 Squadrons were to complete the conversion-to-type training by early 2007. Each regiment was to have two Apache squadrons with a total of sixteen aircraft and a utility squadron with eight Lynx AH.7 or 9.

It was initially planned for Apache pilot conversion courses to last fifteen weeks, but this has been extended to twenty-six weeks. This means that completion of conversion training for 144 pilots slipped from April 2004 to February 2007. As simulator hours are capped under ATIL's contract, the number of pilots trained each year fell from seventy-two to forty-eight.

Once air and ground crew from frontline AAC squadrons passed through the ATIL-run training, each unit then went through a conversion-to-role training package to prepare them to go on operations. This package was prepared by the British Army's Air Manoeuvre Advisory Group and personnel of 9 Regiment in time for when the first conversion-to-type course finished training late in the spring of 2004.

After the full force of six Apache squadrons had been trained, it was intended that ATIL would then move to pumping out a steady stream of new personnel to replace natural wastage of people from the Apache Force. The frontline squadrons were then expected to start being involved in the normal British Army readiness cycle of exercises and deployments, while at the same meeting their training commitments with 16 Brigade. Efforts were begun to investigate the network linking of ATIL's simulators to allow more advanced training profiles and mission rehearsals. The Joint Helicopter Command (JHC), which oversees 16 Brigade's helicopter units and the RAF's support helicopter assets, is also looking at linking Apache simulators to the CAE-run Medium Support Helicopter Training Facility (MSHTF) at RAF Benson to allow mixed-force package training with RAF Puma, Merlin and Chinook helicopter crews.

Live-firing weapons training began at Lulworth in Dorset as part of both the MAR process and conversion-to-type training, but this is limited to only firing helicopters' rockets and guns. There is no range in the UK on which live-laser or RF Hellfires can be safely fired and moves were begun to investigate possible locations for this training. Options under consideration included US ranges in the Arizona desert or at the British Army training centre at Suffield in Canada. The laser-engagement training equipment was expected to fill much of this training gap, allowing Apache aircrew to practise realistic tactics and battle procedure alongside tank and infantry units on Salisbury Plain Training Area in the UK or at Suffield from 2004 onwards.

Through 2003 and into 2004, the first Apache conversion-to-type training course was under way at Middle Wallop and then the first tranche of personnel moved north to join 9 Regiment at its Yorkshire base.

Within days of Britain's first AgustaWestland Apache AH.1 attack helicopter squadron force being declared ready for action in October 2004, the unit found itself being put to

Exercise Eagle's Eye saw 16 Brigade conduct extensive training at West Freugh in south-west Scotland. *(Tim Ripley)*

the test in Exercise Eagle's Eye in south-west Scotland. The focus of this exercise was to test the Apache in a realistic scenario and see if 656 Squadron AAC was up to speed on its new helicopter. The declaration of the squadron's 'initial operating capability' was defined as being ready to deploy a small package of four aircraft anywhere in the world.

The two-week long exercise saw some 4,500 Army and RAF personnel, supported by around thirty helicopters and 1,500 vehicles, moving from assembly areas in south-west England to conduct simulated combat operations in the West Freugh area, which is a few miles to the east of the ferry port of Stranrear. Aviation components included 9 Regiment AAC with eight Apaches of 656 Squadron, along with six Westland Lynx AH.9s and one Westland Gazelle AH.1 of 672 Squadron. A strong contingent of RAF support helicopters, including ten Boeing Chinook HC.2s, from 18 and 27 Squadrons, and four AgustaWestland Merlin HC.3s of 28 Squadron, supported the exercise. They were grouped into a Joint Helicopter Force (JHF) for the exercise. The RAF's air transport force was heavily involved in the exercise, at one point providing eleven Hercules aircraft, which was a significant effort considering the heavy world wide commitments of the RAF's C-130 fleet at the time. Tactical air traffic control, air movements control, tactical communications wing and tactical refuelling elements were also strongly involved to help

Colonel Peter Fraser-Hopewell, Deputy Commander of 16 Air Assault Brigade. *(Tim Ripley)*

establish West Freugh as a forward operating base for Hercules and helicopters. 9 Regiment and the Royal Logistic Corps were heavily involved in establishing forward arming and refuelling points (FARPs) in the exercise area to support helicopter operations in remote regions.

The exercise scenarios involved a fictional former Soviet-style republic invading its neighbour and the UN calling on member states to go the victim's assistance. 16 Brigade was Britain's contribution to the international military campaign. The first phase involved a sustained suppression of enemy air defence (SEAD) effort against the RAF electronic warfare range at Spadeham, involving RAF Tornado GR4s, Dutch and USAF F-16s. With the hostile air defences neutralised, 16 Brigade was able to begin its move from Keevil and

Apache in the rain at West Freugh. *(Tim Ripley)*

Kemble airbases on Salisbury Plain. On the afternoon of 14 October, eleven Hercules from the Lynham Transport Wing flew 706 troops from the 2nd Battalion, The Parachute Regiment, to make a parachute drop north of West Freugh to open the ground phase of the exercise. The paratroopers then launched a ground assault on a small airstrip at Castle Kennedy to drive away a small group of enemy troops. Brigadier Jacko Page, 16 Brigade's Commander, parachuted in with the assault troops to establish a forward tactical headquarters.

With the paratroopers on the ground in the heart of enemy territory, the rest of the Brigade began to move north. Beginning early on the morning of 15 October, the helicopters began leaving Salisbury Plain and via a FARP at RAF Shawbury in Shropshire, they gathered early in the afternoon at another FARP at Kirkbride, a disused airfield west of Carlisle. One Apache pilot described this as a 'massive logistic effort'. 9 Regiment's adjutant, Captain Rob Threapleton, said with all the aircraft arriving at one time the FARPs needed to be very organised.

According to Colonel Peter Fraser-Hopewell, 16 Brigade's Deputy Commander, a key part of the exercise was to test the movement of men and machines over considerable distance.

We put in FOB, refuelling points. Co-ordinating, synchronising the move of Apache, Chinook and Merlins is quite complicated. We set ourselves long distances to move aircraft and men, to set a challenge. This exercise has real moving parts. If you don't get the fuel to the helicopters then they don't arrive on time. It was also conducted in challenging weather conditions.

The afternoon of 15 October saw the first of eight Apaches launch from Kirkbride to lead a formation of six Chinooks and four Merlins carrying the 1st Battalion, The Argyll & Sutherland Highlanders.

About half an hour later, the first pair of Apaches had taken up firing positions behind a ridgeline seven kilometres from the objective – West Freugh airfield – as Tornado bombers swept over the target. The Apache helicopters then started to engage air defence positions and ground troops defending the airfield. Using the Apache's laser-training system, the pilots were able to get reliable feed back to the accuracy of their Hellfire missile, rocket and 30-mm cannon fire.

'We arrived thirty minutes before the Chinooks and controlled fast air on to the air defences – we did airborne forward air control,' said one of the 656 Squadron Apache pilots.

The two subsequent Apaches provided close-in fire support as the Argylls were dropped off at a tactical assembly area south of the airfield by the Chinooks and Merlins. They remained on station as the troops fought their way onto the airfield. The final pair remained overhead to help prevent counter attacks, as the wave of helicopters began to return to Kirkbride to refuel.

Supporting the troops in contact with the enemy involved the employment of a technique known as Close-in-Fire Support or CIFS. According to Apache crews, CIFS is a middle ground between an artillery fire mission and CAS. 'It is available to any soldier on the radio net,' they said. It involves Apaches flying close to the assault infantry wave and putting down fire over the heads of the troops as requested.

One Apache pilot said:

> Our firepower is equivalent to one and half a Harrier per aircraft. This exercise is an education process, demonstrating to the troops what we can do. Unfortunately we don't fire blanks so the exercising troops can't get a real impression of the firepower available to them.

Post mission analysis of the Apache gun camera videos and the instrumented training aids, however, provided ample evidence of the success of the operation. Colonel Fraser-Hopewell said the Apache 'did very well', with only one being glimpsed at a distance by the defenders of West Freugh. He said the Apache had a 100 per cent success rate on all targets. 'We were very pleased at the capability shown yesterday,' he said.

For the Apache crews, their exercise was not yet over. The first wave of crews returned their aircraft to Kirkbride and were soon replaced by new crews who flew protective missions over the forward troops during the night.

During the next phase of the operation, the Chinooks and Merlins deployed forward to West Freugh, while the Apaches flew forward to Castle Douglas to join the paratroopers. Operating from a FARP in a field, the Apaches were on call at one-hour notice to fly CIFS or scout missions at the direction of 2 PARA. West Freugh then became a hive of activity as a shuttle of Hercules aircraft flew in the main Brigade headquarters and more supplies.

The final week of the exercise saw battalion-level operations throughout south-west

Scotland, as the Brigade mopped up small pockets of simulated enemy resistance. One pilot said:

> We were the first AH squadron in the first AH Regiment. As squadron we underwent six months on type-conversion and then conversion to role, where we learned to fight the helicopter. In the first half of the conversion period we worked as pairs, in the last three months we did composite air operations and co-ordination with ground troops is the final bit. Then we tried to make sure we could mesh with brigade.

The Apache crews spent Exercise Eagle's Eye living in the field with the paratroopers and Highlanders of 16 Brigade.

The pilot continues:

> We were living in day sacks, which is fine but you needed to think about how to look after your £20,000 flying helmets [which slave the weapons onto targets]. If they get wet or damaged the helicopter doesn't fly.
>
> The AH is awesome. The night vision FLIR is very sensitive to moisture. That is its biggest limitation and its [performance] drops at night.
>
> We are the first squadron and we have not done less than a 12-hour day yet. The training over the last six months has been excellent. We've hit the ground running at Dishford [9 Regiment's home base] and the momentum has not slowed. You cannot afford to be away from the aircraft for a few weeks – the British Army is definitely getting their money's worth from us.

Although Exercise Eagle's Eye provided the British Army with its first experience of using the Apache in a large scale exercise, many in 656 Squadron were looking ahead to the day when they took their new helicopter into action for real. One Apache pilot commented, 'the real culmination of our training will be when we go on an operation and use the weapon system for real.'

The US and Dutch experience of using the Apache in action in Iraq and Afghanistan over the previous three years was being examined closely by 9 Regiment. 'The Dutch in Iraq advertised what their aircraft could do to the locals and since then not a single one of their convoys being escorted has been attacked,' said a 656 Squadron pilot.

The AAC spent a lot of time talking to its allied counterparts and this led to them looking at how to develop the tactics and procedures to use the Apache in low-intensity warfare. It seemed that the large-scale conventional battles that the British Army had envisaged when they originally decided to buy the helicopter in the aftermath of the 1991 Gulf war were a thing of the past. The trial of the CIFS techniques during Exercise Eagle's Eye was the start of this process and it would accelerate the closer it came to the point when 9 Regiment would be committed to operations.

CHAPTER 12

A Fatal Blow?

As the British Army began, at last, to get its first Apache squadron up and running during late 2003 and early 2004, the Service's ambitions to field full air manoeuvre capabilities by the later half of the decade were coming under increasing pressure from budget shortfalls in the Ministry of Defence. Her Majesty's Treasury (finance ministry) was in the process of deciding the government's overall spending plans for the next three years and word quickly got around Whitehall that it was not going to be generous to the Armed Forces. Pressure from the Chancellor of the Exchequer (finance minister) Gordon Brown to generate resources for election-winning policies was immense and the then Defence Secretary Geoff Hoon was ordered to trim his department's spending plans accordingly.

Central to 'air manoeuvre' concepts being developed in the late 1990s were plans to buy attack and transport helicopters to allow 16 Brigade to operate deep behind enemy lines or across the forward line of own troops (FLOT). These capabilities were also considered very applicable in the peacekeeping or guerrilla warfare scenarios that the British Armed Forces were beginning to face in the US-led 'global war on terror', where there were no fixed frontlines and the battlefield situation was very fluid.

Defence Secretary Geoff Hoon. *(Tim Ripley)*

The fielding of the AAC AgustaWestland Apache AH.1 attack helicopter fleet took up the bulk of the British Army's procurement budget in the first years of the twenty-first century. (*AgustaWestland*)

A four-step development process was under way that moved towards giving the British Army's Apache and air manoeuvre units the ability to fly 150 kilometres beyond the FLOT on deep air manoeuvre or 'deep strike' missions. These could either be direct attacks on enemy positions or escort tasks for transport helicopters carrying a battalion's worth of troops on air assault missions behind enemy lines to seize key objectives. The British Army air manoeuvre project was closely allied with the Royal Marines' littoral manoeuvre effort, which envisaged the conducting of helicopter assaults up to 200 kilometres from an amphibious fleet. The distances involved in both the air and littoral manoeuvre concepts were designed to allow British ground and helicopter forces to decisively defeat opponents in surprise strategic operations. To achieve these objectives required not just helicopter lift capacity, but reconnaissance and surveillance, logistic and refuelling support, communications and fire support.

As a result of the cancellation of the SABR helicopter programme the RAF Chinook had to continue to split its efforts between supporting 16 Air Assault and 3 Commando Brigades. *(Tim Ripley)*

As part of the 1998 Strategic Defence Review (SDR) process, a series of incremental targets were set to bring the full air manoeuvre capabilities on line and remove the UK's helicopter lift shortfalls. By late 2003, Step 1 to field the lead aviation task force was looking like it would almost be complete by the end of the following year. Step 2 involved developing the first elements of the Royal Marines' littoral maritime manoeuvre project. During 2003, work was under way to see if it could afford to buy a replacement for the Sea King Mk 4 from 2010 to meet these requirements. The Royal Navy's force of Sea King Mk 4s was limited in range and could not then achieve the desired 200-kilometre 'ship to objective' range for lifting a battalion's worth of troops ashore. Step 3 was supposed to be the move towards fielding the initial operating capability by 2007 for deep manoeuvre operations of a limited duration, but this was also being reviewed and recosted before it could be given the go ahead. The huge costs involved in fielding Step 4, the full air and littoral maritime manoeuvre capability by 2012, were considered so prohibitive

The RAF's airlift shortages were not resolved by Hoon in his 2004 spending review. *(Tim Ripley)*

that even before the Hoon defence review took place some in the Ministry of Defence suggested it would have to be scrapped. In 2002, the British Army leadership were already starting to focus their attention away from air manoeuvre capabilities to other priorities, including the introduction of the Bowman digital communications system up to 2008 and then the Future Rapid Effects System (FRES) family of armoured vehicles after that.

In the later half of 2003, the British Ministry of Defence launched another major review of air manoeuvre and littoral warfare concepts as part of the looming government spending review and to pick up any lessons from the 2003 Iraq war. Arguments swirled around the Ministry of Defence Main Building in London and at major army, navy and air force headquarters during this period, as Service chiefs battled to protect their budgets from Hoon's spending axe. At the core of these debates were arguments over the purchase of additional transport helicopters to support the Apache force. The National Audit Office produced a report in April 2004, which revealed that the Ministry of Defence was 38 per cent short of helicopter lift capacity across the three armed Services.

Some in the ministry claimed that US experience during the 2003 Iraq war seemed to suggest that the Apache and other helicopters were vulnerable during operations far behind enemy lines. Heavy losses suffered by US Army Apache units during the advance on Baghdad seemed to suggest that deep strike missiles were too costly. Also, counter-insurgency operations required close air support against small groups of enemy infantry, rather than mass attacks against formations of enemy tanks. As Operation Iraqi Freedom progressed, US Army Apaches found themselves increasingly being used for close air support for frontline troops because of a lack of 'depth' targets for them to attack. This has led to suggestions being made that deep manoeuvre operations might not really be necessary or realistic.

There was also growing concern that the AAC and REME would not be able to recruit, train and retain all the personnel necessary to fully man three Apache regiments. Aircrew training courses had been extended, meaning only forty-eight aircrew could be trained each year rather than seventy-two, which has reduced the number of pilots the training system could generate. It was suggested that rather than having forty-eight Apaches ready for action at any one time, only thirty-six would be available, severely curtailing the size and scope of any 'deep strike' operations by the Apache force.

In 1999, the New Labour government had given the go ahead for the first concept phase of the Support Amphibious Battlefield Rotorcraft (SABR) programme to address the helicopter requirements of both 16 Brigade and the Royal Marines late in the first decade of the twenty-first century. This initially set the in-service date for SABR as

AgustaWestland Merlin HC.3 helicopters. (*AgustaWestland*)

2005/06 but the government did not formally launch the project by awarding production contracts.

Initial operational analysis conducted by the SABR integrated project team suggested that up to around seventy new helicopters, in addition to the forty Chinooks and twenty-two Merlin helicopters then in service, were required to deliver the main SABR capability. At the heart of the SABR project was purchasing enough helicopters to allow 3 Commando and 16 Brigades to operate to their full potential at the same time. Without the full SABR purchase, the air assault and amphibious brigades would not be able to conduct operations simultaneously and would continue to share the same small fleet of Chinooks, as had happened in the 2003 invasion of Iraq. It was proposed that a mix of new-build Chinooks and Merlins would be purchased, including a variant of the Chinooks with folding rotors to allow embarked operations from aircraft carriers and amphibious ships. This would have been a unique UK capability that could have cost £100 million to develop.

The estimated cost of developing and building the SABR helicopters was between £3 billion and £6.5 billion, although the latter figure was based on purchasing the hugely expensive American Bell-Boeing V-22 Osprey tilt rotor aircraft. Progression to the next phase of the project, the so-called Assessment Phase, was eventually rescheduled to start in the spring of 2004. The Assessment Phase would aim to reduce risk and uncertainty prior to committing to manufacture or main gate decision in 2007 or 2008, with the first new helicopters in service by 2010.

As well as buying new helicopters, the AAC was looking for additional funding for the personnel to man the forward arming and refuelling points (FARPS) needed to support Apache operations over large areas. Also, the communications equipment for Apaches to allow beyond-visual range transmissions 150 kilometres behind enemy lines had yet to be agreed and funded by the Treasury.

The British Special Forces were also starting to show an interest in utilising the Apaches to support their covert operations and were looking for a flight of four aircraft to be held on alert to support them. This would be on top of the existing commitment to provide a squadron of Apaches to support the Royal Marines during amphibious operations from 2005 and further dilute the availability of Apaches to support 16 Brigade. Arguments raged about whether it was more cost effective to centralise the Apache force or distribute it in small units to the Royal Marines and Special Forces.

These trends were leading some senior British Army officers to consider scrapping the ambitions plans to give 16 Brigade the full 'deep' air manoeuvre capability. If this happened then the three existing Apache regiments could be grouped into a separate US-style 'attack aviation' brigade to operate independently or be divided up between 16 Brigade 1, (UK) and 3 (UK) Divisions. Under some plans being considered at this time it was proposed that 16 Brigade would revert to being an airborne unit for parachute assaults only.

During the first half of 2004, the vicious budget battles being fought within the Ministry of Defence to divide up the shrinking defence budget came to a conclusion. There was some new money for intelligence gathering systems, but any new spending had to be found by cutting spending on existing projects. The battlefield helicopter and air manoeuvre forces took a big hit in the budget battles at the expense of the purchase of new aircraft carriers, fighter aircraft, new light-armoured vehicles and the reorganisation of the British Army. Medium Workstrand 13, as the section dealing with helicopters was code-named, cut the equipment budget for battlefield helicopters up to 2014 from £4.6 billion to £3.1 billion. Spending on helicopter procurement plummeted for the rest of the decade, from an annual spend of £842 million in 2001/02 to only £209 million in 2006/07.

In July 2004, Defence Secretary Geoff Hoon's announcement 'Delivering Security in a Changing World' cut military manpower by 10,000, which was second only in severity to the 10,000 cut in manpower being taken by Ministry of Defence civil servants. Military bases, units and procurement projects were slashed in all three Services.

Hoon told the House of Commons that cuts were needed to re-focus efforts into what were termed 'network-enabled' warfare technologies. The announcement a day earlier at the Farnborough airshow of the selection of Thales as prime contractor for the £800 million British Army's new Watchkeeper unmanned aerial vehicle (UAV) programme was meant to reinforce this message.

Hoon's failure to win a significant rise in funding for his ministry from Gordon Brown was really to be at the heart of the cutbacks. With Brown clearing the decks for the next election and pumping money into vote-winning education, health and other social programmes, defence had to go near to the end of the line. Hoon and the Service chiefs therefore had to rejig their spending plans, accepting cuts in the current force structure to try to keep the future big ticket procurement programmes on track.

In an interview published in *RAF News* after the announcement about cuts, Air Chief Marshal Sir Jock Stirrup, the Chief of the Air Staff, admitted that the increase in the defence budget was not enough to meet all the RAF's requirements. He commented 'given the level of investment we need to make that increase is insufficient to accommodate all we seek to do.'

The Chief of the General Staff, General Sir Mike Jackson, who was the budget holder for SABR and other air manoeuvre projects, did not place them at the top of his list of priorities. He made buying the Bowman digital communications system his top procurement priority between 2004 and 2008. The re-organisation of the infantry and the conversion of armoured and mechanised brigades into light rapid deployment brigades were Jackson's force development priorities. The need to provide forces to garrison Iraq was also starting to become a major drain on the British Army's budget.

Hoon announced he was proposing to spend £3.1 billion on new military helicopters over the next decade but this was some £1.5 billion less than previous plans and at a stroke removed any idea that the full potential of the SABR project would be met. The project was scrapped and helicopter procurement planners were told to go back to the drawing board.

The Ministry of Defence repackaged its helicopter procurement plans as the Future Rotorcraft Capability (FRC) project and very quickly it became apparent that plans to buy new transport helicopters before the end of the decade were dead. Some £800 million was to be spent updating the Royal Navy's AgustaWestland Merlin HM.1 maritime patrol helicopters. More than £1.2 billion was to be spent on buying seventy upgraded Future Lynx helicopters to replace the AAC and Royal Navy's Lynx light-utility helicopters, with only forty-five of these being intended to replace the ninety Lynx AH.7 and AH.9s then in AAC service from 2014. It was proposed to replace the 100 or so Gazelle AH.1 utility and observation helicopters of the AAC with only twenty leased civil-standard machines.

The launching of the Future Lynx project was one of the few bright spots in Hoon's defence cuts package but the helicopters will not enter service until 2014. *(AgustaWestland)*

The remainder of the helicopter budget would be soaked up by Apache and Chinook upgrades. There was the prospect of thirty or so medium-lift helicopters, most likely advanced versions of the Merlin, being purchased but this would not take place until 2015 at the earliest. In the meantime, a series of small-scale upgrades and urgent operational requirement (UOR) enhances would have to suffice to keep the RAF's Chinooks, Pumas and Merlins in operational condition until the middle of the next decade.

One piece of good news from the 2004 defence review was a decision to form an additional AAC regiment to provide extra FARPs, although this would be made up of 'weekend soldiers' of the Territorial Army.

In a bizarre twist, the FRC also set as a priority the upgrading and return to flying status of the eight Chinook HC.3 helicopters that had been ordered in 1995 for £259 million. These helicopters were supposed to be delivered by 1998 and were to have sophisticated night-flying systems to allow them to fly Special Forces troops deep behind enemy lines but the project was a disaster. The contracts were poorly written and to save money there was no designated prime contractor. By 2001, the helicopters had been delivered to the UK but major problems with the night-vision systems were discovered during trials at the Defence Evaluation and Research Agency's (DERA) Boscombe Down test centre. All the companies involved and the Ministry of Defence started to blame each other for the mess and soon the helicopters, which could not fly safely unless the pilot could see the ground, were put into storage until the dispute could be resolved. In the meantime, the Special Forces continued to 'borrow' half a dozen Chinooks from the main RAF fleet and upgraded them under the modest Night Enhancement Programme (NEP), taking them away from tasking to support 16 Brigade or other frontline units. It took another six years of prevarication and delay for the Ministry of Defence to decide, in March 2007, how it would get the HC.3 helicopters into service. The House of Commons' Public Accounts Committee called the debacle 'one of the worst equipment procurement the committee had seen'.

The 2004 defence review did not help other important projects to enhance the combat capability of 16 Brigade. The Indirect Fire Precision Attack (IFPA) project, which was intended to give the British Army's light forces long-range fire power, continued to languish in the pending tray and no production decisions were taken.

Although much fanfare was made by the government of the purchase of the Watchkeeper system, it would not enter service until the end of the decade. The Watchkeeper was a variant of the Israeli-made Hermes 450 UAV. A proposal by the Watchkeeper contractor, Thales, to provide the British Army with an interim capability of base-line Hermes 450s until the enhanced Watchkeeper entered service was not taken up on cost grounds. This meant the British Army would have to continue to use its existing Phoenix UAVs for another five years, even though the air vehicle could not fly in the hot summer conditions found in the Middle East.

To save money the government also ordered the RAF to withdraw its veteran Canberra PR.9 photographic reconnaissance aircraft by early 2006. It had been hoped that the Raytheon Sentinel R.1 airborne stand-off radar (ASTOR) aircraft would enter service in time to take over from the Canberra but a technician dropped the main test radar, causing US$55 million worth of damage and delaying the project by several months. Other technical problems meant the system did not seem likely to enter service until late 2008 at the earliest.

The British Army and RAF's ability to locate and strike at enemy forces outside of the direct line of sight of UK troops was severely limited and did not seem likely to be rectified until the end of the decade.

Scrapping the SABR project meant that any idea of bridging the helicopter lift shortfall was lost for a decade. In the end, 16 Brigade survived the 2004 defence review intact as the British Army's sole air manoeuvre force and the objective of operating 150 kilometres behind enemy lines remained. But there was little prospect that the Brigade would move very far up the 'air manoeuvre' capability stepladder for at least a decade. The RAF transport helicopter force would have to wait at least a decade before it got any more helicopters, while the AAC's ageing Lynx fleet would not be replaced until

2014 despite growing unserviceablity and rising operating costs. The only consolation was that the Apache force was starting to come on line in strength.

A senior Ministry of Defence budget planning official told the media briefing where Hoon announced his cuts package in July 2004 that the 38 per cent shortfall in helicopter lift would not be a problem. 'We've changed the requirement for helicopter lift' he said. 'So there is no longer a shortfall, problem solved.'

CHAPTER 13

Exercise Eagle's Strike, 2005

As dusk fell, the peace and tranquillity of the English west country was broken by the sound of Westland Apache AH.1 attack helicopters of 9 Regiment Army Air Corps (AAC) starting up. Two at a time, the Apaches pulled back from the flight line and taxied down Merryfield's runway before lifting off and heading eastwards for the battlezone on Salisbury Plain.

Down the runway, lines of paratroopers and Territorial Army soldiers could be seen filing towards pick-up points and loading onboard Westland Merlin HC.3 support helicopters. Three Boeing Chinook HC.2s had already lifted off ahead of troop-carrying helicopters, their under-slung 105-mm Light Guns destined to set up a firebase to provide support for the assault troops.

Before very long, a constant stream of helicopters was airborne and the finale of Exercise Eagle's Strike was well under way.

9 Regiment AAC poised for action at RNAS Merryfield during Exercise Eagle's Strike 2005. *(Tim Ripley)*

AgustaWestland Apache AH.1 attack helicopters head for Salisbury Plain during Exercise Eagle's Strike 2005. (Tim Ripley)

For Brigadier Ed Butler, the newly appointed commander of 16 Air Assault Brigade, the exercise was a chance to put his troops to the test and prove that his new attack helicopter regiment was ready for action. This was the biggest British Army field exercise to take place in 2005 and it was the culmination of the decade-long effort by the AAC to field the AgustaWestland Apache AH.1. At a cost of £2.9 billion, the Apache programme had swallowed up the bulk of the British Army's equipment procurement budget during the first half of the decade and a lot was expected of it.

The British Army, RAF and Royal Navy had mustered an unprecedented number of helicopters, aircraft and communications equipment to test the Apache regiment in a realistic combat setting. As well as the fourteen attack helicopters of 9 Regiment, Exercise Eagle's Strike saw some thirty other RAF, Royal Navy and AAC helicopters; there were RAF Lockheed Martin Hercules transport aircraft and fixed-wing combat aircraft participating. These included six RAF Chinooks of 18 Squadron, Odiham, six RAF

Brigadier Ed Butler, Commander 16 Air Assault Brigade. *(Tim Ripley)*

Merlins from 28 Squadron, three Sea King AEW 7s of 849 Naval Air Squadron, a Merlin HM.1 from RNAS Culdrose, four Lynx AH.9s and three Lynx AH.7s from 9 and 4 Regiments AAC.

The exercise in May 2005 saw some 3,000 personnel of 16 Air Assault Brigade deploy by air and land to RAF St Mawgan in Cornwall to establish a forward operating base. Then the Brigade mounted an air assault operation onto Dartmoor before moving to set up another forward operating base at RNAS Merryfield, an outstation of the large Royal Naval Air Station at Yeovilton. This was soon turned into a major helicopter hub with all the Brigade's aircraft lined up on its hardstandings. Hundreds of army vehicles were positioned around the fringes of the airfield under camouflage nets and large antenna farms sprouted from the huge Brigade command post. Amid the throng of vehicles were the twenty or so huge new Oshkosh tankers, which towered above 16 Brigade's old complement of Land Rovers and DAF lorries, and allowed Brigadier Butler to keep his forward arming and refuelling points (FARPS) supplied with fuel to keep his helicopters flying.

There was a lot riding on this test of the Apache but Butler did not display any nerves at an open-air press briefing to introduce the helicopter. Several dozen journalists and television crews crowded around Butler and several of his senior officers. Unlike his secretive predecessor, Butler was clearly comfortable and confident speaking to the media. He radiated calm confidence and his film star good looks were lapped up by several of the television crews who could not get enough sound bites from the Brigadier.

> This exercise is demanding and complex and as a result I am confident the Brigade is ready to go out on operations and do everything I might ask of them. It is designed to push men, organisations and helicopters to the limit. I set the objectives and requirements needed to project brigade operations over sustained distances. It replicates a lot of the conditions we might find ourselves in around the world.

Media interest was high during Exercise Eagle's Strike 2005 because of the Apache's debut. *(Tim Ripley)*

Exercise Eagle's Strike is the culmination of an extended force development process and is the first time we've exercised attack helicopters as a regiment. We are learning a huge amount about it.

The attack helicopter must be useable across the spectrum of operations. I am confident 9 Regiment will deliver all I ask of it if it goes on operations. The Apache represents significant increase in combat power. It brings a significant improvement in our find or search capability – its radar and surveillance systems aid that. There is a huge amount of firepower in the system. We have the newer model with [a] better engine and better defensive aid suite. I have all my logistics, guns, engineers and enabler[s] to deliver attack helicopters, air assault infantry and paratroopers.

There is a real adrenalin buzz around the Brigade. They are excited to be here and have state-of-the-art technology in their hands. They are keen to put it into practice.

The centrepiece of Exercise Eagle's Strike was the presence of 9 Regiment, which was preparing to be declared operational as the British Army's first Apache-equipped Lead Aviation Battle Group. As such, the regiment will be held at high readiness to deploy at short notice to global trouble spots. 'Troops of our brigade are held at high readiness, at

5 and 30 days' notice to move,' said Butler. 'The attack helicopter will be part of that capability.'

'This is a significant moment for us as a Regiment and Brigade,' Lieutenant Colonel Richard Felton, Commanding Officer 9 Regiment, said at the Merryfield briefing. 'This is the culmination of a lot of hard work. When we approach high-readiness, which is imminent, we will be ready to deploy.'

Felton was a key member of Butler's team. He had been handpicked to command 9 Regiment as it moved to become fully operational and would lead it into action in Afghanistan in 2006. Although apparently easy going, Felton was a hard taskmaster of his aircrews, sending them on exercise after exercise until they had fully mastered their new helicopter and its weapon system.

Felton said:

> The soldiers are very proud that they have a capability that delivers. The technology in the Apache is expensive but you get payback of utility across different type of operations. The Apache is a revolution in terms of capabilities.

9 Regiment had been building up its aircraft strength and training its personnel for over a year. In autumn 2004, its first Apache sub-unit, 656 Squadron, was declared battle-ready during Exercise Eagle's Eye in south-west Scotland, giving the British Army its attack helicopter initial operating capability (IOC). The regiment's second sub-unit, 664 Squadron, then came on line after a similar work-up period.

Felton said:

> I now have 600 soldiers, 16 attack helicopters and eight Lynx AH.9 battlefield utility helicopters and 300 vehicles. That includes 150 technicians and 120 people in the command and control element.

Felton praised his support personnel for ensuring almost all the regiment's helicopters

Exercise Eagle's Strike 2005 saw the debut of 16 Brigade's new Oshkosh fuel tankers. *(Tim Ripley)*

Royal Navy Westland Sea King AsaC.7 airborne command and control helicopters supported 9 Regiment's Apaches during Exercise Eagle's Strike 2005. *(Tim Ripley)*

RAF Boeing Chinook HC.2s provided vital logistic support during Exercise Eagle's Strike 2005. *(Tim Ripley)*

could take part in the exercise. 'I have 90 per cent availability rates due to the foresight of my technicians,' he said.

The culmination of Exercise Eagle's Strike was a night-time air assault operation aimed at capturing Imber village, over 70 miles to the east inside the huge Salisbury Plain Training Area.

This complex operation involved all elements of 16 Air Assault Brigade and its success was dependent on the Apache during several phases of attack. Preparations for the operation began well ahead of assault and involved placing enabling troops forward towards the battlezone.

Immediately before the attack, Felton said:

I have sent 200 troops out enabling me to set up FARPs 50 miles from here. I have radio sites deployed to extend my communications. My helicopters will first isolate the village and then disrupt enemy forces in the village before supporting the infantry assault.

The first thing we will do tonight is destroy an enemy air defence site to create the freedom of movement for the rest of the brigade to insert troops. From then the attack by the ground forces will go into [the] village, my helicopters will then switch to destroying any enemy armour trying to reinforce the village and doing disruption

The flightline at RNAS Merryfield saw the largest concentration to date of AAC Apache helicopters. *(Tim Ripley)*

tasks in [the] village with close in fire support (CIFS) when called for by the ground troops.

Working in pairs, the Apaches of 9 Regiment were all allocated specific tasks during the operation. To ensure constant coverage of the objective with surveillance equipment and weapons, pairs of Apache were cycled through the network of FARPs.

By dawn, after the initial attack, the first pairs of Apaches were starting to return to Merryfield to allow their crews to rest, although a small number of aircraft remained in the station ready to support the continuing ground operation to clear Imber village of hostile forces. This phase of the operation saw the Chinooks and Merlins ramp up their efforts flying in reinforcements and building up supplies in the forward area. One lift saw five Chinooks simultaneously underslung the vehicles of the Brigade tactical headquarters from Merryfield to Salisbury Plain.

During the exercise, the performance results of the Apache air strikes were recorded by its instrument training system, which activated transponders on the Challenger 2 tanks used by the enemy forces when the helicopter crews scored a hit.

Royal Navy Westland Sea King AEW.7 radar helicopters flew in a ground surveillance role in support of 16 Air Assault Brigade for the first time during Exercise Eagle's Strike to expand the network-enabled capability of the Brigade and give the senior commander 'real-time' control of air and ground operations.

The use of airborne early warning helicopters to identify hostile armoured vehicles for attack helicopters builds on the employment of 849 Naval Air Squadron in a 'mini Joint-STARS' role during the invasion of Iraq in 2003. The Sea King's Thales Searchwater radar proved able to provide effective overland moving target indicator (MTI) coverage of Iraq troop movements, allowing air and artillery strikes to be directed against them.

Three of 849 Squadron's helicopters were used to support 9 Regiment, culminating in the night-time air assault operation launched from RNAS Merryfield on to Salisbury Plain. Throughout this operation, two Sea Kings were airborne providing coverage of the objective and surrounding area, while the third aircraft acted as a spare.

Felton said:

> The Sea Kings gave me an Airborne Command Element (ACE), a UHF strike primary radio net and an air mission command radio net. I used two Sea Kings' MTI to track moving vehicles and then to cue my attach helicopters to destroy the enemy armour. The Sea King's radar has a far wider coverage than the Longbow radars on our Apache.

Senior commanders in 16 Brigade's headquarters were able to watch an 'air picture' of the operation showing the position of all helicopters down-linked in real-time by the Link 16 Joint Tactical Information Distribution System (JTIDS) on the Sea Kings throughout the assault on Imber. Individual attack missions by the Apaches had to be cued verbally over radio nets by operators on the Sea Kings or by Brigade headquarters because the British attack helicopters do not have Link 16 fitted to allow their aircrews to monitor the radar

Apaches return to Merryfield to re-arm and re-fuel after the opening phase of the air assault on to Salisbury Plain. *(Tim Ripley)*

Lieutenant Colonel Richard Felton, Commanding Officer 9 Regiment AAC. *(Tim Ripley)*

tracks from the early warning helicopters.

Royal Navy Merlin MH.1 helicopters also joined the exercise to supplement the airborne early warning coverage of the Sea King AEW.7s and feed additional information into the 'air picture'.

'Our Apaches don't have Link 16 but we do have the Improved Data Model (IDM) that allows us to track the position of all the other attack helicopters,' said Lieutenant Colonel Felton.

During the fielding of the Bowman digital communications system to 16 Brigade in 2006 a network of 'gateways' or rebroadcast systems was delivered to allow improved data-communications traffic to be routed to and from airborne Apaches and ground headquarters. Dubbed the Apache Bowman Connectivity (ABC) project, the gateways allow Apache crews to download 'snapshots' of Longbow radar into 16 Air Assault Brigade's headquarters.

The successful completion of Exercise Eagle's Strike was not the end of the British Army's efforts to field its full complement of sixty-seven Apaches. Brigadier Butler said work would start soon after the exercise to 'prove' the Apache in the special forces support role. 9 Regiment's 664 Squadron practised its special forces support role during Exercise Chameleon in the summer of 2005.

Details of the special forces training for Apache crews were sparse but it involved practising strike missions with special forces forward air controllers and flying escort missions for helicopters carrying special forces troops deep into hostile territory. Dedicated Apaches would not be permanently assigned to the UK's Joint Special Forces Aviation Wing based at RAF Odiham but a pool of specially trained aircrew was be held at high readiness at 9 Regiment's Dishforth base to support special forces missions.

This was a follow-on from an effort late in 2005 to embark eight 'marinised' Apaches on Royal Navy amphibious warfare ships to support littoral operations by the Royal Marines 3 Commando Brigade. During the summer of 2005 a handful of the specially modified Apaches was in the process of being returned to 9 Regiment ahead of an

RAF Merlins and Chinooks were deployed in strength during Exercise Eagle's Strike 2005. *(Tim Ripley)*

amphibious exercise in the autumn. The modifications include anti-corrosion measures. By the end of the 2005, nine Apache crews of 9 Regiment were qualified to fly from the helicopter carrier HMS *Ocean* and the two amphibious assault ships, HMS *Bulwalk* and *Albion*, to provide an initial maritime operating capability by the end of the year. During 2006, the number of maritime qualified crews grew and the Apaches were cleared to fly from Invincible class aircraft carriers.

Exercise Eagle's Strike was a major boost for 16 Brigade but the Apache fielding programme was still not going to plan because of delays in training enough attack helicopter aircrew. Wastage rates on the demanding training courses at Middle Wallop were proving to be higher than expected and extra courses had to be organised. This led to the third reorganisation of the AAC's attack helicopter fielding plans in four years. It led to the public announcement that the full force of sixty-seven Apache AH.1s was not now expected to be fully manned until 2010.

UK Armed Forces Minister Adam Ingram revealed details of the new plans during a

16 Brigade's headquarters is moved by air to Salisbury Plain under-slung beneath RAF Chinooks. *(Tim Ripley)*

parliamentary answer in August 2005.

> At this stage it is envisaged that all three [Apache] regiments will be manned with
> 42 Apache attack helicopter-trained aircrew, which represents 87.5 per cent of the
> final manning requirement. There will then follow a period where all three
> regiments will be brought up to full-manning by September 2010.

Difficulties in recruiting and training sufficient numbers of aircrew are proving more of a
problem than was expected, according to AAC officers. The British Army's Air
Manoeuvre Working Group set out a new plan in 2001 to reorganise Apache aircrew
training after delays in getting the helicopter's simulators operational, with the objective
of having 144 aircrew fully trained by February 2007. Under the new plans announced by
Ingram, only 126 aircrew would be ready for action by 2009.

These problems are also understood to be behind a rescheduling of dates for 3 and 4
Regiment AAC to be declared operational. Ingram said:

> The conversion of the second [Apache] regiment is under way and is due to be ready
> for operations by September 2007. The third regiment is programmed to [begin]
> converting from October 2007 and should be ready for operations by October 2009.

One question on everyone's lips at Merryfield was when the British government would
unleash its Apache on a foreign battlefield.

During the summer and autumn of 2005, a light-role rapid reaction brigade-sized force
was in the process of being selected for a new British operation in Afghanistan. A logistic
support package was also being finalised. The deployment of 9 Regiment was considered
during this force generation process.

Ingram said at Merryfield that debates were still on going as to whether or not the
Apache would go to Afghanistan. 'It is in the process, being examined and looked into,'
he said. 'We need to balance Afghanistan and Iraq with other commitments.'

The newly formed 19 Light Brigade – led by former 2 PARA commanding officer
'Chip' Chapman – and 16 Air Assault Brigade were both in contention to be selected to
go Afghanistan, to work in southern Afghanistan under the command of the UK-led Allied
Rapid Reaction Corps (ARRC) headquarters.

Planners at the British Army's Land Command Headquarters and the UK Permanent
Joint Headquarters (PJHQ) were juggling a number of equipment and training issues
before they could select the brigade for the Afghan mission. According to officers close
to the planning, these included the fact that 19 Light Brigade had only converted to its
rapid reaction role from being a mechanised brigade at the start of 2005. It was still in the
process of receiving its new equipment, in particular communications equipment and 105-
mm Light Guns.

However, 16 Air Assault Brigade was well established and proven from recent
operational deployments to Macedonia, Afghanistan and Iraq. It was due to begin
conversion to the Bowman digital communication system in 2006 and this could have
complicated preparations for any Afghan mission.

A further issue being addressed by UK planners was the size and cost of the logistic
support package, including a substantial force of Chinook transport helicopters, needed to
sustain the British force in land-locked Afghanistan for its six-month long deployment.

9 Regiment conducted maritime exercises on Royal Navy aircraft carriers and amphibious ships in the aftermath of Exercise Eagle's Strike. *(AgustaWestland)*

Brigadier Butler and Lieutenant Colonel Felton stressed that any deployment decision would be taken by the government. 'Where we go is up to the politicians,' said Felton. But Butler added 'If [the politicians] want us to go, we can.' When asked what his helicopters might contribute to any new UK peacekeeping mission, Felton replied 'Clearly it doesn't hand out sweets. It reassures local population, shows UK resolve and provides a deterrence.'

CHAPTER 14

Afghanistan, 2006

The aim of the operation was to relieve the UK Pathfinders who were still in the Musa Qalah district centre after several weeks of heavy fighting. The first couple of attempts from the west failed due to heavy Taliban resistance at the chokepoint where the road from the desert meets the build-up area in the infamous 'Green Zone' separating the wadi from the desert. Even with heavy cover from jets and attack helicopters we weren't able to push through the 'Green Zone'. We changed tactic and moved north around Musa Qalah and finally got into the compound early

morning on the 26th July and thereby gave the brave Pathfinder Platoon a much-needed rest after several weeks of fighting. To ease our advance into the district centre we got excellent attack helicopter support from the Kandahar-based UK Apache – Callsign Wildman. They escorted us all the way inside the town and put down powerful 30-mm suppressive fire on Taliban ambush points along the route, including taking out a sniper in position waiting for us to arrive. This wouldn't be the last time Callsign Wildman saved the day for the Danes. All we saw in the early morning light in the district centre were dirty, skinny,

Fighters of the Afghan Taliban movement proved to be tough and determined opponents for 16 Air Assault Brigade. *(US DoD)*

The government of Afghan President Hamid Karzai had little influence or control in the lawless south of its country. *(NATO)*

heavily-armed, bearded rock-hard British soldiers. All of them smiling like seven-year-old schoolboys on Christmas morning. They were happy to see us, and we were happy to join them.

> *Forward Air Controller, Callsign Norseman 21, of the Danish Recce Squadron*

The summer of 2006 saw 16 Air Assault Brigade fighting thousands of heavily armed guerrilla fighters of the Taliban. For five intense months combat raged across southern Afghanistan as troops of 16 Brigade and other NATO forces tried to help prop up the rule of the Kabul government in the lawless region.

This fighting was of an intensity that few had expected and it came as a surprise to the senior leadership of NATO and British forces in Afghanistan. The Taliban not only proved to be present in far greater numbers than had been predicted, but they proved far more skilful and determined opponents than anyone had imagined. For the soldiers and airmen of 16 Brigade, the Taliban were the most skilled opponents that they had ever faced. This was a type of warfare they had never experienced before. Time and again, the tide of battle was turned by 16 Brigade's helicopter crews – both Apache attack and Chinook transport machines – as well as fixed-wing air support by the RAF and United States Air Force.

When the fighting eased in September 2006, the Taliban had been fought to a standstill across southern Afghanistan. However, the laudable ambitions of NATO leaders to begin reconstruction and humanitarian projects to win over the region's population to the Kabul government looked hollow. Several major towns across the region were devastated by fighting; thousands of refugees fled their homes and the production of illegal heroin surged ahead.

Southern Afghanistan has been described as the unfinished business of the 2001 US-led invasion that toppled the Taliban regime in Kabul and installed the pro-western government of President Hamid Karzai. His government, while overseeing progress around the capital and in the north of the country, had not been able to establish any kind of control over the provinces that straddled the Afghanistan–Pakistan border. This was a wild and inaccessible region, where real political authority lay in the hands of a network of tribes and clans. Although Karzai was a Pashtun, his government was seen in the south

AAC Apaches received their combat debut in Afghanistan in the summer of 2006. (*AgustaWestland*)

as being dominated by Tajiks from the north. More importantly, he had few Pashtuns in his government whom he could rely upon to work for him in the south and east. Crucially, a high percentage of the billions of dollars of international aid money that poured into Afghanistan after 2001 ended up in the hands of Tajik ministers and their families. Little of it reached the people of southern Afghanistan.

In this vacuum, the Taliban had been steadily regrouping and rebuilding its forces ready to attempt to strike back. The unpopularity of corrupt governors imposed by the Kabul regime and the haphazard brutality of the detachments of police and soldiers sent from the capital added to the Taliban's confidence that they could soon stage a comeback in the south. The Taliban movement had its origins in the religious schools of southern Afghanistan, which it then evolved into a group of amateur policemen who helped local people drive off corrupt officials. This eventually helped it seize power and, in 2006, the Taliban were keen to repeat this process. By seizing control of large tracts of the south, the Taliban hoped to prompt a collapse of the Kabul government, which would then allow them to drive out US-led occupation forces. The Taliban operated largely in the shadows and rarely did any concrete news of their activities reach the US military in Kandahar or Kabul. Taliban fighting units were made up of groups of twenty to thirty fighters, usually led by veteran commanders. These leaders used their local contacts to recruit scores of village militia men to bolster their fighting strength, either by promising to protect poppy

RAF Lockheed TriStar transport aircraft flew 16 Brigade's troops to Kabul, where they were then shuttled by Hercules aircraft to Kandahar airbase. *(Tim Ripley)*

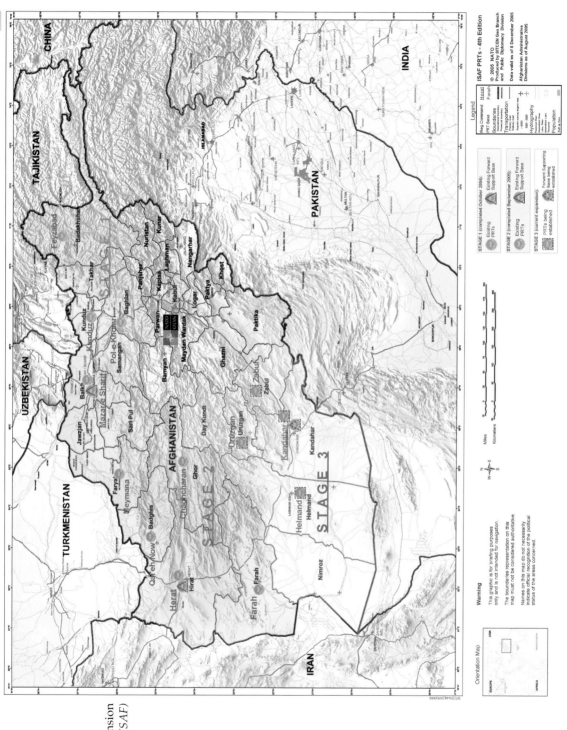

NATO expansion
(NATO/ISAF)

Brigadier Ed Butler led British forces in southern Afghanistan in the summer of 2006. *(Tim Ripley)*

fields or by direct payment of around $100 a month to each local fighter. This was the best pay on offer in southern Afghanistan in 2006.

The south of Afghanistan was also the heartland of the country's heroin industry, which by 2005 was its main export. In the Helmand, Kandahar and Uruzgan provinces the poppy – the raw material of heroin – was the main crop of the peasant farmers and this generated almost 90 per cent of Afghanistan's $2 billion foreign currency earnings in 2006, according to UN experts who monitored the global heroin industry. Heroin production involved huge networks of farmers, landowners, processors and foreign buyers. This resulted in the peasant farmers who cultivated poppy crops being indebted to their landlords. If their poppy crop was lost then they forfeited their land or other property. As a result, Afghan farmers would fight any attempt by the Kabul government, backed by the US and UK, to eradicate the poppy crop. This was exploited ruthlessly by the Taliban.

Four years on from their initial operation to depose the Taliban and hunt down Al Qaeda chief Osama bin Laden, the American military was beginning to tire of the operation in the country and looked to NATO as a way to draw down its troop numbers. Its main effort was in Iraq and Afghanistan seemed peaceful enough to allow NATO allies to expand their operations beyond the capital and the north of the country. The US Army had maintained roughly 20,000 troops in Afghanistan since 2002, including a brigade of combat troops in southern Afghanistan backed up by an army aviation task force at Kandahar airfield (known to all who served there as KAF). The brigade staged occasional demonstrations of force across the south's five provinces – Nimroz, Helmand, Kandahar and Uruzgan and Zabul – but its troops rarely left the main roads or large urban areas. The Taliban nearly always melted away when American GIs moved around the countryside and gave the US Army leadership a slanted view of their opponents. During 2005, the US Army leadership in Afghanistan was convinced that the Taliban were defeated and the mission could be safely handed over to NATO peacekeeping troops to do 'nation building' and other not very macho-type tasks.

NATO forces in Afghanistan during 2006 were commanded by Lieutenant General David Richards. *(NATO)*

The US Army's position was diametrically opposed to the view of the US Special Forces who had continued to maintain a 2,000-strong Combined Joint Special Operations Task Force (CJSOTF) in Afghanistan to hunt down the remnants of Al Qaeda. This force operated closely with paramilitary operatives of the Central Intelligence Agency (CIA) and the UK's MI6 or Special Intelligence Service and Special Forces. These organisations had decades of experience in Afghanistan, stretching back to when they helped the Mujahideen fight the Soviets. They had operatives who were very knowledgeable about the Taliban's cross border tribal links with Pakistan. By 2005, the CJSOTF was the only western military force that routinely operated in the rural regions of southern Afghanistan and it was convinced that the Taliban were up to something, although no one was quite sure what. Throughout the summer of 2005, the CJSOTF troops were regularly engaging small groups of Taliban fighters across southern Afghanistan, although many in the US and NATO high command in Kabul dismissed these incidents as a 'little local difficulty'. The US Army even proposed pulling out the bulk of CJSOTF's field detachments that were working with local Afghan National Army (ANA) forces. These provided some of the only 'on the spot' intelligence from much of the countryside. The job was done, or so said the conventional soldiers in the Pentagon. By the summer of 2006, the US Army high command was pushing to reduce its presence in Afghanistan by half to free up troops for Iraq. The US Special Forces managed to stage a rear-guard action and gained permission to stay in Afghanistan until the end of 2006 and another battalion of 'Green Berets' rotated into the country in the spring of that year.

Little was known about the disposition, morale, weapons or tactics of the Taliban before British troops deployed to Helmand province. *(NATO)*

NATO leaders decided that this was the moment for the alliance to fill the breach being left by withdrawing US forces and expand the zone controlled by the International Security and Assistance Force (ISAF) to cover all the country. US troops would remain in the east of the country, but would be placed under NATO command. This project, dubbed 'NATO expansion', would be a chance for NATO's European members to contribute to the US-led 'global war on terror' without having to send troops to fight alongside the Americans in Iraq.

During the summer of 2005, NATO planners set about asking for nations to contribute troops for the new mission in southern Afghanistan. British Prime Minister Tony Blair was a long-time supporter of Karzai and was keen to support the new NATO plan. By early 2006, Britain, Canada and the Netherlands had all signed up to provide the bulk of the forces for the new NATO regional command. The British offered 3,000 troops, while the Canadian and Dutch governments would each provide enhanced battalion-sized task forces of around 1,000 combat troops backed by their own air, combat support and logistic forces. The British would run Helmand, the Canadians would take on Kandahar and the Dutch were to take over Uruzgan. A US task force would remain in Zabul for most of 2006 until a replacement could be found from other NATO nations. Britain, Canada and the Netherlands would take turns commanding the new Regional Command South (RC South) Headquarters at Kandahar, which would be led from the spring of 2006 by a Canadian Brigadier or one star general. The three nations involved committed themselves to the operation for three years. At the same time, NATO's Allied

Karzai's men in the south in April 2006. The governors of southern Afghanistan's provinces meet the Canadian commander of Regional Command South. Left to right: 2nd Mr Jan Muhamad Akbari (Daikundi Province), 4th Brigadier General David Fraser (Regional Command South Commander), 5th Mr Dilbar Jan Arman (Zabul Province), 6th Mr Abdul Hakim Munib (Uruzgan Province), 7th Major General Benjamin Freakly (Commander of Combined Joint Task Force-76), 8th Mr Asadullah Khalid (Kandahar Province), and 10th Mr Daoud (Helmand Province).*(Canadian Ministry of National Defence)*

Command Europe Rapid Reaction Corps (ARRC) would take over command of ISAF for the crucial period of the transition from US to ISAF command. Britain as lead nation in ARRC would have a vital role in controlling military operations across Afghanistan during 2006, with Lieutenant General David Richards set to become a key player in what was soon to become the most high profile military operation in the world.

While this NATO force generation process was under way, the UK Ministry of Defence was making its own plans. Almost 8,000 British troops were still committed to the occupation of Iraq and senior officers in the Ministry of Defence were not very enthusiastic about taking on another major commitment. Planners at the Permanent Joint Headquarters at Northwood, which controlled UK military operations around the world, were convinced that the Iraq commitment was winding down after the successful elections in early 2005 and this would free up resources for this new mission. Blair and his new Defence Secretary, Dr John Reid, were very keen on the Afghan mission and pushed hard for Treasury (finance ministry) funding approval. The Chancellor of Exchequer (finance minister) Gordon Brown was approached with presentations suggesting an innovative 'cross department' approach would be applied to win over the population of Helmand province from the 'Islamic fascists' of the Taliban and the so-called 'narco warlords' who dominated it. This would see the Ministry of Defence, the Foreign and Commonwealth Office (FCO) and the Department for International Development (DfID) join forces on the ground to drive development and prosperity, and root out corruption. The idea was for

International Security Assistance Force (ISAF) badge. (*NATO*)

British troops to guard aid projects being set up by DfID, while FCO officials reformed local administration to root out the drugs dealers. An added bonus would be the ending of Afghan heroin production as the drug was making its way to Britain in increasing quantities. Dr Reid stressed that if the mission failed Osama bin Laden could return to his Afghan hideouts. It all sounded too good to be true when Dr Reid announced the details of the British troop deployment in January 2006.

As a result of his cross-department sales pitch, Dr Reid was keen to stress that he did not envisage the British Army storming into Helmand with all guns blazing. Instead, he wanted to build up the trust of the local people and gradually win them over to the side of the Karzai government. At the press briefing to announce the British deployment, Dr Reid specifically disowned the firepower-heavy approach then being used by US Special Forces to fight the Taliban, particularly the use of B-52 heavy bombers. This view was popular within the British Army and it seemed to chime with its traditional approach to peacekeeping. Dr Reid continued with his campaign to portray the Afghan mission as an aid and reconstruction effort over the next couple of months and in April made his much quoted comment that he hoped British troops would 'not fire a shot' during their new mission. At several media briefings in the run up to the Afghan deployment he stressed the dangers of the mission, although media commentators at the time generally considered that the coming campaign would face a similar type of insurgency to that found in Iraq, where road-side bombs were the main threat.

The size of the force package Dr Reid announced in January 2006 was also controversial as a result of the subsequent need to reinforce the Afghan garrison after intense fighting irrupted in the summer. Senior advisors of the former Defence Secretary say he approved every request for troops he received from the British military. 'Dr Reid ensured that the Chiefs of Staff were satisfied that they had sufficient forces for the operation as planned and that this was put on record.' said one of the Defence Secretary's advisors.

At the start of the UK force generation process, ideas were floated to send three battalions of infantry (including hundreds of Gurkhas), more than three dozen helicopters, E-3D AWACs radar aircraft, heavy artillery, Sea King Airborne Surveillance and Control (ASaC) 7 helicopters equipped with ground surveillance radar and the purchase of Predator unmanned aerial vehicles through urgent operational requirement funding.

USAF RQ-1 Predator unmanned aerial vehicles provided real-time video feeds to US and NATO commanders of Afghanistan's battlefields. *(USAF)*

According to officers involved in the planning process these ideas all fell by the wayside within the Ministry of Defence planning process. A senior official in the ministry at this time said:

> Half of this has to do with many in the ministry, particularly on the civilian side, being afraid to ask the Treasury for money. They had been conditioned over the years not to rock the boat and were afraid to ask for things. They did not realise what a powerful position they were in at the start of the operation.

Senior army officers involved in the force generation process said the Treasury held the Ministry of Defence to its initial bid made in early 2005 for a force of 3,150 troops to be sent with a budget of £1 billion. One of these officers said:

> We had to live with the Treasury's cap on the number of troops until after we were fully engaged with the Taliban in Helmand in the summer. Because this bid was made at the start of the force generation process the tactical level commanders who went out to Helmand later in 2005 on reconnaissance missions had less influence on the process than was desirable. Subsequent force packages deployed to Afghanistan in 2007 and 2008 had more realistic numbers of troops and greater quantities of equipment.

The other major problem for the planners of the Afghan mission was the 'incomplete

A RAF Boeing Chinook HC.2 heads north from Kandahar airfield to deliver supplies to British troops in Helmand province. *(Tim Ripley)*

intelligence picture' about conditions in Helmand province, according to one participant in this process. 'This not only affected the intelligence on the Taliban but also economic conditions and other factors affecting what type of aid projects were needed.'

Just like the Americans, there were considerable differences of opinion in London about the situation on the ground in Helmand. The Defence Intelligence Staff (DIS), drawing heavily on reports from British operatives working with their US CJSOTF counterparts, was convinced the Taliban would relish the chance to take on NATO forces. Its assessment concluded that once the first Chinook landed in Helmand to drop off British soldiers they 'would be engaged before the helicopter's ramp touched the ground'. At the other extreme was a view, based on reports by a recent visit to the province by UN aid workers, that the poverty-stricken peasants of Helmand would welcome any chance to improve their lives. One of the senior officers involved in the planning process suggested that small groups of paratroopers should be posted around Helmand in so-called 'Platoon Houses' to protect grass roots development projects with farmers. This had been tried in Bosnia with some success, suggested the officer. The experience of the British-run provincial reconstruction team (PRT) in northern Afghanistan from 2003 where troops helped in many humanitarian projects also shaped perceptions of planners in London. This operation faced little hostility from the local population and this made some of the civilian

Taliban Forces, Southern Afghanistan, Summer 2006

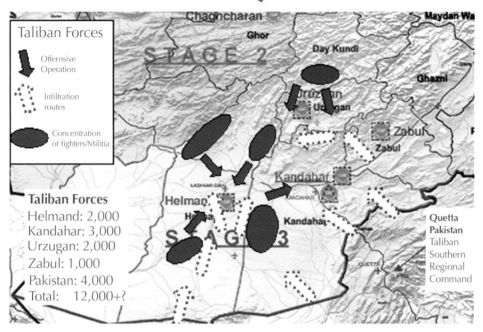

Estimated Taliban dispositions, summer 2006 *(Background map: ISAF/NATO, Data: Tim Ripley)*

officials in the British government think that only a small military force would be required for security. The involvement of DfID and FCO in the force generation process added to what some military officers dubbed the 'institutional naivety' of some of the planning for the Afghan mission.

The planning was bedevilled by the almost total lack of tactical intelligence on the strength, location, weaponry or leadership of Taliban forces in Helmand province. The best guess was that the Taliban could draw on 6,000 fighters in southern Afghanistan and maybe 1,000 of them were thought to be in Helmand. This problem would continue to bedevil 16 Brigade's operations throughout the Afghan campaign.

With the intelligence picture so vague, it was difficult for the Afghan planners to pin down exactly their troop and equipment requirements. The result was a compromise force package. Military planners hoped it would be big enough to look after itself but was also not too large to impose a drain on the already overstretched British Army and RAF. The major factor in this planning was to ensure that so-called 'high demand low density' units, such as helicopter crews and maintenance technicians, were not overused to allow the UK to sustain its forces in Afghanistan for at least three years. The proposed force totalled some 4,500 troops, of whom 1,000 were earmarked to go Kabul with the ARRC headquarters for only nine months. The bulk of the troops was to make up the UK force

AAC Lynx AH.7s at Kandahar airfield prepare for night-time missions over Helmand. The hot climate meant the small helicopters found it difficult to operate in the daytime in the Afghan summer. *(Tim Ripley)*

in Helmand province. As had been heavily leaked, the job was given to 16 Air Assault Brigade. Its main infantry element was based on the 3rd Battalion, The Parachute Regiment (3 PARA), and it would for the first time see the deployment of UK Apache attack helicopters. RAF Chinook transport helicopters and Hercules transport aircraft would support the mission. The three-year mission had a budget of £1 billion.

16 Brigade's commander, Brigadier Ed Butler, who was no stranger to Afghanistan, had to craft a plan that took account of all the divergent threat assessments as well as meeting the requirements to begin some sort of reconstruction activity as soon as possible. He determined that the centre of gravity of Helmand was its capital Lashkar Gar and the heavily cultivated Helmand River valley. This was where the bulk of the province's million or so population lived. It was also the centre of the Afghan heroin industry and the river provided the water required to irrigate the poppies needed to produce the billions of dollars-worth of heroin manufactured in the country every year. The main effort of the UK force would be to secure what became known as the 'triangle' or 'lozenge' between Lashkar Gar, the province's second town of Gereshk and the soon-to-be built British base out in the desert known as Camp Bastion. Only once the full force was in place in July

The RAF's Lockheed Martin C-130J Hercules force came of age in Afghanistan, where the aircraft's more powerful engines and longer range came into its element. *(Tim Ripley)*

2006, and the 'lozenge' was secure, with development projects well under way, would UK troops transition to a more offensive mode to launch 'search and destroy' missions against groups of Taliban. This phase was expected to last months not weeks.

When Butler presented his plans to the British Chiefs of Staff they endorsed this cautious approach. With little hard intelligence on the Taliban, the Chiefs were apparently keen for the British forces to get firmly established before they undertook any ambitious operations. The Ministry of Defence's political leadership was also paranoid about a repeat of the media coverage of the build-up to the Iraq war in 2003, which highlighted poor equipment and living conditions for troops. Realisation that the campaign could last a number of years prompted the ministry to order that the construction of Camp Bastion be completed before the main combat elements of the 16 Brigade arrived. The Afghan government also objected to the British force being based in Lashkar Gar or Gereshk to keep western forces largely out of sight of the civilian population. The Americans also advised that a desert location was easier to secure.

A so-called enabling force of more than 850 Royal Engineers protected by hundreds of Royal Marine Commandos was dispatched in February 2006 to start building the camp. Thousands of containers of equipment and suppliers were shipped to Pakistan for movement by huge convoys of local trucks, known as jinglies, into Afghanistan. It would be three months before the camp was ready and 16 Brigade could begin moving to

British paratroopers sweep through Musa Qalah during Operation Snake Bite, which brought in supplies to the British garrison in the town's district centre. *(KAF Pool/Tim Ripley)*

Afghanistan. One of Dr Reid's senior advisors commented that this might have been a mistake and handed the Taliban the strategic initiative. They now knew when the British were coming and where their main bases would be. The main British combat power – 3 PARA and the Apaches – would be some of the last units of 16 Brigade to arrive in country. One British officer who served in Afghanistan at this time described the building of Camp Bastion as an 'act of strategic naivety', which ignored the ability of the Taliban to pre-empt the British deployment. More junior level British commanders wanted to put their combat troops in ahead of the logistic support to allow them to engage the enemy at a time and place of their choosing but they lost this argument with the Ministry of Defence.

While Camp Bastion was being built, the remainder of 16 Brigade was kept busy in a series of pre-deployment exercises. These aimed to build up the Brigade's experience at small unit level, then move to more complex operations. Cultural training played an important part in this training, with Afghans living in the UK being hired to play the part of tribesmen and to act as interpreters for the British troops. Commanders were taught

NATO air power in action against Taliban fighters taking cover in a village compound. *(Canadian Ministry of National Defence)*

This sign in the Regional Command South Headquarters compound tries to foster cultural understanding of Afghanistan among NATO personnel. *(Tim Ripley)*

It is better to let them do it themselves imperfectly, than to do it yourself perfectly. It is their country, their way and our time is short. T.E. Lawrence

how to conduct *shuras* or meetings with tribal elders. The bulk of 16 Brigade's artillery unit, 7th Parachute Regiment Royal Horse Artillery (7 RHA), was also re-roled to be responsible for training ANA units. It would only take one of its three gun batteries, with only six 105-mm Light Guns, to Afghanistan. Known as Operational Mentoring and Liaison Teams (OMLT) these troops, which were inevitably nicknamed 'omelettes', would play a key role in building up the three ANA battalions that were supposed to be in Helmand. The OMLT teams were heavily reinforced with volunteers from other British Army units. A camp was in the process of being built with US funding next to Camp Bastion to be the base for the ANA brigade being formed to operate in Helmand. Denmark and Estonia offered to provide small detachments to the UK force.

The force package included a detachment of Desert Hawk handheld mini-unmanned aerial vehicles (UAVs) to provide local reconnaissance around British bases and there was also a small signals intelligence team to listen in on Taliban radio communications. However, 16 Brigade did not have any large wide-area surveillance systems that would be under its direct control. The Americans promised to allow British commanders to access its big RQ-1 Predator UAVs. The RAF also offered to make its Nimrod MR2 patrol aircraft, which were fitted with night vision video cameras, and its Canberra photographic reconnaissance aircraft available. These were powerful systems but crucially other forces, such as the US military or the British Special Forces, had first call on them, which would hinder 16 Brigade's ability to build up a full picture of what was happening in Helmand away from its fixed bases. The Canberras would also only be available until June 2006 when they were due to be scrapped to save money. The Brigade's conversion to the Bowman battlefield internet communications system was delayed until after the Afghan deployment and scores of satellite radios were transferred to the Brigade to allow it to communicate over long distances.

The culmination of this training package occurred in April 2006 when 3 PARA and 9 Regiment, AAC, were flown to Oman for a huge live-firing exercise. This put the Apache to the test for the first time in desert conditions and allowed the Royal Electrical and Mechanical Engineers (REME) to develop a fix to clean out sand that jammed the helicopter's 30-mm cannons.

Joint Helicopter Force (Afghanistan)

The Afghan operation saw the creation of a unique British aviation unit that combined attack, transport and observation helicopters under a single commander. Dubbed Joint Helicopter Force (Afghanistan) (JHF(A)), it provided the UK Task Force with a powerful rotary wing force to conduct combat operations, fly re-supply missions and casualty evacuations.

The JHF(A) had its headquarters at Kandahar Airfield and provided helicopters to work under the tactical command of the 3 PARA battlegroup at Camp Bastion. On each day during the summer of 2006, JHF(A) had to provide basic casualty evacuation and medical coverage for the British force and a reserve or reaction force element to respond to unforeseen events such as a helicopter crash. Any extra capacity could be made available for deliberate or pre-planned British operations. Other NATO nations and the Afghans could also request British helicopter support.

RAF and AAC officers took turns to lead JHF(A), with the commanding officer of 9 Regiment, AAC, Lieutenant Colonel Richard Felton, running it during the summer of 2006 before handing over to a RAF Wing Commander from the Chinook Force.

An RAF Flight Lieutenant who flew in Helmand during this period said:

On a typical day, two Apache and two Chinook were deployed with the Immediate Reaction [medical] Team (IRT) and the [platoon-sized] Helmand Reaction Force (HRT) on stand-by at Bastion, 24/7. IRT/HRF were our priority and had to be sustained. They brought out wounded troops and responded to crisis.

An AAC Apache pilot recalled:

We used Kandahar as our maintenance area and the remainder of our force was based [at Bastion]. Of our eight aircraft, four were up at Bastion at any one time. The Apache main effort was forward [at Bastion].

The threat determined that we had to work as a team. The Chinook was the army's lifeline but because of the threat and the fact that Apache provide fire support and eyes on target with its sensors we did joint-planning and preparation. You couldn't do it separately. To have any effect we worked closely as a team.

The Chinook pilot reinforced this point, 'Working with Apache was routine. There was no RAF/army divide here. We just have different types of aircraft. We planned and briefed together.'

British Paratroopers wait to be lifted by RAF Chinooks after an operation to bring supplies into Naw Zad's district centre. *(KAF Pool/Tim Ripley)*

On the ground in Afghanistan, unusually mild weather allowed the Taliban to launch a series of attacks on Canadian troops in the first three months of 2006. This included a full frontal assault on a joint US-Canadian forward operating base just outside Sangin. In the brief but bloody battle, more than a hundred Taliban fighters charged the base only to be cut down by US Army Apaches, air strikes and heavy machine-gun fire.

Elsewhere in Helmand, an advance team from 16 Brigade had taken over the organisation of the Provincial Reconstruction Team (PRT) in Lashkar Gar from the US Army. These soldiers from 21 Air Battery Royal Artillery were some of the first 16 Brigade troops on the ground in Helmand in early April and they soon attracted two Taliban suicide bomb attacks on their positions in the provincial capital. At this time, the Pathfinder Platoon had also deployed and was conducting reconnaissance patrols throughout Helmand. It fought a brief firefight with Afghan National Police (ANP) in the town of Now Zad but the province seemed quiet.

On the ground in Helmand, 16 Brigade's commanders and units were to be used to fill out a command structure initially dubbed the Helmand Task Force (HTF), which had its command post in the provincial capital Lashkar Gar. It was led by a former commanding officer of the Irish Guards, Colonel Charlie Knaggs. His main job was to 'hand hold' the new provincial governor 'Engineer' Daoud. He had been appointed by Karzai earlier in the year in a bid to clean out the old provincial leadership, which was heavily implicated in the drugs trade. Daoud soon set about putting men loyal to him in place in the districts of his province. He also tried to put loyalists into key posts in the local police. This 'clean out' campaign did not win Daoud any friends around Helmand and in particular it made many local drugs traders think that their business might be endangered by the new regime and their British supporters.

Knaggs, as senior British officer in Helmand, reporting to the Canadian-run RC South

Efforts to build up the strength, equipment and motivation of the Afghan National Army proved slower than NATO leaders expected. *(NATO/ISAF)*

Headquarters in Kandahar, had tactical control of the PRT and the 3 PARA battlegroup.

Because of NATO politics, the UK decided not to put Brigadier Butler's headquarters in Helmand. From April until July, he had to stay up in Kabul in his capacity as Commander British Forces or COMBRITFOR in Afghanistan and could only make brief visits to forward units, although he did have secure satellite telephone communications with the major British and NATO headquarters. At this crucial part of the campaign, the command of British forces was spread across five headquarters: COMBRITFOR in Kabul where Butler was based; the Canadian-led RC South Headquarters at Kandahar where a British officer was the Chief of Staff; a UK logistic headquarters at Kandahar, the HTF in Lashkar Gar where Knaggs co-ordinated British operations with Daoud and at Camp Bastion where the combat forces centred on 3 PARA were to be based. Although in a crisis Butler could speak directly to the commanding officer of 3 PARA, Lieutenant Colonel Stuart Tootal, this command set-up created much 'multi-national command tension'. One British staff officer who worked in RC South Headquarters during this time recalled that the proliferation of headquarters meant coalition and NATO operations across southern Afghanistan were bedevilled by 'national caveats and differing objectives'. Senior British officers described this command set-up as 'confusing and sub-optimal'.

An even more complicating factor was the looming switch of RC South from US to

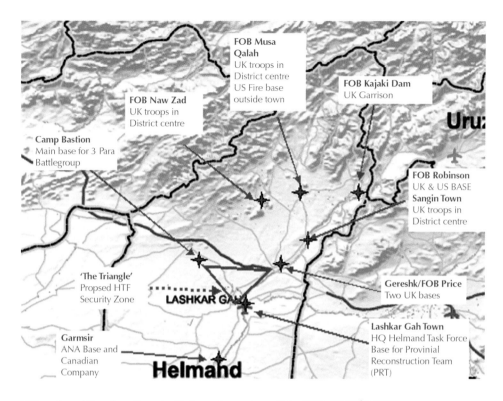

UK and coalition locations in Helmand province, July 2006 *(ISAF/NATO)*

NATO command at the end of July. Until then, RC South and hence the UK-led HTF, was under direct US command and Major General Ben Freakley of the US Army's 10th Mountain Division who had a very different approach to peacekeeping to the British Army. On top of this, the US Special Forces and their British Special Forces colleagues had their own very separate chain of command that seemed to be a law unto itself.

Into this maelstrom of Afghan political manoeuvring and differing western military agendas, 16 Brigade started to arrive in Afghanistan in strength during the later half of April. This flow of troops became a torrent in early May. First came the support troops of 13 Air Assault Regiment, RLC, and 16 Close Support Medical Regiment. Headquarters staff and signallers then arrived, along with the OMLT troops of 7 RHA. The RAF Chinooks had been in place since March helping to build Camp Bastion. 18 (Bomber) Squadron had just swapped over to the new arrivals of 27 Squadron who would serve for the next four months. The main body of 3 PARA and the Apaches of 9 Regiment's 656 Squadron arrived at Kandahar in early May but it took a couple of weeks for them to get up to Camp Bastion, unpack their equipment, draw ammunition and prepare for action. The guns of 7 RHA's I Battery and the reconnaissance vehicles of the Household Cavalry Regiment (HCR) would not arrive until the middle of June.

Flying in Afghanistan

Afghanistan has a well-deserved reputation for being one of the world's most demanding environments to fly helicopters in.

A combination of Afghanistan's hot temperatures, height above sea level and desert dust means helicopter pilots can take little for granted. The country's high mountain ranges and vast deserts offer very different challenges to aviators.

A highly experienced USAF Sikorsky HH-60 Blackhawk pilot who flew in southern Afghanistan during the summer of 2006 rated the country's environment as a far more dangerous threat to helicopter crews than the enemy. 'The enemy are number eight on my list of threats,' said the pilot. 'The biggest threat is Afghanistan itself – the altitude, heat, darkness, brown out and weather.'

The centre of Afghanistan is dominated by a series of mountain ranges that rise to more than 10,000 feet above sea level, which makes it very difficult for even the most powerful helicopter to operate over, particularly in the country's hot summer heat. In such conditions, helicopter pilots have to carefully judge their speed to ensure they have the power to rise above dangerous terrain. It also greatly limits the cargo that can be carried in summer months.

Down in the desert of Helmand, the fine dust that is thrown up by landing helicopters' rotor blades can blind pilots just as they are about to touch down, causing a dangerous loss of situational awareness and even the most experienced pilots can accidentally fly into the ground. Known as 'brown outs' these conditions mean helicopter pilots have to carefully judge their final approaches to landing zones. The risks involved are greatly complicated if the enemy opens fire and prompt helicopter pilots to take rapid evasive action.

Afghanistan's darkness was also a major threat to nocturnal helicopter operations because of the lack of ambient light from towns or street lighting. This seriously degrades the performance of the night vision goggles used by many helicopter pilots in Afghanistan to fly at night by making it difficult for them to spot the ground.

The Taliban were not standing by to allow the British to move peacefully into Helmand. They were determined to drive out Governor Daoud's men and police from the northern districts of Helmand and then push southwards to raise their black flag over the provincial capital. This offensive coincided with similar drives by the Taliban in Kandahar and Uruzgan provinces. NATO forces were going to be stretched to the limit, just as they were deploying into unfamiliar territory. The Taliban also realised that they had to stop any of the promised reconstruction and other humanitarian projects being launched by NATO and the Kabul government if they were to retain the loyalty of the population. If NATO troops responded to Taliban attacks with overwhelming firepower, this would play into their hands and turn the local population against western forces. On top of this, Taliban propaganda played up the rhetoric of senior NATO leaders, such UK Defence Secretary Dr Reid, saying that the alliance wanted to put Afghanistan's heroin industry out of business. This seemed a direct attack on the economy of Helmand and the other southern provinces.

The first phase of the Taliban offensive was against a small contingent of French and US Special Forces who were training ANA troops near the Kajaki Dam in the far north of

RAF BAE Systems Harrier GR7s based at Kandahar airfield were the nearest strike aircraft to Helmand province and aircraft were held on 24/7 alert to respond to calls for assistance from NATO troops. The aircraft is taxiing past an Estonian armoured vehicle. *(Tim Ripley)*

Helmand province. Fear of the sudden arrival of hundreds of Taliban led the handful of Frenchmen and Americans to form up their Afghan allies in a convoy of trucks and head south to the NATO base outside Sangin on 20 May. The convoy had barely gone a few miles when it was ambushed. Hundreds of Taliban and their local allies subjected the convoy to a sustained attack over several dozen miles of road. Heavy fire broke up the convoy and the Frenchmen, along with dozens of Afghans, were isolated. Their unarmoured pick-up trucks and jeeps were riddled with bullets. The Americans had armoured Humvees and were able to escape to Forward Operating Base (FOB) Robinson. Later, the remnants of the convoy limped into the base, leaving behind two dead Frenchmen and fifteen Afghans. A Company of 3 PARA was scrambled from Camp Bastion in Chinooks, escorted by Apaches, to search for missing Frenchmen and ANA troops. The Apache squadron had only just got up and running and was in the process of making its final Hellfire missile qualification firings when the call to Kajaki came. This was the first combat mission of the UK Apache Force.

The paratroopers found the abandoned vehicles and an AAC Apache was called up to destroy one of the French jeeps in order to stop its highly secret position-tracking equipment falling into Taliban hands. It later emerged that the local villagers had joined

USAF aircraft, including Boeing F-15E Strike Eagles, performed the majority of air support missions over southern Afghanistan during 2006. *(USAF)*

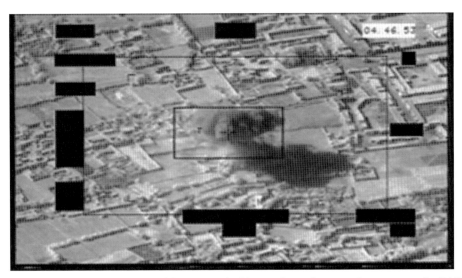

Imagery of an air strike on a Taliban stronghold seen from the targeting system of a RAF
BAE Systems Harrier GR7. *(KAF Pool/Tim Ripley)*

the ambush and helped mutilate the bodies. News of the Taliban 'victory' spread quickly.

In Lashkar Gar, Governer Daoud was by now in a panic. He was telephoning Karzai on
an hourly basis asking what to do. The Taliban appeared to be rolling across northern
Helmand unopposed and his political position, as governor, appeared to be collapsing
with each Taliban advance. He turned to Colonel Knaggs and demanded that the newly
arrived British help stop the Taliban offensive. District centres in Musa Qalah, Now Zad,
Sangin and Baghran appeared to be about to fall, or so claimed Daoud. Knaggs, RC
South, Butler and planners at PJHQ in Northwood debated what to do. British officers in
Afghanistan stressed that they appeared to have little choice but to help Daoud. It was
decided that the call for help from Daoud now had priority. The UK force still did not have
all its major units or logistic support in place and they would not all arrive until early July.
At the time, this seemed like a short-term mission that would not impact on the long-term
British strategy.

At Camp Bastion, Tootal and his senior commanders were ordered to ride to the rescue,
even as they were in the middle of preparing to move the bulk of their forces to FOB
Robinson and Gereshk to begin securing the 'triangle'. 7 RHA and an ANA company had
already moved into FOB Robinson.

To help hold Musa Qalah, a patrol of the Pathfinder Platoon drove into the town and
found it relatively quiet after a gun battle between the Taliban and local police holding the
district centre. These walled compounds were the centre of government power in Afghan
towns and were usually garrisoned by a few dozen badly armed and poorly motivated
policemen. The Pathfinders pulled out of Musa Qalah when a company of US troops arrived
to occupy the district centre. The US troops set up a fire support base outside the town.

When the district chief of Baghran called Daoud to say his district centre was about to
fall, A Company of 3 PARA mounted an evacuation mission. The town was too far in the
north of the province to be held so Chinooks loaded with paratroopers flew up and

Maintenance of the AAC's Apache fleet was carried out in the relative safety of Kandahar airfield. *(Tim Ripley)*

evacuated the chief and his entourage. Not a shot was fired. Tootal's B Company was then flown into Now Zad to hold the district centre after more panicked calls from Daoud. Again, there was little sign of the enemy.

Up in the north of Helmand, the large Kajaki Dam was also now under threat and the engineers who were trying to repair its hydroelectric generators were threatening to leave. An OMLT team and detachment of ANA were despatched to guard the site. When a Taliban mortar team started to harass the remote dam site, 3 PARA's mortar platoon and a platoon from B Company were sent to beef up the defences. This set the stage for several months of cat and mouse gun battles and mortar duels around the barren hills of Kajaki.

Just as 3 PARA's troops were completing these missions, the US command in Afghanistan was ramping up another of its countrywide offensives, dubbed Operation Mountain Thrust. This was billed as 'setting the conditions' for the transfer of authority from US to NATO command. Senior British commanders in southern Afghanistan were not enthusiastic about the aggressive firepower-heavy tactics the Americans wanted to employ. These were seen as being counter-productive and bound to turn the population against the British. When British commanders protested, the Americans threatened to conduct the operation anyway. So it was decided that it was better to go along with the Americans to try to mitigate the worse effects of their tactics. The result was Operation Mutay on 4 June.

This operation saw Tootal leading A Company on a heli-borne raid on what was described by US intelligence as a 'high value Taliban target' living in a compound outside Now Zad. The bulk of the RAF Chinook Force was mustered for the raid and Apache

An RAF Chinook lands at the NATO forward command post in the desert of Kandahar province during Operation Medusa. *(Canadian Ministry of National Defence)*

escort helicopters were on hand, as well as USAF A-10A Warthog tank buster jets.

What began as a straightforward insertion to set up a cordon and search operation soon turned into a six-hour long firefight. Dozens of heavily armed Taliban were waiting for the Chinooks. As the first paratroopers emerged from their helicopters, heavy fire raked the landing zones. They had to fight their way into the compound. Apache gunships were called in to strafe a Taliban machine-gun nest and then the A-10As were ordered in to deal with stubborn resistance. Eventually, the paratroopers managed to sweep through the compound but the 'high value target' had long gone. Everyone in the Company had engaged the enemy during the bitter battle that left up to three dozen Taliban dead. The heavy resistance and the skill of their opponents had been a bit of shock to the men of 3 PARA but they had overcome the enemy and had not suffered any casualties. When the Chinooks returned to lift the company back to Camp Bastion, the morale was sky high.

For senior British commanders the results were seen as mixed. The helicopters and fixed wing air support worked well and their men put up a good fight but the abilities of the Taliban were worrying.

Over the coming months a series of incidents would start to divert 3 PARA further away from its main mission to secure the 'triangle' and begin reconstruction tasks with aid experts from DfID and the FCO.

On 11 June, a Royal Artillery OMLT patrol was ambushed in Sangin and a British officer killed, prompting a major rescue mission by A and B Companies. Two days later,

A Canadian Joint Terminal Attack Controller directs a NATO air strike in southern Afghanistan during September 2006. *(Canadian Ministry of National Defence)*

A Company was flown north to Musa Qalah to extract a US Army supply convoy that had been ambushed. When the Taliban killed a political ally of Daoud and several of his bodyguards near Sangin, A Company moved into the town to secure the district centre on 21 June. Senior British officers and Daoud then flew into the town to meet tribal elders to talk about starting aid projects. They considered the offers of assistance and asked the British to hold off from heavy patrolling of the town for three days while they tried to persuade the Taliban not to attack.

Knaggs and Tootal had also managed by now to get C Company of 3 PARA into Gereshk in a bid to kick start aid operations. 3 PARA started patrols around the region trying to set up *shuras* with tribal elders to build up relationships and win friends.

On the evening of 27 June, the war in Helmand would ignite and all of the British bases there would come under sustained attack. Outside Sangin, a British Special Boat Service (SBS) team raided a 'suspected Taliban compound' on the orders of the US Special Forces command. The assault met heavy resistance and two SBS men were killed in a firefight with a large group of Taliban. The survivors called in USAF air support to extract them from the battle.

A few miles away in Sangin, the paratroopers of A Company had no idea this operation was about to happen. A patrol of Gurkhas from FOB Robinson outside the town was sent to help the SBS force move to safety but not before one of their Snatch armoured Land Rovers was hit by a rocket-propelled grenade (RPG). The pin-downed troops called up artillery fire from 7 RHA's I Battery in turn to help them return safely to base. They could not find the two dead Special Forces operatives so at first light B Company was flown out by Chinook from Camp Bastion, under the control of Tootal's tactical headquarters, to put in a large cordon and search operation to try to find the missing men. They were soon discovered, along with four dead Taliban fighters.

Further south on the same day, another British patrol was ambushed outside Gereshk as it tried to establish contact with local elders. The platoon from 3 PARA's C Company was lured into the village of Zumbelay by Taliban supporters and then had to fight its way out after the ambush was sprung. The paratroopers were accompanied by a reporter from *The Sunday Times*, Christina Lamb. Her report of the incident, which said she and the troops ran for their lives through fields until other British troops could provide covering fire, caused consternation in the UK and the government was attacked in the media for not sending enough troops to Afghanistan. The reaction of the Ministry of Defence was simple. Media visits to the frontline were banned until further notice.

Across Helmand the reaction was more dramatic. Over the next week British bases in Musa Qalah, Sangin and Now Zad came under sustained attack by large groups of heavily armed, skilled and determined Taliban fighters, backed by hundreds of less motivated

Scimitar CVR(T) vehicles of the Household Cavalry Regiment were grouped in Manoeuvre Operation Groups to interdict Taliban supply lines in the deserts around Musa Qalah and other Afghan towns. *(BAE Systems)*

fighters recruited from the local population. British intelligence officers were convinced that the Taliban offensive had been long planned, but the events in Sangin provided them with a 'legitimacy' in the eyes of the local population, particularly the apparent breaking of the 'truce' in patrolling agreed at the *shura* with the town's elders. This made it easier for the Taliban to stir up popular opinion against the British and recruit local fighters.

Order of Battle of the British Forces in Southern Afghanistan, July 2006

Headquarters Regional Command South – Kandahar Airfield

HQ Helmand Task Force – Lashkar Gar
216 Squadron Royal Signals
Provisional Reconstruction Team (based on 21 Battery RA)

HQ BRITFOR, Camp Souter, Kabul

Joint Helicopter Command – Afghanistan

(UK helicopters operated from Kandahar Airfield and Camp Bastion)
27 Squadron RAF with 6 x Chinook HC.2
656 Squadron, 9 Regiment, Army Air Corps, with 8 x AgustaWestland
    Apache AH.1 attack helicopters
672 Squadron with 4 x Westland Lynx AH.9 utility

Camp Bastion

3 PARA BATTLEGROUP

(detachments FOB Price, Gereshk district centre, Sangin district centre, FOB Robinson, Kajaki Dam, Now Zad district centre, Musa Qalah district centre)

Major combat units:
3rd Battalion, The Parachute Regiment
D Squadron, Household Cavalry Regiment
I Battery, 7th Parachute Regiment, Royal Horse Artillery, 6 x 105-mm
    Light Guns
18 Battery, 32 Regiment, Royal Artillery with Desert Hawk mini
    unmanned aerial vehicles
D Coy, 2nd Battalion, The Royal Gurkha Rifles
9 and 51 Parachute Squadron, Royal Engineers deploying late July/August
A Company 2nd Royal Regiment of Fusiliers (150 troops)
1st Battalion, The Royal Irish Regiment (two platoons and mortar platoon,
    100 troops)

Camp Tombstone

Operational Mentoring and Liaison Team Headquarters, 7th Parachute
   Regiment Royal Horse Artillery
1st Battalion, 3rd Brigade, 205th Corps, Afghan National Army
2nd Battalion (under training)

Kandahar Airfield/Camp Bastion

National Support Element, based on:
   13 Air Assault and 29 Regiments, Royal Logistic Corps
   7 Air Assault Battalion, the Royal Mechanical and Electrical Engineers
   16 Close Support Medical Regiment
   47 Air Despatch Squadron, RLC
   156 Company, Royal Military Police

Kandahar Airfield

904 Expeditionary Air Wing
RAF C-130 Detachment, led by 24 & 30 Squadrons, 4/5 x C-130Js
   Hercules
RAF Harrier Detachment, led by 3 (Fighter) Squadron, 6 x Harrier GR7
34 Squadron, RAF Regiment Kandahar Airfield (130 troops)

Over the next month, fighting intensified as the British troops holding district centres came under hourly sniper, machine-gun, mortar and rocket fire. Casualties mounted as the troops holding these exposed positions found themselves pinned down and unable to move outside their bases except in large patrols. They traded fire around the clock with Taliban fighters and often the only way to diminish the enemy fire was to call up US or RAF jets to bomb the suspected firing points. Each British base had a Fire Support Team (FST) inside it, made up of RAF Regiment forward air controllers (also known by the US term Joint Terminal Attack Controllers – JTACs) and 7 RHA artillery observers, who day after day kept a constant stream of air support overhead during these desperate battles. The huge distances that the British forces were operating over meant that the six guns of 7 RHA could not provide anywhere near the required level of fire support so air power was the only way to rapidly being firepower to bear in a crisis.

The shortage of surveillance and reconnaissance systems available to 16 Brigade was now being felt. With fighting raging across southern Afghanistan, the HTF only had use of the USAF Predators and RAF Nimrods for a few hours a day and the Taliban were operating across a huge area. The best intelligence source available to the British forces was the eavesdroppers of the joint Royal Signals and Intelligence Corps Light Electronic Warfare Team (LEWT). One of its detachments in Sangin was hit by Taliban fire and a member, a British soldier of south Asian origin, was killed in early July.

3 PARA undertook one last major strike mission at the request of the Americans in the middle of July to hunt down another 'high value Taliban target' near Sangin. Operation

Canadian Light Armoured Vehicles were deployed in southern Helmand in July 2006 to shore up the defences of Garmsir. *(Canadian Ministry of National Defence)*

Augustus was the biggest 3 PARA operation to date and involved lavish air support, including AC-130 Spectre gunships and Predator UAVs, as well as the usual Apaches and RAF Harriers. A Canadian Light Armoured Vehicle (LAV) company joined the assault. Taliban fighters put up fierce resistance and the paratroopers came under fire again as they tried to get off the Chinooks.

An RAF Chinook helicopter pilot who flew during the operation recounted:

> When we go into a hot landing zone the paratroopers had 20 seconds to get off the aircraft and they are conditioned to do this. We were going into a landing zone when a paratrooper was waiting to get off the aircraft. He was shot but just kept moving to try to get down the rear ramp. The crew had to restrain him, telling him 'you're not going anywhere.'

Again, the high value target was nowhere to be found but the large cache of arms was discovered and destroyed in the compounds secured by 3 PARA and the Canadians.

Under its original logistic plan, 16 Brigade had envisaged only conducting two four-to-five day major battalion-sized cordon and search operations each month. These were envisaged as being launched from Camp Bastion or Gereshk and then the troops would return to base to recuperate. Now the bulk of the Brigade's combat troops were fighting on a 24/7 basis in six isolated garrisons.

With British and NATO road convoys still liable to be ambushed or hit with improvised explosive devices, the safest way to re-supply the troops in the district centres and bring out wounded was by helicopter. This was not as easy as it seemed. The district centres were in the centre of urban areas and they did not have enough room for helicopter landing sites, so it was not possible to land the big Chinooks safely inside them. The British troops had to mount patrols out of the district centres on to open ground to secure landing sites for any in-bound helicopters. This meant every helicopter mission into the district centres was high risk for both the ground troops and helicopter crews alike. Often, only the presence of Apache gunships circling above the landing sites allowed the Chinooks to get in and out safely.

For senior British commanders, it meant the nature of their operation in Helmand had fundamentally changed. Any idea of trying to conduct reconstruction or humanitarian operations was gone.

The bulk of the HTF's combat troops was committed in the district centre and the troops were fighting for their lives. With the summer heat pushing above 50 degrees, food and water scarce and the troops fighting around the clock, senior officers wondered how long their men could keep fighting. Without the Chinooks and Apache bringing in supplies, or protecting road convoys, the troops would not have been able to hold on.

Brigadier Butler said 3 PARA could not have held out without the efforts of the RAF Chinook crews.

> They carried the most risk of anyone here – they can have 40 to 50 guys on board their helicopters. I must praise them for keeping going back, it was pretty close at times. They have done some awesome flying.

By moving his troops by air, the Brigadier said the Chinooks 'saved many lives'.

Towards the end of July, the supply situation was getting desperate so a series of battalion-sized deliberate operations were conducted around the district compounds to allow road convoys to get into the beleaguered troops. The bulk of the British Chinook and Apache Force was massed for these operations to saturate the local area with more than 400 troops at a time. The first operation around Sangin in mid-July involved two companies of paratroopers, with lavish air support, so the Taliban kept out of the way long enough for a large supply convoy to get into the district centre. Similar events followed in Now Zad and Musa Qalah over the next four weeks. These temporarily relieved the situation but the troops in the district centres were still calling up daily Apache and fixed-wing air strikes to neutralise Taliban rocket and mortar positions.

Helicopter Strike

When the UK helicopters were concentrated for a deliberate operation, considerable planning and preparation was involved over a forty-eight-hour period. An AAC Captain who served in Helmand in the summer of 2006 said:

> There was massive co-ordination of the many moving parts, not just aviation. We used fast jet in support because we were the Airborne Forward Air Controllers in the fight. During deliberate operations we would talk in fast jets, monitoring the territory as the Chinook land.

An Apache pilot said:

> We were busy but it ebbed and flowed. In general our tactics were very different from the Chinooks, they had to go to lower levels but there was still the RPG threat and terrain [problems]. The enemy usually knew we were coming so we were always evolving our tactics. Ideas were always coming from the ground troops on better ways to flush out the enemy. Finding them in the first place was most the difficult thing. This was very small-scale stuff but highly dangerous.

A Chinook pilot recalled:

> Things were constantly changing, what you expect would not happen. Big multi-ship operations were hairy. The locals expected us and so you had to do it fast. There was a real risk. You needed speed. We had a few hits when we had to go in and land. The Apache stayed in the overhead but we had to descend into the threat area.

Apache crews said they only used close-in fire support (CIFS) procedures under the direct control of paratroopers on a limited number of occasions. The AAC Captain recalled:

> In district compounds they had Joint Terminal Attack Controllers (JTAC) (which were formerly Forward Air Controllers) and they would call us in. We used CIFS in one operation when the paratroopers were moving through an area flushing the [bad] guys out when they came up on [radio] net asking us to engage enemy in wood line – it did work. The enemy ran when we appeared. If they did not and were seen, they went to pieces – literally. The gun was our weapon of choice, it can be engaged quickly and accurately. You just kept your eyes on target. You only got a 10- to 15-second glimpse of the bad guys. If you chased them into a building then you put in a Hellfire and if they were hiding in a field you would use rockets.
>
> We did not use the Longbow radar to find targets, we used it to deconflict with other aircraft, to co-ordinate where everyone was coming in – Chinooks and jets. If we'd scattered behind terrain after a contact then we could quickly work out where everyone was. Aircraft serviceability was very good. The forward looking infra-red [night sight] was epic – the clarity was good.

The end of July finally saw the US transfer command authority to NATO. This meant Butler was given a formal place in the NATO chain of command, with tactical control of UK forces in Helmand. He move down to Kandahar from Kabul and he pulled much of the HTF headquarters back from Lashkar Gar and set up what became known as the UK Task Force headquarters at Kandahar Airfield to better control the fight in Helmand province. Lashkar Gar was considered too small to safely accommodate all the headquarters personnel and it had only one small helicopter pad, which made it difficult to move people and supplies in and out.

The combination of determined resistance in the district centres by the troops of 3 PARA, The Royal Irish Regiment, Royal Regiment of Fusiliers, Gurkhas, Pathfinders and the Danish Reconnaissance Squadron, along with air support from the Apaches, Chinooks and fast jets were inflicting heavy losses on the Taliban. Some 250 air strikes were called down by 7 RHA's FSTs alone during 16 Brigade's time in Helmand.

Even though the efforts of the Apaches and Chinooks to re-supply the district centres gained great prominence during this period, other innovative tactics were being used to defeat the Taliban. The RAF Hercules detachment at Kandahar teamed up with 47 Air Despatch Squadron, to begin air-dropping supplies to the beleaguered troops in the district centres. While one supply-drop famously went astray and landed among the Taliban, the drops eventually proved an efficient way to get supplies to the troops. Some disgruntled paratroopers recalled the siege of Arnhem when the RAF parachuted supplies onto drop zones controlled by the Germans.

The 105-mm gunners of 7 RHA's I Battery were also grouped with the Scimitars of the Household Cavalry to form what was termed a Manoeuvre Operations Group (MOG) to patrol in the desert outside Musa Qalah. Their aim was to intercept Taliban re-supply columns and bring heavy firepower to bear to help the defenders of the district centre inside the town. Ultimately 7 RHA would fire more than 4,000 rounds during their time in Helmand. The employment of the MOG at last gave 16 Brigade the tactical initiative and allowed it to take the fight to the Taliban at places and times they were least expecting. The MOGs were supplied by helicopter or air drop to make them more difficult for the Taliban to track.

It was very difficult for British commanders to build up the MOG because of the demand for troops to hold the district centres. 3 PARA proposed to add to the Taliban's problems by launching surprise parachute drops but on the three occasions operations were developed, there proved to be insufficient C-130s available. One senior officer attached to the HTF headquarters in the summer of 2006 recalled, 'The Commanding Officer of 3 PARA had far more tasks than he had troops for. Once many of the troops were in forward posts they were unavailable. So there was no spare infantry manpower.'

The fighting in the north of Helmand was only part of a wider battle that stretched across southern Afghanistan. South of Lashkar Gar, the Taliban stormed into the town of Garmsir in the middle of July, routing the ANA contingent sent to hold the town. Garmsir lay astride the main Taliban supply route from Pakistan and was also a key hub in the heroin export trade. HTF had no reserves left and had to call upon the services of a Canadian Light Armoured Vehicle (LAV) company, backed by air power to hold the ring. After a few weeks they were needed in Kandahar province to counter the Taliban build-up there and had to pull back. The Taliban were back again a month later and this time the Canadians could not spare any extra troops. Daoud threatened to resign if it was not

An RAF Chinook swoops down to deliver supplies to an isolated NATO outpost.
(Canadian Ministry of National Defence)

retaken. The job of pushing back the Taliban fell to a newly trained ANA battalion and an OMLT team in early September. When the Afghan battalion commander refused to lead his men south, a Royal Irish Regiment captain took over command of the operation. The Afghans and a handful of British and Estonian troops fought to drive back the Taliban, amid scenes of vicious close quarter fighting. This scratch force, backed by British Apache and NATO air power, held the town for two weeks before being pulled back to base exhausted. No more troops could be spared to try to hold back the Taliban in the south of Helmand for several weeks.

In neighbouring Kandahar province, the Canadians launched a major offensive, dubbed Operation Medusa, at the start of September to drive lack the Taliban from the outskirts of the provincial capital. UK Special Forces were dispatched to seal Taliban escape routes from this battle zone. In an operation to support this mission, an RAF Nimrod MR2 aircraft caught fire and exploded, killing all fourteen personnel on board. RAF Regiment troops from Kandahar airfield were scrambled on board British Chinooks to secure the crash zone and recover the remains of the crew before Taliban fighters threatened to overrun the site.

The British had not envisaged this level of combat before 16 Brigade deployed and it was placing a huge drain on the resources of the UK Armed Forces. The RAF Harrier detachment at Kandahar airfield almost ran out of bombs at the start of September and emergency re-supply flights were ordered to re-stock the KAF bomb dump. Particularly worrying was the surge in flying by the Apaches and Chinooks. The eight Apaches in Helmand alone were now flying more than 400 hours a month, which was more than double the scheduled peacetime flying rate of 180 hours a month for the whole of the sixty-seven-strong UK Apache fleet. This severely depleted the flying programme of the Apache Force back in the UK and made many AAC officers wonder if they could keep up this level of flying for many more months. There were barely enough trained Apache technicians to keep up with overhauling the growing number of worn-out helicopters starting to be flown back to repair centres in the UK from Afghanistan. The same problem affected the Chinook Force, although to a lesser degree, and an extra airframe was flown out to Afghanistan at the end of the summer after media criticism in the UK.

Throughout August, the fighting continued at the alarming level of intensity. By late August, British officers were claiming that around '1,000 Taliban' had been killed in fighting in Helmand but the enemy seemed to be still fighting with a degree of determination and effectiveness that astounded the British. If 1,000 Taliban had been killed, then the pre-deployment estimate of 1,000 enemy fighters in Helmand must have been hopelessly short of the mark, given the continuing level of combat in the province. The other conclusion was that support for the Taliban was growing. By the autumn of

The UK Apache Force was averaging more than 400 hours of flying a month in Afghanistan during the summer of 2006. *(Tim Ripley)*

RAF Nimrod MR2 patrol aircraft provided surveillance support for UK and NATO forces in southern Afghanistan, including monitoring Taliban activity on the ground with video cameras. One was lost in an accident near Kandahar on 2 September 2006. *(Tim Ripley)*

2006, ISAF intelligence officers were estimating that the Taliban could draw on around 12,000 fighters across southern Afghanistan – more than doubling the estimates made earlier in the year – with some 6,000 in Helmand.

Butler was by now becoming increasingly concerned at the vulnerability of the casualty evacuation helicopters to Taliban fire and the possible effect on morale in the UK if a Chinook were lost with major loss of life. The dramatic flight into Musa Qalah district centre by a Lynx to pick up a casualty only highlighted the precarious position of the garrison. The loss of the Nimrod further intensified this thinking and worries were rising in the British command in Afghanistan that public opinion might not survive the loss of a Chinook with twenty or more passengers on board. Senior officers thought this might set back the British campaign in Afghanistan irrevocably.

A stream of senior officers visited Afghanistan to gauge the progress, or lack of it. In London, the situation was monitored on a daily basis, with growing concern. General Richards in Kabul was equally concerned and wanted Butler to pull his men out of the district centres in such a way that did not hand a propaganda victory to the Taliban. He wanted more MOGs to take the fight to the Taliban, rather than having the bulk of the British forces bogged down in the district centres. Moves were made to prepare to withdraw the British garrison from Musa Qalah. Daoud and Karzai strongly protested about the idea of a British withdrawal, which they said would undermine their authority.

In mid September, the tribal elders in Musa Qalah gave the British the excuse they needed to pull out of the town, which had now been heavily damaged during three months of intense fighting. Most of its population had fled to the countryside. The failure of the Taliban to live up to their promises to force out the British undermined their support among the local population and emboldened the elders to ask the Taliban to cease-fire. The elders approached both the British and the Taliban to ask for a cease-fire to allow them to rebuild their town. Both sides had been exhausted by the fighting in northern Helmand and jumped at the chance to pull back when the elders made their offer. Butler flew up to the desert outside Musa Qalah for a *shura* to broker a deal with the elders. The town was soon quiet and the deal seemed to stick. Elsewhere around Helmand fighting also seemed to subside.

By the end of September, Butler declared 'tactical success' in the battle for the district compounds. He called them a 'breakwater' and said that the Taliban tide had been smashed. This had brought a 'pause' in fighting in Helmand, which ISAF commanders hoped to exploit by the delivery of humanitarian aid during the winter months.

During early October, 3 Commando Brigade, Royal Marines, began replacing 16 Brigade but it still had a strong contingent of RAF and AAC helicopters deployed in support. 9 Regiment was to continue providing Apaches to the UK Task Force until May 2007, with its squadrons rotating every three to four months. The RAF Chinook squadrons continued to take turns to serve in Afghanistan, deploying a flight's worth of aircrew every four months.

The bulk of 16 Brigade's troops was home by the middle of October and the Brigade's tour in Afghanistan was hailed as the most intense period of combat faced by the British Army since the Korean War in the 1950s. Between June and September, nineteen members of the UK Armed Forces were killed on the ground and fourteen personnel died in the Nimrod crash. The UK Task Force suffered a total of 170 casualties during this phase of the fighting.

The level of firepower employed was staggering. Some 260 air strikes were called in by British troops in Helmand between June and August. 3 PARA fired 450,000 rounds of small arms and machine-gun ammunition, as well as 750 mortar rounds, in some 498 individual engagements. Butler commented that the level of air support used was not what had been originally envisaged. 'We did not want to do this but we needed it for protection,' he said.

During the summer of 2006 phase of the Afghan campaign the British Army relied on helicopters to an unprecedented degree, according to Major General Gary Coward, who headed the UK's Joint Helicopter Command at the time. 'In Iraq the deployed commander saw helicopters as one of his key enablers, whereas in Afghanistan, because of the nature of the operation, terrain and the enemy, helicopters were the critical enabler,' he said. He added that even ground convoys did not move around the south of the war-torn central Asian country without top cover from helicopters.

Praise for the high level of integration between land forces and helicopters was repeated by Brigadier Ed Butler, who said '3 PARA would not go anywhere without attack helicopters because of the effect they had on the enemy. There is an unprecedented bond between 3 PARA and the helicopter crews.' Other British officers described the level of cohesion between aircrew and ground troops as similar to that in the UK's Special Forces helicopter wing.

With only some eighteen helicopters – eight Apaches, six Chinooks and four Lynx –

RAF Regiment personnel from 34 Squadron secured the Nimrod crash site until a Taliban attack threatened to overrun their positions. *(Tim Ripley)*

deployed to Kandahar and Camp Bastion during the summer of 2006, the number of helicopters in Afghanistan became a subject of great controversy. British troops regularly complained to the few journalists who managed to get to Camp Bastion that there were not enough helicopters. As serving officers, Butler and Richards could not publicly say they did not have enough helicopters, but diplomatically commented in public that 'they could have done more, faster' if they had had more resources. The real issue was not the number of helicopter airframes, but the amount of spare parts and the number of trained helicopter pilots and technicians available in the UK Armed Forces. To generate the hundreds of flying hours a month needed in Afghanistan, the helicopter forces left in the UK were largely denuded of spares, severely limiting aircraft availability for army exercises and aircrew training. The need to sustain British forces in Afghanistan over several years meant the Joint Helicopter Command had to husband its personnel and valuable spare parts. Some AAC and RAF officers worried that the lack of flying hours could prevent them training crews sufficiently to man subsequent rotations of British troops to Afghanistan during 2007 and 2008.

The summer's fighting devastated several of Helmand's major towns and created thousands of refugees. Ambitious plans to kick-start reconstruction and humanitarian aid projects just did not happen. British soldiers were scathing about FCO and DfID officials who left Helmand as soon as the fighting started in June. No poppy fields or heroin factories were destroyed. The so-called 'cross department' approach was just irrelevant. The effort to build up the Afghan armed forces was also uneven, with only two poorly trained ANA battalions up and running by September instead of the planned three. The Afghan police added little to the fight against the Taliban. In the summer of 2006, Helmand was a battlefield, plain and simple. It would be up to follow-on British forces to start winning the hearts and minds of Helmand's population.

A phrase common among senior British officers in the autumn of 2006 was 'the enemy has vote on the Afghan battlefield'. This was a reference to the fact that the Afghan campaign was not going to be a walkover and British forces would have to get used to dealing with unexpected turns of events. The Taliban were clearly determined, skilled and numerous opponents. They had significant backing from a sizeable chunk of the local population in Helmand province. Unlike in Kosovo in 1999, Sierra Leone in 2000 and southern Iraq in 2003, the Taliban did not fold within a few days or weeks after British troops appeared in southern Afghanistan. A much larger force than was sent in the spring of 2006 would be needed to defeat the Taliban, who could be relied upon to try their best to confound the British. This was a real war of a kind not faced by the British Armed Forces since the Korea War in the 1950s or the Falklands in 1982. In the autumn of 2006, the outcome was clearly still in the balance.

The lack of troops, helicopters, UAVs and other resources that bedevilled 16 Brigade

In October 2006 Royal Marines of 3 Commando Brigade replaced the paratroopers of 16 Air Assault Brigade in Helmand. This required complex relief in place operations, such as this one at Kajaki, to be carried out with troops being moved by Chinooks with strong Apache escorts. *(Patrick Allan)*

during its tour would need to be addressed in follow-on force packages as the real scope of the Taliban threat became apparent. The insertion of 16 Brigade in Helmand could be characterised as a 'reconnaissance in force' that revealed the true size and nature of the Taliban's fighting machine, their strategy and tactics.

Senior officers of 16 Brigade, however, say their fight to hold the district centres formed a 'breakwater', which protected the provincial capital of Lashkar Gar and nearby Gereshk from being overwhelmed by the Taliban wave. Butler described this as 'Phase 1 of the campaign', commenting that it was 'a five month break in battle – which we won'. British troops held their ground and the Taliban failed to seize control of Helmand's main population centres.

Butler attributed this [success] to the fighting spirit of his paratroopers who fought for weeks in desperate conditions, spending twenty-two hours a day in firing positions in the district centres. 'Morale was sky high,' he said. 'They were still running to [the] sound of gunfire [even at the end]. The Airborne ethos and the self belief that comes from jumping out of aircraft delivered this.'

CHAPTER 15

The Future of
16 Air Assault Brigade

In the nine years since its formation in 1999, 16 Air Assault Brigade has secured its place in the British Army's order of battle as the UK's specialist air manoeuvre formation.

As well as proving itself on operations in Macedonia, Iraq and Afghanistan, major units of the Brigade have provided air manoeuvre expertise and capabilities to other parts of the UK Armed Forces on numerous other operations.

The 2006 campaign in Afghanistan was graphic proof that the British Army and RAF have at last mastered the use of helicopters in combat, fifty years after the first employment of helicopters by British forces during the Suez crisis.

Helicopters were central to all British combat operations in Afghanistan during the summer and autumn of 2006. Air manoeuvre enthusiasts in the British Army and RAF could feel vindicated that their efforts over the previous decade had created a powerful and effective combat force. The long-delayed combat debut of the Apache has transformed the capability of 16 Brigade. 'Going by air to battle' proved itself in the deserts and mountains of Afghanistan as British troops fought the Taliban during 2006.

As this volume goes to press, 16 Brigade is preparing to return to Afghanistan to take up the battle against the Taliban again in May 2008. This time the Brigade will go to central Asia with more than double the number of troops it took in 2006. Its two Parachute Regiment

The Future Lynx will provide 16 Air Assault Brigade with its utility and manned aerial surveillance capability from 2014.
(*AgustaWestland*)

Upgrades to the AAC's Apache fleet are scheduled to take place over the next decade.
(AgustaWestland)

battalions, along with the 1st Battalion, The Royal Irish Regiment, and the 5th Battalion, The Royal Regiment of Scotland (Argyll & Sutherland Highlanders), are to spearhead the new Afghan mission. Territorial volunteers from the Parachute Regiment are being mobilised to fill out manpower shortages in the Regular battalions. The Brigade will also take many new weapons and have other advanced capabilities at its disposal. It will deploy for the first time with the new Bowman digital communications system. Commanders will have access to real-time surveillance of the Taliban through US-supplied Reaper and Israeli-made Hermes 450 unmanned aerial vehicles. Re-supply convoys will have dozens of heavily armoured Mastiff trucks. Warrior and Viking armoured vehicles will also be available to move troops around the Afghan battlefield. Long-range firepower has been enhanced through the deployment of Guided Multiple Launch Rocket Systems (GMLRS) to Afghanistan. Royal Navy Sea King HC.4 helicopters have augmented the helicopter force in Afghanistan and additional spares have been purchased to extend the flying hours of the Apache and Chinook fleets.

This is an impressive force and Parachute Regiment officers say it will be by far the most powerful combat force the British Army has ever put into the field in Afghanistan. Some military sources suggest that if this force can not inflict a decisive defeat on the Taliban then the British campaign in Afghanistan could be in serious trouble.

While the insertion operation into Afghanistan in 2006 was tailor-made for 16 Brigade, the subsequent continuation of the campaign over the past two years has had major implications for the British Army's air manoeuvre forces. When the Brigade was established, it was envisaged that elements of it might be employed on an *ad hoc* basis for other short duration operations but continuous employment of key parts of 16 Brigade on back-to-back tours are clearly taking their toll, with highly trained personnel leaving the military early and recruitment is difficult. The Apache aircrews of AAC and maintenance technicians of the Royal Electrical and Mechanical Engineers have been on operations in Afghanistan continuously for almost two years. This is making it very difficult to retain key personnel and bring the Apache Force up to its full strength of six squadrons from the current four. The same problems are affecting parts of the RAF that are essential to 16 Brigade, such as the Hercules and Chinook Forces, to a lesser degree.

With the Apache, Chinook and Hercules Forces committed almost fully to the Afghan operation, 16 Brigade's core air manoeuvre capabilities are suffering. For example, during a Lead Airborne Task Force exercise in the summer of 2007, not enough Hercules could be mobilised to meet the full fifteen aircraft requirement to deliver the force in one parachute drop. Instead, the drop had to be spread over several days.

A purchase of extra medium-lift helicopters has been delayed until the middle of the next decade. (*AgustaWestland*)

Real-time sensor surveillance sensors, such as the Raytheon Sentinel R.1 Airborne Stand Off Radar (ASTOR), offer the prospect of transforming 16 Brigade's operations. *(Raytheon)*

Many British Army and RAF officers are clearly worried that if the Afghan campaign continues at its current level of activity for many more years, 16 Brigade could turn into a 'hollow force' that might not be able to meet it core commitment to be ready at short notice to react to unexpected events. It seems this issue has been recognised and plans are being prepared to 'rest' the Brigade from six-month tours in Afghanistan for a two-year period.

This is not just a problem affecting 16 Brigade but is a symptom of the over commitment of the British Armed Forces to conflicts over the past decade. The under-resourcing of the British military during this unprecedented period of operational activity has clearly been highlighted by the experiences of 16 Brigade.

A decade ago, the New Labour government's Strategic Defence Review (SDR) set out an ambitious vision for transforming the British Armed Forces into a highly effective expeditionary force. Unfortunately, the resources needed to execute this vision were never forthcoming. Plans to more than double the number of Chinooks and Merlin heavy-lift helicopters were dumped unceremoniously in Defence Secretary Geoff Hoon's 2004 cutbacks package. Likewise, efforts to provide 16 Brigade and 3 Commando Brigade with a new family of Indirect Fire Precision Attack artillery and rocket weapons have fallen victim to spending cuts and delays. The RAF's Airborne Stand Off Radar (ASTOR) and the British Army Watchkeeper real-time surveillance systems have been delayed through budget shortfalls and technical glitches and will not be fully online until the end of the decade.

16 Brigade has only just taken delivery of the Bowman digital radio systems and, perhaps more importantly, plans to modify the Apache fleet to be fully connected to the British Army's battlefield internet have been delayed until well into the next decade. This

The Chinook will continue to be the mainstay of the RAF transport helicopter force for at least twenty years. *(Tim Ripley)*

potentially limits the ability of the Service's main offensive weapon system to connect to British and allied data networks and exploit advances in real-time surveillance systems that are coming online.

The RAF's air transport force has similarly suffered from under-investment and apart from the acquisition of four C-17s in 2001, it has fewer aircraft than it did in 1997. The Airbus A400M is now delayed and will not enter service until 2012 at the earliest.

This sorry tale has meant that 16 Brigade and other parts of the British Armed Forces have continuously suffered from a lack of key battle-winning capabilities. The Macedonian crisis, the 2003 Iraq invasion and the 2006 Afghan campaign all highlighted shortages of helicopters, airlift, long-range weapons and surveillance systems. The formation of the Joint Helicopter Command has streamlined the command of UK

The RAF RQ-9 Reaper armed unmanned aerial vehicles will be on station over Afghanistan when 16 Brigade deploys to the country again in mid 2008. *(USAF)*

battlefield helicopters and significantly reduced the inter-Service rivalry that previously bedevilled joint helicopter operations. The close co-operation of RAF and AAC helicopters during Afghan operations is testament to this. However, it is clearly impossible for a helicopter to be in two places at once. The rationing of helicopters between 3 Commando and 16 Brigade during the 2003 Iraq invasion demonstrated graphically that the British Armed Forces were critically under-equipped with heavy-lift helicopters. The scrapping of plans to expand helicopter procurement in 2004 meant this 'helicopter gap' has not been filled.

It took the shock of the resistance put up by the Taliban in 2006 to shake the government out of its complacency and this opened the doors to several hundred millions pounds of spending on new helicopters and other weapons. The cost of the UK's Afghan operation surged to almost £800 million during its first year and UK military operations in the central Asian country were projected as costing £964 million in the year up to April 2008. This was compared with the original projection of £1 billion over three years.

Whether or not the government of Prime Minister Gordon Brown will reserve the long-term decline in investment in defence is not clear as this volume goes to press. The UK Ministry of Defence and the Treasury were in the process of finalising spending plans for the next three years in the final months of 2007. Initial reports are not encouraging. In September 2007 it emerged that the Ministry of Defence had scrapped plans to replace the

The Parachute Regiment continues to provide the core of 16 Brigade's fighting infantry strength. *(Tim Ripley)*

105-mm Light Gun with a 155-mm artillery piece that would have dramatically extended the range of 16 Brigade's artillery and given its guns the ability to fire precision-guided munitions. Likewise, plans to buy a lightweight truck-mounted GMLRS launcher that can be carried inside a Hercules have yet to be confirmed and contracted.

Improved night vision systems are now in widespread use with 16 Brigade. *(Thales)*

For the soldiers of 16 Air Assault Brigade, the next five years clearly hold the prospect of spending many more tours of duty in crisis zones around the world. Although it will be well into the next decade before much of the new equipment they require will come online, there seems to be no change in the British government's inclination to send its Armed Forces into action around the world.

The Afghan campaign in 2006 show the risks that are being run by not equipping the British Armed Forces properly. Until 16 Brigade engaged the Taliban in June 2006, the British Armed Forces had been lucky in the opponents they had faced since 1997. The Airborne fighting spirit of 16 Brigade and lavish air power saved the day but it was touch and go at times.

Network communications systems are now in widespread use with 16 Brigade. *(Aerosystems International)*

INDEX

British Army Brigades

4 Armoured Brigade 83, 88, 91

5 Airborne Brigade 12, 16, 30, 46, 49, 56, 70, 74, 77, 86, 88, 90, 92, 93, 99, 100, 115, 123

6 Airmobile Brigade 43, 47-49

7 Armoured Brigade 50, 155, 160, 170, 171, 176, 177

19 Mechanised Brigade 177

24 Airmobile Brigade 12, 16, 49, 55-57, 59, 61-69, 74, 77, 88, 115, 123, 160

British Army Regiments and Battalions

1st Battalion, The Parachute Regiment (1 PARA) 28, 88, 92, 97-99, 105, 108-111, 122, 123, 164, 167, 171, 177

2nd Battalion, The Parachute Regiment (2 PARA) 28, 105, 113, 118, 135, 137-141, 143, 144, 147, 151, 152, 158, 192, 193, 217

3rd Battalion, The Parachute Regiment (3 PARA) 28, 155, 164, 169, 173, 176, 177, 232, 234, 236, 238, 241, 243, 244-246, 249-251, 253, 257

1st Battalion, The Royal Irish Regiment (1 R IRISH) 30, 107, 11, 164, 169, 177, 253, 254, 262

5th Battalion, The Royal Regiment of Scotland (Argyll & Sutherland Highlanders) 30, 193, 262

1st Battalion, The Royal Gurkha Rifles (1 RGR) 31, 88, 97, 99

2nd Battalion, The Royal Gurkha Rifles (2 RGR) 253

1st Battalion, Royal Welsh Fusiliers (1RWF) 60

2nd Battalion, Royal Regiment of Fusiliers 253

3 Regiment AAC 24, 57, 158, 160, 162, 164, 170, 171, 173, 189

4 Regiment AAC 24, 49, 50, 113, 118, 121, 189, 207, 239

9 Regiment AAC 189, 194, 205, 207, 208, 209, 212-216, 217, 236, 257

22nd Special Air Service Regiment (22 SAS) 45, 111, 139, 254

13 Air Assault Regiment, Royal Logistic Corps 39, 239

23 Engineer Regiment 39

7 Parachute Regiment Royal Horse Artillery 31, 122, 137, 138, 152, 153, 164, 169, 172, 175, 178, 235, 239, 243, 247, 249, 253

29 Regiment Royal Artillery 45

Other British Units & Military Organisations

Land Command 63, 71, 104, 217

Joint Rapid Reaction Force 16, 112, 123, 124

HQ ARRC 85, 217, 227, 231

Joint Helicopter Command 13, 36, 71-74, 76, 77, 79, 81, 83, 104, 189, 190, 257, 258, 265, 266

Defence Helicopter Flying School 74

1 (UK) Armoured Division 49, 77, 114, 160, 177, 178, 200

3 (UK) Mechanised Division 77, 200

3 Commando Brigade 43, 46, 50, 70, 146, 152, 169, 177, 257, 266

Directorate of Special Forces 63, 66, 225

Special Forces Aviation Wing 47, 214, 257

7 Air Assault Battalion, REME 39

Joint Helicopter Force – Afghanistan 236

Joint Helicopter Force – Iraq 160, 169, 171

D Squadron, Household Cavalry Regiment 32, 34, 153, 164, 173, 176, 239

156 Provost Company, Royal Military Police 39, 177, 178

47 Air Despatch Squadron, Royal Logistic Corps (LEWT) 237 Squadron, Royal Signals 34, 81, 249

654 Squadron AAC 49, 50, 133, 189

657 Squadron AAC 133, 137, 138

659 Squadron AAC 49, 95, 97

9 Para Squadron, RE 114

51 Para Squadron, RE 169

69 Squadron, Queen's Gurkha Engineers 100,

5 & 16 Brigade Pathfinder Platoon 34, 99, 108, 109, 113, 138, 143, 144, 153, 164, 172, 173, 175, 176, 219, 243, 253

Special Boat Service (SBS) 50, 246, 247

DERA/QinetiQ 80, 185, 203

RAF Units and Squadrons

7 Squadron 38, 46, 47, 50, 108

18 Squadron 37, 171, 190, 239

24 Squadron 37

27 Squadron 37, 190, 239
28 Squadron 38, 190, 207
30 Squadron 37
33 Squadron 133
47 Squadron 37, 107
70 Squadron 37, 107
99 Squadron 133
230 Squadron 38
SHF HQ 49, 90-92, 99, 100, 123

Non-UK Military Forces & Organisations
UNPROFOR (Bosnia) 60, 62, 63
UN RRF (Bosnia) 57, 61, 63
UN MNB (Bosnia) 62, 66
IFOR (Bosnia) 69
KFOR (Kosovo) 91, 99, 132
TFH (Macedonia) 132, 137, 138, 142, 144
ISAF (Afghanistan) 147, 151, 226, 227, 257
Kabul MNB 148, 149
RC-South (Afghanistan) 238
TF Hunter (US) 137, 142
CJSOTF (US) 225, 230
I Marine Expeditionary Force (I MEF) (US) 163, 164, 176
3rd Marine Air Wing (USMC) 160, 163, 166
10th Mountain Division (US) 138
82nd Airborne Division (US) 49, 159
101st Air Assault Division (US) 49, 123, 133, 134, 141
5th Marine Regimental Combat Team (US) 163, 169
Kosovo Liberation Army 84, 85, 98, 99
National Liberation Army (Macedonia) 127, 129, 133, 143, 144
Afghan National Army (ANA) 157, 225, 235, 243, 254, 259
Taliban (Afghanistan) 152, 220. 224, 227, 231, 233, 240, 241, 243, 245-250, 253-256, 259, 261, 266
Al Qaeda 143, 145-147, 152,

224, 225
6th Iraqi Armoured Division 173, 175, 176, 178
CIA (US) 176, 225

EQUIPMENT
HELICOPTERS
AgustaWestland Apache AH.1 16, 22, 53, 69, 72, 73, 80, 81, 115, 124, 179, 180, 184-187, 189, 190, 193, 194, 199, 202, 203, 205, 206, 212, 214, 215, 217, 220, 236, 241, 252, 253, 255, 258, 263
AgustaWestland Merlin HC.3 12, 35, 38, 56, 73, 190, 193, 200-202, 212, 214
AgustaWestland Future Lynx 201
Bell AH-1W Cobra 52, 171
Boeing Chinook HC.2 12, 29, 32, 36, 43, 44, 46, 48, 51, 56, 69, 70, 72, 73, 81, 90, 91, 93, 95, 99, 104, 107-109, 111, 113, 127, 131, 133, 138-141, 143, 144, 160, 167, 171, 176, 189, 190, 193, 200, 202, 203, 205, 212, 220, 230, 236, 241, 244, 245, 247, 250-256, 258, 263
Boeing AH-64D Apache 12, 52, 93, 95, 179, 180, 237
Bell-Boeing V-22 200
Bristol Belvedere 42, 43
McDonnell Douglas AH-64A Apache 51
Sikorsky HH-60/UH-60 Pavehawk/ Blackhawk 137, 139, 240
Westland Gazelle AH.1 24, 44, 49, 69, 72, 73, 80, 133, 139, 153, 160, 164, 171, 201
Westland Lynx AH.7/9 23, 25, 43, 47, 49, 52, 56, 57, 69, 72, 73, 76, 80, 95, 97, 111, 113, 133, 153, 160, 164, 171, 173, 189, 201, 203, 209, 236, 256, 258
Westland Puma HC.1 29, 36, 43, 48, 49, 70, 72, 73, 76, 91, 93, 95, 133, 139, 189

Westland Sea King HC.4 29, 43, 49, 51, 69, 76, 80, 197, 262
Westland Sea King AEW.7 207, 213, 214, 228
Westland Scout 42, 44
Westland Wessex 42, 43

AIRCRAFT
Airbus Military Company A400M 80
Antonov An-124 89, 109, 136, 150
BAE Systems Harrier GR7 49, 167, 250, 255
Boeing C-17 Globemaster 25, 38, 124, 133, 134, 144
Boeing B-52 Stratofortress 228
Boeing E-3D Sentry (AWACS) 113, 228
English Electric Canberra PR.9 235
Fairchild A-10A Warthog 173, 176, 245
Hawker Siddeley Nimrod MR.2 235, 249, 254, 257
Lockheed C-5 Galaxy 65
Lockheed C-141 Starlifter 65
Lockheed Martin C-130 Hercules 12, 29, 30, 31, 32, 37, 38, 80, 81, 107-109, 113, 114, 116, 117, 123, 124, 134, 137, 158, 160, 164, 167, 190, 206, 232, 253, 263
Lockheed Tristar 38, 39, 107, 135
Raytheon Sentinal R.1 (ASTOR) 81, 203, 264
Vickers VC-10 38, 39, 89, 134, 135

UNMANNED AERIAL VEHICLES
Elbit Hermes 450 203, 262
GEC-Marconi Phoenix 173, 203
General Atomics RQ/MQ-1 Predator 229, 235, 249, 250
General Atomics MQ-9 Reaper 262

Lockheed Martin Desert
   Hawk 235
Thales WK450 Watchkeeper
   81, 201, 203, 264
IAI/TRW Hunter 137, 142,
   144

**VEHICLES AND
   ARTILLERY**
CVR(T) Scimitar 32, 109,
   137, 153
Challenger 2 tank 212
Warrior infantry fighting
   vehicle 262
T-55 tank 50
LAV 250, 253
AS-90 self-propelled gun 164
105mm Light Gun 29, 31, 37,
   45, 60, 109, 164, 172, 175,
   205, 235
Indirect Precision Fire Attack
   81, 203
155mm M777 howitzer 81
Milan missile 27, 48
Javelin missile 27
MAMBA radar 81, 164
Land Rover 19, 138, 154, 164,
   171, 175
Bowman Radio 13, 19, 81,
   184, 198, 201, 214, 262
HVM Starstreak missile 34

Ships
HMS Albion 215
HMS Bulwark 215
HMS Illustrious 109
HMS Ocean 41, 109, 215
HMS Theseus 41

**PEOPLE
BRITISH ARMY**
Field Marshall Sir Peter Inge
   63, 65, 67
General Mike Jackson 78, 85,
   88, 89, 93, 94, 97, 100, 201
Lieutanant General Rupert
   Smith 63, 67-68
Lieutenant General David
   Richards 102, 104, 105,
   108, 227, 256, 258
Lieutenant General John Reith

100, 159
Major General Robin Brims
   63, 65, 159, 171
Major General Garry Coward
   257
Major General John McColl
   147
Brigadier Adrian Freer 89,
   94, 95
Brigadier Ed Butler 9, 206,
   207, 209, 214, 218, 232,
   238, 251, 256-258, 260
Brigadier Mark Carleton-
   Smith 15, 16
Brigadier Jacko Page 158,
   159, 176, 192
Brigadier Andrew Pringle 63,
   67
Brigadier Peter Wall 114,
   115, 121, 122, 126, 127
Brigadier Barney White-
   Spunner 127, 131, 137,
   148, 149
Colonel Simon Barry 63
Colonel Fraser-Hopewell
   192, 193
Colobel Charlie Knaggs 237,
   238, 243
Lieutenant Colonel Chip
   Chapman 97, 141, 144, 217
Lieutenant Colonel Tim
   Collins 169, 176
Lieutenant Colonel Paul
   Gibson 107-109
Lieutenant Colonel Richard
   Felton 209, 211, 214, 218
Lieutenant Colonel Duncan
   Francis 138, 144
Lieutenant Colonel Jonathan
   Riley 68
Lieutenant Colonel Mike
   Rose 45
Lieutanant Colonel Stuart
   Tootal 238, 244, 247
Major Richard Leakey 97

Royal Air Force
Air Chief Marshall Sir Jock
   Stirrup 201
Air Vice Marshall David
   Niven 71, 73, 74, 76

Group Captain Al Campbell
   90
Wing Commander Gavin
   Davey 116, 117
Wing Commander Wayne
   Gregory 91, 92, 99
Squadron Leader Paul Bartlett
   93, 94
Flight Lieutenant Jeff Lindsay
   92, 94
Flight Lieutenant Andy
   Lawless 45
Flight Lieutenant Al Ritchie
   140

United States
George W Bush 156, 157
Richard Holbrooke 85
Donald Rumsfeld1 145, 177
General Wes Clark 93
General Tommy Franks 157,
   163
Liuetanant General James
   Conway 166
Maj Gen Ben Freakley 238
Lieutenant Colonel George
   Bilafer 93, 95
Major Dennis Griffin 142

OTHERS
Chemical Ali 176
Tony Blair 70, 83, 87, 101,
   130, 146, 226
Osama bin Laden 144, 156, 24
Gordon Brown 195, 227, 266
Alistair Campbell 166
Geoff Hoon 195, 198, 201
Saddam Hussein 49, 51, 156,
   168, 169
Hamid Karazi 146, 147, 150,
   220, 226, 228, 237, 256
Major General Gunnar Lange
   137
John Major 61
General Ratko Mladic 67, 68
Dr John Reid 227, 228, 234,
   240
Simon Wren 166
Governor Daoud 237, 243,
   244, 246, 256

LOCATIONS
UK
Aldershot 77, 105
RAF Benson 38
RAF Brize Norton 26, 27,
    38, 39, 107, 117
Castle Douglas 193
Canterbury 162
Colchester 19, 55, 62, 68, 77,
    162
Dishforth Airfield 19
RAF High Wycombe 117,
    179, 186, 188
RAF Lyneham 37, 38
NAS Merryfield 205, 207,
    212, 213, 217
Middle Wallop 179, 186, 187,
    189
RAF Odiham 37, 38, 90, 107,
    214
RAF Shawbury 189
Wattisham Airfield 19, 162,
    188, 192
West Freugh 190-193
Wilton 63, 66, 117

IRAQ
Amara 13, 160, 167, 175,
    176-178
Baghdad 155, 159, 160, 162,
    172, 175-177
Basra 157, 170, 171, 175-177
Ad Dayr 174, 176
Al Faw Peninsula 157, 167,

169
Al Hammar Canal 169, 173
Maysan Province 176, 177
Nasariya 160, 170, 172
Qalat Sakir 154, 160, 167,
    171, 172, 178
Qurnah 176
Rumaliya 163, 169, 170, 175,
    177, 178

AFGHANISTAN
Baghran 243
Bagram 148, 152
Garmsir 253
Kabul 145, 146, 148, 149,
    151, 152, 220, 221, 224,
    231, 238, 253, 258
Kajaki 241, 244
Kandahar 9, 219, 221, 226,
    236, 238, 253, 258
Lashkar Gar 232, 237, 238,
    243, 253, 260
Musa Qalah 219, 243, 246,
    247, 251, 253, 256, 257
Now Zad 237, 243, 245, 247,
    251
FOB Robinson 241, 243, 247
Sangin 237, 245-247, 249
Zumbelay 247

BALKANS
Camp Able Sentry 134, 137,
    138
Gorazde 61, 65, 68

Kacanik Gorge 83, 89, 94, 96
Ploce 13, 63, 68
Pristina 95, 99, 100
Sarajevo 60, 61, 66
Srebrenica 65, 66
Skopje 85, 92, 95, 97, 129,
    131, 133, 134, 137, 139
Tetovo 143

OTHERS
Al Ali Salam, Kuwait 171
Freetown, Sierra Leone 105
Mount Kent, Falklands 44, 45
Thumrait, Oman 149, 150
Port Stanley, Falklands 44, 45

Exercises
Corsican Lanyard 88
Eagle's Eye 2004 190, 194
Eagle's Strike 2000 113-126
Eagle's Strike 2005 205, 206,
    208, 211, 213, 215
Nap Archer 43
Purple Star 70
Sky Warrior 43

Operations
Essential Harvest 131, 143
Fingal 145
Fresco 157
Haven 51
Medusa 9, 253
Mountain Thrust 244
Quick Lift 63